CHARLES O'BRIEN

# Cinema's Conversion to Sound: Technology and Film Style in France and the U.S.

INDIANA UNIVERSITY PRESS
*Bloomington and Indianapolis*

This book is a publication of

Indiana University Press
601 North Morton Street
Bloomington, IN 47404-3797 USA

http://iupress.indiana.edu

*Telephone orders*   800-842-6796
*Fax orders*   812-855-7931
*Orders by e-mail*   iuporder@indiana.edu

**Library of Congress Cataloging-in-Publication Data**

O'Brien, Charles, date
  Cinema's conversion to sound : technology and film style in France and the U.S. / Charles O'Brien.
      p.  cm.
Includes filmography.
Includes bibliographical references and index.
    ISBN 0-253-34463-8 (alk. paper) — ISBN 0-253-21720-2 (pbk. : alk. paper)
  1. Sound motion pictures—History. 2. Motion pictures—France—History. 3. Motion pictures—United States—History. 4. Sound—Recording and reproducing—France—History—20th century. 5. Sound—Recording and reproducing—United States—History—20th century. I. Title.
PN1995.7.O27 2005
791.43′09—dc22

                                                                    2004009891

1  2  3  4  5    10  09  08  07  06  05

For Madeleine Nelleke

# Contents

# Acknowledgments

Given the length of time involved in work on this book, the list of people and institutions deserving thanks is similarly lengthy. At the outset a Chateaubriand Fellowship awarded in 1995 allowed me to gather archival materials in Paris that later proved essential. Also foundational was support from the Social Sciences and Humanities Research Council of Canada which helped fund additional research trips to Europe. I must also state my gratitude to the Camargo Foundation, located in the breathtaking setting of Cassis, France, where, under the skilled direction of Michael Pretina, the book's first draft was written. Several grants from the Faculty of Arts and Sciences at Carleton, headed by Dean Aviva Freedman, proved very helpful at key points in the research and writing.

Thanks also to Hubert Dreyfus and David Hoy for admitting me into their NEH Summer Institute in 1994, where illuminating, multidisciplinary discussions of Heidegger, Merleau-Ponty, and Wittgenstein proved unexpectedly relevant to the attempt in this book to examine technology's interface with filmmaking practices. I am grateful to Alan Williams for inviting me to Rutgers University in 1996 for his conference on the French cinema of the German occupation. The response at Rutgers to my paper on film sound helped me decide to write a book on national sound-film style, while leaving me with no illusions concerning the difficulty of what I was taking on.

Once the writing was underway, bits of this book were presented in the form of works-in-progress at the Screen Studies Conference in Glasgow, the International Film Studies Conference in Udine, Italy, and the conference of the Film Studies Association of Canada. Deeply felt thanks to Leonardo Quaresima, Francesco Casetti, Laura Vichi, Francesco Pitassio, and others involved in organizing the International Film Studies Spring School in Gradisca, Italy, who invited me to lecture there on conversion-era sound film in 2003 and 2004.

With respect to intellectual inspiration, Rick Altman's encouragement of this project and the crucial example of his own achievement in the domain of film-sound research were invaluable. To the extent that this book counts as a contribution to film-sound study, Rick's intellectual example and kind support have been decisive.

At various stages of the research and writing, in North America and in Europe, I received crucial support, in one form or another, from Richard Abel, Dana Polan, Susan Suleiman, David Rodowick, and David Bordwell. Timely communications from Janet Bergstrom and Barry Salt helped improve two chapters. Thanks to Chris Faulkner for creating a space at Carleton University for French film study. Although this book was conceived subsequent to the completion of my graduate work at the University of Iowa, it indirectly owes a great deal to people I encountered there, both personally and intellectually. In this regard, the list of names is virtually endless; nonetheless, at the risk of omission, I'd like to mention in particular Dana Benelli, Janette Bayles, Carol Donelan, Nataša Ďurovičová, Caryl Flinn, Jim Lastra, Claire Fox, Jim McLaughlin, and Steve Ungar—for their profound generosity at times when it really counted.

My deepest, most incalculable debt is owed to Dudley Andrew. Beyond the example of his own extraordinary scholarly commitment and courage, Dudley's unwavering support during my years as a graduate student at the University of Iowa was essential to my pursuit of an academic career. With regard to French film history specifically, I must mention in particular Dudley's decision to send me to Paris in 1988 as his research assistant, which, among other benefits, introduced me to the Paris archives later mined for the materials cited in this book.

Work on the book depended on a variety of archives, libraries, videotheques, and research institutions. Particularly important were the Bibliothèque Nationale de France, and especially its Département des Arts et Spectacles; the Forum des Images in Paris; Harvard's Widener Library; the Nederlands Filmmuseum; the library of the Universiteit van Amsterdam; the Cinémathèque Québecoise; and Carleton University's MacOdrum Library. Special thanks go to the staff of the excellent Bibliothèque du Film in Paris and to its director Marc Vernet, who, besides providing a research environment rich in resources, showed exceptional hospitality during my visits there.

Michael Lundell at Indiana University Press was supportive of my work on this book from its early stages, which, given the unorthodox topic, provided the welcome reassurance needed to push onward without a second thought. This book's existence owes much to Michael's support.

Thanks also to Karen Kodner, Dawn Ollila, and Richard Higgins for their helpful copy-editing and editorial work on the manuscript, and to the two anonymous readers of the manuscript for their well-informed comments and criticisms. Needless to say (and the same applies to all other names mentioned in these paragraphs), any errors and excesses in this book are solely the author's responsibility.

My years in Carleton University's School for Studies in Art and Culture, with its degree programs in film studies, art history, and music, have shaped my examination of film relative to the visual and sonic arts in ways as important as they are difficult to pin down. In light of the pleasure I've had in teaching at Carleton, I'd like to thank my Carleton colleagues—faculty, students, and staff, past and present, with special tribute to Laura Marks and Will Echard, who read and commented on drafts of particular chapters.

Finally, I struggle to put into words my gratitude to Randi Klebanoff, whose steadfast willingness to discuss drafts of the manuscript, not to mention perpetual wisdom and goodheartedness, gave me the sense of perspective needed to keep the project on track. Thanks, too, for our daughter Madeleine Nelleke, who provided her dad with delight and wonder daily throughout the research and writing.

Cinema's Conversion to Sound

# Introduction: National Cinema after Recorded Sound

The conversion to sound cinema is commonly characterized as a homogenizing process that quickly and significantly reduced the cinema's diversity of film styles and practices. The analysis in this book offers an alternative assessment of synchronous sound's impact on world cinema through a shift in critical focus: in contrast to film studies' traditional, exclusive concern with the film image, the investigation here centers on national differences in sound-image recording practices. Through an analysis juxtaposing French and American filmmaking, the following investigation reveals the aesthetic consequences of fundamental national differences in how sound technologies were understood and used—differences that endure today, distinguishing French and American films from each other, and also setting apart French and American films from the films of India, Italy, and other countries.

Such differences can be located in basic aesthetic and technical norms. The American and French cinemas, in contrast to numerous other national cinemas, place a strong emphasis on a tight synchronization of the actors' voices with their images. At the same time, the American and French cinemas also differ from each other in important respects. Most fundamentally, whereas the emphasis in 1930s Hollywood was on sound's intelligibility within a film's story-world, French filmmaking implies an alternative model, whereby sound serves to reproduce a performance staged for recording. This difference found its fundamental technical manifestation in the French preference for *son direct*—the recording of sound simultaneously with the image. In the United States, simultaneous sound-image recording, except for dialogue, was largely abandoned by 1932. Instead of the recording of actors' performances, sound-film work in 1930s Hollywood was understood in terms of a process of assembly, whereby scenes were constructed from separate bits and pieces—shot by shot, track by track. In France, sound cinema developed differently, according to a recording-based conception, whereby scenes were understood as the reproduction of actors' and singers' performances. Symptomatic of the national difference was the French cinema's divergence technically from the American cinema, with the standardization of "re-recording" and other multi-track techniques occurring in France only in the 1940s, during the German occupation—a decade later than in Hollywood. Moreover, even then, direct sound remained unusually common in French filmmaking.

Foundational for the subsequent history of sound-film practices were developments during the 1950s and 1960s, when, with the film-industrial adaptation of magnetic sound, direct-sound methods came to define the work of certain of the most important alternative filmmakers of the time. From Jean-Marie Straub and Danièle Huillet to Jean-Luc Godard, Jacques Rivette, and Jean Eustache, filmmakers in France during the 1950s and 1960s, while working with new portable technologies, experimented with direct-sound techniques familiar to the national cinema of the 1930s. In the decades since, direct sound has endured in French filmmaking to the point of defining the national film style.[1] According to Larousse's *Dictionnaire du cinéma* (1986), "The French cinema, if it often resorts to a partial postsynchronization for practical reasons, retains a preference in principle for direct sound."[2] As during the 1930s, direct sound is believed to enable superior performances from actors. Michel Chion observes, regarding French film practice in the 1990s: "Most French directors persist, as much as possible, in preferring direct sound, which they regard as more authentic and honest with regard to actors' performances. Thus, they post-synchronize only scenes that seem inaudible, or whose conditions of shooting prohibited the possibility of an acceptable direct recording."[3]

The analysis in this book explores direct sound in France as the fundamental national film technique—the filmmaking method that has distinguished the French cinema stylistically from other national cinemas, beginning during the conversion years and continuing, in one form or another, up through the present. In the remaining pages of this introduction, the book's investigation into sound's significance for the history of national film style is outlined in three stages. First, key issues are raised concerning the effects of sound-era technological change on film style, with a focus on the familiar notion that film style became homogenized worldwide during the 1930s. Second, I explain briefly how research for the book evolved, and how the focus on sound-film technology and style required re-conceptualization of French cinema history through (1) an examination of mainstream film-industry practice, and (2) an explicitly comparative study of the French cinema relative to the American cinema. Finally, a chapter-by-chapter breakdown presents the ideas and arguments of each chapter corresponding to issues in this introduction.

## Sound Technology's Impact on Film Art

With synch-sound films offering a moviegoing experience notably different from that of "silent" films, the impact of synchronous sound's introduction to cinema was sufficiently powerful to draw strong responses from critics, both for and against. Regardless of these various judgments, there was no question concerning the radical nature of the change wrought by synchronous sound on films as art and entertainment. Synchronous sound was not simply an extra feature that supplemented the film image; it wholly transformed the phenomenology of film. Although attempts to link motion pictures and phonographs dated from the late nineteenth century, the new sound films, with their powerful electronic amplification and, in the case of films with optical soundtracks, their lock-tight synchronization, impressed viewers as absolutely novel. Essential in this regard was the strong sense of the clarity and immediacy of actors' performances enabled by electronic sound recording and reproduction, with its vastly expanded frequency range. In the United States, the film industry's conversion had been motivated by the goal of producing sound films as low-cost substitutes for live musical, stage, and radio acts. A salient feature of these films was their simulation of the experience of the popular stage, the concert hall, and the radio broadcast. Many of the first sound films looked like recordings of stage and radio routines, and film critics were often disparaging. In contrast to the "poetic" transcendence of the everyday associated with auteur films of the silent era, synchronous sound seemed limited to the brute reproduction of performances originating in other media. Prominent commentators, including Charlie Chaplin, Sergei Eisenstein, Erich von Stroheim, René Clair, Fernand Léger, and Luigi Pirandello, spoke for many in the artistic community in characterizing sound cinema as a recording medium rather than an art form.[4]

The sound cinema's capacity for recording was indeed impressive.

Like the first motion pictures of the 1890s, the sound films of the late 1920s offered a unique perceptual experience, manifest in a fascinating enlargement of aspects of everyday phenomenal life that ordinarily went unnoticed. Foremost here were the revelatory effects of electronic sound technology on the human voice. In France, critics coined the term "*phonogénie*" to refer to aspects of an actor's voice that became evident only when electronically recorded and reproduced. As one critic observed, "A recorded voice is no longer an ordinary human voice but an articulated sound, endowed with powers, properties, and faculties of expression that we had not known, while also deprived of certain of its former qualities."[5] In light of its singular capacity to reveal the fullness of phenomenal experience, to suggest a co-presence between viewer and actor, sound cinema was frequently discussed in connection with developments pending in film color, 3-D, and television—all heralded as contributions to humankind's ever-growing mimetic capability.[6] But just as the association with "realism" ensured sound cinema's status as a technological achievement, it served to exclude it from the realm of art. Rather than transforming reality into art, sound films made ordinary reality salient in unexpected ways. If sound films displayed artistry, it was in the recording of stage-derived art, rather than in creating art unique to cinema. Thus, as the cinema's conversion unfolded, silent films began to appear in a new context. Now juxtaposed against the new, astonishingly realistic sound films, silent films began to acquire the historicity associated with works of art. By the mid-1930s, film archives and cinematheques, devoted to film preservation and restoration, were founded in Europe and in the United States, thus laying foundations for subsequent film historiography.[7] The emergent sound cinema cast retrospective light on the cinema's past, to the point that the distinction between silent and sound film as understood today must be seen as a product of the changes wrought by the film industry's conversion.

An indication of sound technology's challenge to the idea of film as art can be found in a basic continuity in historical writings on the early sound period. The essential concern of much of this writing has been filmmakers' attempts to overcome the aesthetic limitations imposed by new technologies. For instance, to cite one prominent tendency, film-history surveys, since the 1930s, have emphasized the success of gifted directors—such as Rouben Mamoulian, Fritz Lang, René Clair, King Vidor, and Ernst Lubitsch—in harnessing sound technologies artistically. In these accounts, the heroic protagonists are exceptional artists who enabled the triumph of film art over advanced technology's resistance to aesthetic purposes. In recent decades, an alternative, academic historiography of film has situated the heroic achievements of extraordinary directors within the effects of broad, long-term industrial trends on film practice. Thus, in contemporary scholarly studies of sound conversion, the focus is on a relatively impersonal techno-industrial process, whereby synchronous sound is redefined; from its initial status as a wondrous technical novelty, synchronous sound has come to function as another narrative film technique—comparable to mainstream approaches to editing, cinematography and mise-en-scène. In any case, whether examined in terms of the achievements of exceptional artists or as an anonymous film-industrial process, conversion is widely seen as a development whereby sound technology was eventually brought into the fold of an aesthetic project unique to cinema.

The histories of earlier technologies of representation can likewise be understood in terms of the technologies' assimilation to artistic purpose, as has been the case with photography, the phonograph, and motion pictures of the 1890s—all of which contributed to as well as transformed the domain of art in ways that the technologies' inventors, as well as earlier user groups, could not have imagined. If the case of sound cinema seems unique, it is perhaps in the rapid, unidirectional nature of conversion and the uniformity of its impact worldwide. Rather than opening up aesthetic possibilities—as new technologies are sometimes credited with doing (e.g., magnetic-tape recorders circa 1960)—synchronous sound, a big-business monopoly, seemed to close them down, raising costs, mechanizing the studios and laboratories, and ultimately rendering the cinema less rather than more varied stylistically.[8] Moreover, the reduction in diversity appears to have occurred globally. By the mid-1930s, the majority of the world's films, regardless of where they had been made, came to exhibit the same basic conventions of film narration and style—the same sort of character-driven plots; linear, cause-and-effect successions of scenes; and continuity editing. Even the Soviet Union, famous during the 1920s for the radical montage experiments of Sergei Eisenstein, V. I. Pudovkin, Dziga Vertov, and other filmmaker-theorists, began producing conventional, character-centered narrative films by the mid-1930s.

The French cinema provides a particularly dramatic case in this regard, given the impressive field of styles that defined French filmmaking in the years prior to conversion. Paris, where the French film industry was based, functioned during the 1920s as one of the world's major film capitals. France was a favored destination for émigré artists and was unusually receptive to the notion of film as art, with an abundance of ciné-clubs, film journals, and art-house theatres. Moreover, in contrast to the situation in the United States, where a single, "classical" film style reigned as the industrywide norm (with established exceptions, such as slapstick comedy), the French film industry, with its fragmented production sector, produced films exemplifying a more profound stylistic diversity. Whereas institutionally integrated Hollywood was known for its capacity to assimilate international aesthetic and technical influences into a single trademark style, the French cinema's sprawling variety of small producers opened out onto a field of multiple styles, some jostling in self-conscious rivalry with others.[9] These styles encompassed the *impressionism* and *cinégraphie* identified with directors such as Germaine Dulac, Abel Gance, Jean Epstein, and Marcel L'Herbier, who pioneered modernist forms of cinematographic "writing"; an indigenous European classicism, familiar, for instance, in the serials directed by Louis Feuillade, defined by long takes and a deep-staged mise-en-scène; local, piecemeal adaptations of Hollywood's editing-based narrative style; and various fringe movements, ranging from the abstract, music-based *cinéma pur* of Henri Chomette, with its uncompromising formalism, to the countercultural surrealism of Luis Buñuel and its ironic subversion of narrative-film grammar. Compared to this extraordinary range of options, the new sound cinema looked monotonously uniform, as if to confirm that the new technologies permitted only one way of making a film. In France, the effects of the artistic constraints were dramatic. As film historian Colin Crisp puts it, the French cinema of the sound era, with its proliferation of stage-derived scripts and performances, seemed to rest on a rejection of "nine-tenths of the aesthetic possibilities open [to French filmmakers] and regularly practiced in the 1920s."[10]

Proponents of modernist and avant-garde filmmaking disparaged the evident theatricality of the sound cinema's stage-based scripts, studio sets, long takes, and distant camera positions. Also subject to criticism was the patently theatrical acting, evident, for instance, when actors performed as if framed by a stage proscenium, facing an auditorium of fans. (See Figure I.1.) Given the many films based on stage sources, sound cinema was commonly characterized as a return to the "famous-actors-in-famous-plays" narrative cinema that modernist and avant-garde filmmakers of the 1920s struggled to supersede. No longer the most sophisticated of the arts, French cinema in the sound era looked like a throwback to the filmed theatre of the years prior to World War I, as if the notion of film as a recorded performance had suddenly returned to prominence in France, to permeate the national film industry's output.[11] Moreover, the change appeared permanent, as a "filmed theatre" approach to sound cinema persisted in the French film industry through the 1930s, nearly a decade later than in Hollywood. As late as 1936, French film actors were said to engage in a theatrical playing style, adopting the theatrical convention of *l'aparté*, ("the aside") when "the protagonist suddenly testifies to the public, winks an eye in its direction, or tosses off a phrase as if to confide in it."[12] From the standpoint of the avant-gardist film culture, the new sound cinema, with its many moments of stage-inspired direct address, exhibited a virtually pre-cinematic character.

Sound-era commercial pressures were clearly unfavorable to the cinema's modernist and avant-garde movements—and to independent film production as a whole. For film historian Jean Mitry, conversion-era cinema was essentially an industrial rather than an aesthetic phenomenon, and thus, in contrast to the cinema of the 1920s, conversion-era cinema invited analysis in terms of large production companies rather than individual auteur directors.[13] Beyond the pervasive commercialism of sound-era film culture, the formal properties of the synch-sound image inhibited the development of idiosyncratic, personal styles—as filmmakers and theorists of the time were well aware. When sound and image were recorded at the same time—as in the highly popular talkies and *films parlants* ("talking films")—certain cinematographic and editing effects familiar to silent-era cinema became difficult or impossible to duplicate. Multiple superimpositions, lens-filtered images, color tinting and toning, and other cinematographic techniques with tendencies toward two-dimensionality, which had been a hallmark of silent-era cinema, proved incompatible with the phenomenology of the synch-sound film. Inevitably three-dimensional and relentlessly linear in temporality, synch-sound images entailed a straightforward, naturalistic narration and visual style. As one critic wrote, "The silent film, despite the excess of intertitles, had a power of suggestion, leaving the viewer

Fig. I.1. The conversion-era cinema's close links to the popular stage find an invocation in the tableau-like mise-en-scène of films such as *Il est charmant* (Louis Mercanton, 1931), a Paramount-Paris adaptation of a popular stage operetta. In light of the prevalence of this quasi-theatrical sort of mise-en-scène in French films of the early 1930s, sound cinema was frequently characterized in France as an aesthetic retreat to the "filmed theatre" of the 1900s.

open to the realm of dreams. The talking film offers a concrete world [*le film parlant precise*]."[14] The impact on editing was devastating; in many cases, shots in synch-sound films no longer connected according to established silent-era precedents. Many prominent montage innovations of the 1920s remained feasible in sound filmmaking only when the image was post-synchronized. For Abel Gance, René Clair, Marcel L'Herbier, and other film modernists, the mainstream film-industry approach to synch sound, with its emphasis on direct-recorded speech, counted as a repudiation of the figurative and "poetic" art-house films of the late silent era; hence, the familiar notion that sound cinema's technical advance had created an aesthetic backslide.[15]

Characterizations of the early sound cinema as aesthetically regressive typically approach the period solely from the perspective of the 1920s art cinema. Expanding the context for studying sound film to include not only the silent-era auteur cinema but also cognate media, such as the popular stage, radio, and the phonograph, illuminates the films of the early sound years differently. Cinema during conversion incorporated conventions borrowed from the new electronic media of radio and the electric gramophone, at a time when these conventions had just taken form. Thus even in its most commercial aspects, conversion-era cinema was itself highly experimental, and once sound's effects on the image are accounted for, can be seen to have exhibited a nearly bewildering diversity stylistically.[16] (See Figure I.2.) It wasn't until the mid-1930s that sound-film conventions became stabilized, and a single form of classicism began to define film practice worldwide; even then, sound-film practices seen today as alternatives to the mainstream survived throughout the 1930s and into later decades. The aim of this book is to analyze the founding moment in this ongoing history of aesthetic and technical diversity, and also to create a conceptual framework—via demonstrations of certain research methods and historiographical rules of thumb —that might assist the work of scholars concerned with national cinemas during the sound era, and with questions concerning technology's impact on cinema generally.

### The Comparative Project of This Book

The project of this book began with a set of questions raised by preliminary research into 1930s French filmmaking. Guiding these early explorations was the working hypothesis that the French cinema's distinctiveness relative to other national cinemas rested on a unique approach to sound-film technique. Work on this book began in earnest in 1997, when a research grant from Canada's Social Sciences and Humanities Research Council allowed me to visit Paris to examine numerous films and print documents relating to French sound-film technology and technique during the 1930s and 1940s. Viewing dozens of films at the Paris Vidéothèque, and study of the period's film-trade press, film journals, sound-film technical manuals, and film scripts at the Bibliothèque Nationale and Bibliothèque du Film, helped confirm my sense that film-sound techniques distinguished French films relative to contemporaneous Hollywood films—enough so, at least, to take on the task of writing a book on the topic. At the same time, evidence pertaining to

Fig. I.2. While the sound-era French film industry often relied on imported technologies and techniques, it did so in ways that sometimes departed radically from the precedent in other countries. One example concerns the practice of recording sound on location simultaneously with the image—a practice that was common in France but rare in the United States, Germany, Britain, Italy and other film-producing countries. In this production still for *Les amours de minuit* (Genina, 1930) mobile sound trucks outfitted with RCA Photophone equipment are shown being loaded onto a ship for location-shooting purposes. The same trucks were also used for the making of Pathé-Natan's newsreels, which, in contrast to those produced in other countries, featured direct-recorded rather than post-synchronized sound.

the diversity of conversion-era film practices pushed me ultimately to rethink certain assumptions, familiar to the discipline of film studies, which had shaped my initial approach to the topic of recorded sound's impact on national film style.

The modifications to my approach can be summarized in terms of two departures from the customary way of studying national cinema. First, rather than emphasize the work of a select group of canonized art-cinema filmmakers—as has been traditional in studies of the conversion years and in studies of national cinema generally—the examination undertaken here aims for inclusiveness, covering both auteur films *and* the bulk of France's mainstream popular cinema. As my research revealed, unusual sound techniques such as location-recorded sound, associated with auteur directors such as Jean Renoir and Marcel Pagnol, had permeated French film production of the 1930s. Hence, this book encompasses a relatively large sampling of the national output of the time, that is, some sixty French feature films made between 1930 and 1933. In the following chapters, dozens of forgotten films are examined; familiar auteur masterpieces are also situated in unfamiliar contexts of mainstream film-industry practices of their time and place.

The second modification concerns the decision to approach French film in an explicitly comparative framework, whereby French film style is contrasted to contemporaneous American practice. Initially, I had thought of my project as a history of French film that would analyze conversion-era filmmaking relative to the national film practices of later decades. It seemed to me that a study of conversion-era film practice might open an important new context for seeing, and hearing, the French films of subsequent periods—such as the *nouvelle vague* (new wave) of the late 1950s and early 1960s, in which certain of the most innovative films were defined by sound techniques familiar to the national cinema of the 1930s. Through my work on this book, I have been persuaded that a full-length study of the postwar history of French sound-film practice will be rewarding, and in this book's conclusion I offer suggestions concerning how such a study might be constructed. But as my research into the conversion period evolved, I found it increasingly difficult to separate the conversion-era French cinema from analogous developments in other countries. In short, it seemed that to make sense of what had happened in France, it was necessary to consider what had been happening simultaneously outside of France. Particularly relevant were developments in the United States and in Germany, the countries providing much of the world's film-sound technology, whose film industries competed intensely for shares of the French film market. I eventually decided that before undertaking a full-scale examination of the history of French film practice since the 1930s, a study situating French practices relative to contemporaneous practices in the United States and Germany was needed. In light of this shift in perspective, I began to see my research into conversion-era filmmaking in France both as a contribution to French film history and as a case study on sound conversion worldwide. By now, the key questions concerned less what happened in France over the course of historical time (however pertinent and intriguing this study may be) than what happened across geographical space, in the French and American cinemas particularly, during a decisive, transitional period in film and media history.

This shift in thinking is manifest most clearly in this book's openly comparative approach to the historical evidence. My analysis juxtaposes research into French filmmaking with recent scholarship on sound practice in the contemporaneous American cinema, situating the French cinema in the context of national differences in how filmmakers coped with the artistic and technical challenges posed by sound technology. My hope is that this book's analysis of national film-sound practice—though immersed in the particularities of the French case—might provide a historiographical and methodological point of reference, or at least an inventory of research questions and examples, for scholars working on the early sound years in other film-producing countries, who, while confronting substantially different empirical phenomena, must also contend with questions relating to the national adaptation of imported technologies, techniques, and films and to cinema's links with other media.

## Summary of Chapters

In the following overview, the analysis of the early sound years within a framework of national comparisons is presented in terms of the investigations undertaken in specific chapters. In chapter 1, the key issue concerns the familiar claim that film practice and style became homogenized worldwide during the 1930s. When it is agreed that homogenization occurred, what exactly is being agreed to? The question arises in light of sound conversion's multifacetedness as an object of study, encompassing industrial, aesthetic, social, technological, and cultural-political aspects, and offering multiple forms and methods of analysis. Aiming to clarify claims regarding sound technology's effects on film style, chapter 1 attempts to disaggregate sound conversion as an object of study, separating out six topics in conversion-era film culture familiar to the homogenization account. These topics include the standardization of the technology, the worldwide popularity of the first sound films, the trend toward film-industrial integration, new exhibition practices, Hollywood's hegemonic capacity to inspire emulation in other countries, and sound-era changes in film style. The investigation examines the case for homogenization critically, although its basic objective is less to disprove the case than to bring about a change of perspective that allows for a new interpretation of the historical evidence. As a juxtaposition of the French and American cases suggests, sameness at the level of technologies, techniques, and filmic exemplars may nonetheless coincide with diversity in how those exemplars were interpreted. Resting on the principle that study of the worldwide diffusion of sound-era films, technologies, and filmmaking methods must include inquiry into the place-specific ways in which those methods were understood, the chapter surveys international trends, while foregrounding national differences in conversion-era film practice and style.

Whereas chapter 1 surveys evidence concerning conversion's effects on film style, chapter 2 examines alternative approaches to how the evidence has been understood. The investigation begins with the observation that although initially sound conversion was defined exclusively in terms of dramatic, crisis-like events, in the most important studies of recent years the focus has shifted toward film-industrial and aesthetic structures that remained constant over decades of historical time. Yet in contrast to current scholarship on Hollywood's conversion, with its emphasis on aesthetic and industrial continuity, the French cinema's conversion continues to be understood as a radical break from the national cinema's past. The objective in chapter 2 is to show that when the French cinema is defined inclusively, to encompass the mainstream popular cinema and its decades-old notion of a scene as the recording of a performance, then sound conversion's impact in France begins to show up differently, as important aesthetic and industrial continuities between French silent-era and sound-era practices become evident. A case in point is provided by the sound-era French cinema's close relations with popular theatre, which marks both a break from the film modernism of the 1920s and a return to the stage-allied, long-take style of the French cinema of the 1910s. As critics stressed, the sound cinema seemed both new and old, with the theatrical adaptations of the *révolution du parlant* ("talkie revolution") exhibiting what amounted to a counterrevolutionary aspect, whereby an evidently outdated, supposedly theatre-bound film style unexpectedly acquired a second life in the national cinema, to the point of becoming the latter's dominant style in the sound era.

Following on chapter 2's emphasis on film technology's embeddedness in local, place-specific contexts of understanding, chapter 3 pursues questions of national film practice from a reception-oriented angle, via an inquiry into the significance of imported films for the French film community during conversion. National cinemas are customarily defined in terms of films made in a country rather than films shown there. But in the case of conversion, when Europe's film-producing countries relied on imported films to fill the new sound theatres, especially in 1929 and continuing through 1930, an investigation into technology's impact on film style, benefits from an expanded definition of national cinema, with domestic productions situated within the range of films shown in a country. The chapter's investigation centers on French critical commentary concerning two key films of the early sound years: *The Jazz Singer* (dir. Alan Crosland, 1927), the legendary Vitaphone film that was released in Paris in January 1929; and *Le chemin du paradis* (*The Road to Paradise,* dir. Wilhelm von Thiele and Max de Vaucorbeil, 1930), a highly successful French-language version of a German-made operetta, which premiered in Paris in November 1930. In examining these exemplars as rival sound-film styles, chapter 3 explores the logic governing the distinctive manner in which sound cinema was understood in France, as well as the latter's implications for the nature of the viewing experience. Chapter 3 concludes with an inquiry into the unexpected fate of the two predominant styles in French filmmaking. Although often denigrated by critics, the filmed-theatre style associated with *The Jazz Singer* soon came to dominate France's mainstream cinema of the 1930s; in contrast, the music-based style of German operettas such as *Le chemin du paradis,* and the early sound films directed by René Clair, inspired minimal emulation in France, notwithstanding the fervent support for this style from film modernists and its impressive commercial and critical success, both at home and internationally. The mainstream French cinema was oriented toward the production of "national" films for domestic consumption, and hence via diverse invocations of the actors' profiles in other national media, toward a very different, evidently "theatrical" film style.

The book's remaining chapters analyze the mainstream filmed-theatre style through a series of investigations into the singular manner in which imported techniques and technologies were adapted in the French film industry. In terms of historical method, a principle similar to that of chapter 3 applies: just as a film must be examined relative to how it was understood by critics in particular places and times, film technologies and techniques must be understood according to the variety of context-dependent ways in which they were interpreted by filmmakers. This principle informs chapter 4's use of statistical analysis to illuminate editing-related differences between French and American filmmaking. On the one hand, Hollywood-identified editing techniques became increasingly widespread by the late 1930s, practiced in film-producing countries throughout the world—including France. On the other hand, as shown in chapter 4, French films, products of the national film industry's highly fragmented production sector, ended up looking and sounding differently from Hollywood films. Concerning editing specifically, continuity rules proved far less determinate than in Hollywood; montage techniques characteristic of the modernist and avant-garde cinemas of the late silent era resurfaced in modified form; and, most fundamentally, scenes were often filmed in long takes rather than constructed out of separate shots. As the chapter's analysis reveals, even in cases where the editing techniques were similar, the viewer's understanding of filmic space and time may have varied significantly, depending on the nature of the sound accompaniment.

In chapter 5, the French cinema's distinctiveness relative to the Hollywood cinema is situated at the level of recording methods. Here, the fundamental issue concerns the emphasis in French filmmaking on sound's fidelity as a reproduction of a performance. Long after Hollywood had switched over to a basically different conception of film sound, which stressed sound's contribution to a film's illusion of story-world wholeness, sound filmmaking in France continued to be understood in terms of the task of recording actors' performances. An intriguing circumstance behind this basic national difference in sound-film practice is the use in the two film industries of identical technologies—the same sound recorders, ribbon microphones, blimped cameras, and other devices. A methodological implication, supported by a close examination of conversion-era film practices, is that an assessment of sound technology's impact on film style must contextualize technologies and techniques in terms of how the latter were adapted in specific localities, where they may well have served novel purposes.

In chapter 6, topics covered in previous chapters are brought together in a study of production practices at a particular studio in Paris: the Joinville facility of Pathé-Natan, the largest production firm in France during conversion. Pathé-Natan emulated Paramount's "vertically integrated" coordination of production operations with the market demands of a large theatre chain, making Pathé-Natan atypical of the internally divided French film industry of the 1930s, whose production and exhibition sectors worked in conflict with one another rather than in the coordinated fashion associated with Hollywood. Nonetheless, given the centrality of Pathé-Natan's Joinville facility for French film production as a whole, the entirety of the contemporaneous French cinema was affected by Pathé-Natan's industrial concentration. In subsequent historiography, Pathé-Natan has been denigrated for allegedly lowering the national cinema's quality. But as this chapter shows, the kind of filmmaking practiced at Joinville—a studio complex oriented mainly toward making films for the French market—proved foundational for the sound-era French cinema. The chapter concludes with an inquiry into multiple-camera shooting at Pathé-Natan's studio complex at Joinville. At issue is the case of a Hollywood technique that ended up functioning differently in French filmmaking. Discontinued in Hollywood by 1931, multiple-camera shooting endured at Joinville, and in French filmmaking generally, throughout the 1930s. Moreover, the technique was occasionally used in a highly innovative way, as in the many scenes in numerous films made at Pathé-Natan's Joinville studios featuring discontinuous cuts, including those involving total reversals in screen direction. In short, whereas Hollywood films subordinate editing technique to storytelling objectives, the films made at Pathé-Natan's Joinville studios suggest an alternative approach, whereby editing serves not just to construct a story but to inject kinesis into a mise-en-scène that might otherwise seem insufficiently cinematic.

The book's conclusion returns to the question of the significance of French practices for sound conversion worldwide through a brief examination of the legacy of conversion-era film practice in contemporary cinema. At issue is a question that has surfaced intermittently throughout the preceding chapters: How has the direct-sound approach of French films of the 1930s affected filmmaking in later periods, including the present? Or, put otherwise, how have later generations of filmmakers used, and transformed, the national cinema's foundational sound-film techniques? As the conclusion shows, old sound-film techniques endure into the present, where, in new industrial and aesthetic circumstances, they continue to distinguish French films relative to those from other film-producing countries.

# 1 Sound's Impact on Film Style: The Case for Homogenization

As an object of film-historical study, sound conversion, with its outstandingly complex mix of forces and conditions, imposes formidable demands. In accounting for the effects of sound-film technology's diffusion across national borders, the challenge of understanding and explanation is extraordinary enough in the case of the Hollywood cinema; it may seem overwhelming when the inquiry is extended beyond the United States.

Nonetheless, an overall pattern of change appears evident internationally, to the point that film historians are largely in agreement regarding sound conversion's impact on film style worldwide. The consensus, in broad outline, is that the cinema's stylistic range was significantly reduced after sound conversion, so by the mid-1930s narrative films everywhere exhibited the same basic norms of narration and style.

This familiar narrative of homogenization can be elaborated as follows. With respect to film-industrial change, sound conversion served to concentrate power in cartels of vertically integrated film companies, whose unprecedented dependence on financing from large banks imposed new needs for cost-efficient production methods. As film-production practices became increasingly preplanned, budgeted, and standardized, control over the filmmaking process shifted away from film directors and toward cost-conscious, studio-employed producers. Although first evident in the United States, a standardized approach to filmmaking soon became manifest internationally, as Hollywood's studio system inspired emulation in Germany, Great Britain, France, the Soviet Union, and other film-producing countries. The key result with respect to film style, evident by mid-decade, was a drastic reduction in the cinema's range of stylistic options, as the variety of national film styles that had coexisted during the 1920s ceded place to a single, editing-based style, practiced in the majority of the world's film-producing countries—from the United States to France, Germany, the Soviet Union, Japan, India, and Mexico.

In this chapter's analysis, the homogenization narrative is examined relative to the substance of the French case. A critique is undertaken of certain familiar claims regarding the sound cinema's alleged uniformity internationally; the objective, however, is less to refute the familiar account than to construct a new framework for the study of sound cinema, one enabling a more differentiated, fine-tuned assessment of sound conversion's effects on world cinema. Sound-era homogenization could be said to have occurred in a variety of domains—including film styles, film-exhibition practices, modes of industrial organization, film-production methods, and design of sound-film technologies. Separating the topic of sound conversion into subtopics, the following survey distinguishes among domains of film-historical change and discriminates among claims regarding the cinema's sound-era convergence. In thus disaggregating the conversion period as a research topic, this chapter foregrounds the period's internal contradictions in ways that complicate familiar assumptions concerning sound technology's impact on film style. It demonstrates that homogenization in one domain did not necessarily entail it elsewhere, that advances in one area sometimes produced retreat in another, and that particular national cinemas converged in some respects with Hollywood practice while diverging in other ways. The basic historiographical implication is that the impression of homogenization reflects not the realities of sound conversion so much as the established way in which those realities have been understood.

In what follows, six aspects of conversion-era cinema important to the homogenization thesis are briefly examined: (1) the effect of corporate patent ownership on technological standardization; (2) the worldwide notoriety of the first sound films; (3) the trend toward film-industrial concentration; (4) new exhibition practices; (5) Hollywood's hegemonic capacity to inspire emulation by filmmakers in other countries; and (6) the homogenization of film style. The examination of each domain is selective, with a focus on aspects relevant to the general topic of sound technology's impact on film style. The examples refer mainly to American and French practices, though in ways intended to bring out their significance for sound conversion globally.

## Technological Standardization

The claim that world cinema became homogenized during the 1930s finds support in the successful efforts of a few large conglomerates to control worldwide ownership of the basic technologies of sound recording and reproduction. In their negotiations with one another, the major technology suppliers treated technological standardization as a principal goal. Thus, the Paris Sound-Film Peace Treaty of June 1930 (the Paris Treaty), which effectively set in place the economic framework for sound conversion worldwide, stipulated that film-sound technologies be made "interchangeable" so that a film produced by any of the Paris Treaty's parties could be recorded and shown using any patented equipment. As a matter of survival, non-signatories to the Paris Treaty were required to conform to the pact, as in the case of the French firm Gaumont, whose projector, the "Idéal Sonore" (patented in 1929), was designed in line with Treaty standards but in conflict with Gaumont's earlier patents.[1]

The standards were set by a small group of large electronics conglomerates: Western Electric, the well-financed manufacturing subsidiary of American Telephone and Telegraph; RCA (the Radio Corporation of America), a new subsidiary of General Electric and Western Electric's main rival in the United States; and Tobis-Klangfilm, a Dutch-German combine, financed by Dutch and Swiss sources and backed by research and technical support from the Allgemeine Elektrizitäts Gesellschaft (AEG), Germany's largest electrical manufacturer. Just as RCA had been formed to compete with Western Electric in the United States, Tobis-Klangfilm had been formed to block Western Electric's potential monopoly on patents in Europe.[2] Comprising an American-German cartel, these three companies, via the Paris Treaty, effectively redrew the map of world cinema, partitioning the globe into thirty-three countries and regions, with designated cartel members allowed to charge film companies royalties within designated territories.[3] The United States, Canada, India, Australia, New Zealand, and the Soviet Union were assigned to Western Electric and RCA, whereas Germany, Austria, Switzerland, Holland, the Dutch East Indian colonies, Scandinavia, and the Balkan countries were put under the dominion of Tobis-Klangfilm. The lucrative

British market, with its large number of sound-ready theatres, was split one-third for Tobis-Klangfilm and two-thirds for Western Electric and RCA. The rest of the world was declared an arena of direct competition, with France, the largest of the sixteen open countries, serving as the principal contested zone in the global struggle over sound-film profits. For the export-oriented American and German film industries, both of which invested heavily in the making of French-language films, France was a crucial market.

Business agreements such as the Paris Treaty imposed new limits on the cinema's basic technological parameters, with profound consequences for film exhibition and film style. Issues relating to technology owner-ship were formidable in France, where foreign companies controlled the majority of the key sound-film patents, and local companies, with the partial exception of Gaumont, were only minimally involved in agreements such as the Paris Treaty. In France during the early 1930s, numerous small and medium-sized local companies marketed up to forty sound-film systems—the majority of which involved disc-playing phonographs.[4] With a few important exceptions such as Radio-Cinéma (founded in 1929), which had been developed by the T.S.F., the national French radio company, these devices did not use French patents. In any case, in the Paris Treaty's aftermath, sound-on-disc projection became obsolete, and the number of French sound-film-technology companies dropped radically within a few years, leaving the three conglomerates of the American-German cartel to dominate the sound-film-technology market in France.[5]

Insofar as stylistic homogenization can be said to have occurred, tech-nological standardization must be seen as an important condition. But is the former to be seen as an inevitable consequence of the latter, as if, given technological standardization, a flattening of stylistic differences must necessarily result? One holds off from answering yes to this ques-tion insofar as it requires an assumption that the technologies somehow determined their own applications—so that the diffusion of the tech-nologies was enough to ensure sameness in their use. In fact, however, basic sound technologies—disc players, loudspeakers, microphones, tube amplifiers, photo-electric cells, and so on—had all been developed out-side the film industry, in the context of diverse communications-related endeavors, and thus had to be adapted, and even remade, for filmmaking purposes. Considerable trial-and-error efforts were involved, whereby technologies were reinterpreted in light of film-cultural concerns and activities, redesigned for film-specific tasks, and then put to use in ways that the technologies' inventors, and their earlier user-groups, could not have anticipated. Moreover, the film-cultural conditions shaping the adaptation effort were by no means uniform from one national film industry to the next—particularly during the conversion years, when multiple approaches to sound-film practice coexisted in a state of rivalry. In sum, to assess the technologies' impact on filmmaking requires examining the diverse ways in which technologies were used, in specific times and places.

One can begin by drawing a basic distinction between how conversion unfolded in the United States and how it occurred in other national film industries. In the United States, the film industry was uniquely characterized by institutional integration, which enabled coordinated efforts to ensure that new technologies in the national film industry were adapted according to established aesthetic and technical norms. Working together within the context of a common, industrywide project, via film-industry institutions ranging from special committees to professional organizations and trade journals, personnel from different studios collaborated with equipment supply companies, devising ways to soundproof sets, cameras, and lamps.[6] These organized, coordinated efforts ensured an industrywide uniformity in Hollywood's conversion that was unique among the world's film industries. In many countries, propitious circumstances were lacking for the sort of coordinated, industrywide effort characteristic of Hollywood's conversion. In the institutionally fragmented French film industry, for instance, structural conditions ensured perpetual conflict between the film industry's production and exhibition sectors, and sound-film practices varied from studio to studio, and from one small-scale production team to the next. As a consequence, sound technologies were generally used in France in a selective and piecemeal fashion, and in ways informed by a wide variety of aesthetic norms—some of which differed radically from Hollywood's norms.

The conversion to sound illustrates a familiar phenomenon in the history of media technology, whereby major media-technological changes tend to occur only when conditions limit the changes' capacity to threaten established business activities and interests. One way to characterize this circumstance is in terms of what media historian Brian Winston refers to as "the 'law' of the suppression of radical potential," a historiographical rule of thumb according to which a technology's commercialization becomes likely only when established economic powers are confident of controlling the commercialization's potential disruption of the economic status quo.[7] A similar point has been made by Douglas Gomery, who sees film-technological change in terms of a three-stage process whereby the crucial movement from a technology's invention to its more costly innovation and diffusion—that is, its commercialization and adoption throughout the film industry—can occur only when the change appears favorable for the industry's long-term financial stability.[8] In Gomery's account, sound conversion, after a protracted, decades-long period of invention, was innovated and diffused relatively quickly during the late 1920s, when industrial conditions in the United States had evolved so that the sound cinema's potential profits seemed likely to exceed the costs of upsetting established film-industry practice. What must be stressed in the context of this book's comparative project is the extent to which the sort of constraints stressed by Gomery and Winston were place-specific, varying substantially from one film industry to the next. If all conversion-era film industries, newly indebted to large banks, approached the new technologies in a fundamentally conservative manner, so as to limit the disruption of business-as-usual and ensure necessary returns on their investments, the conservatism nonetheless became manifested in highly localized forms. In film-producing countries other than the United States, where conditions for sound-technological adaptation were sometimes fragmentary, ad hoc, and provisional, new technologies were open to interpretations that diverged from norms of the American film industry. For instance, as will be detailed in later chapters, important French production companies such as Pathé-Natan and Braunberger-Richebé, while relying on technologies from RCA and Western Electric, did so in ways that often departed substantially from Hollywood precedents, with significant stylistic consequences.

## International Notoriety of the First Sound Films

Also contributing to the impression of sound-era homogenization was the universal popularity of the first sound films, which generated media hype, critical interest, and ticket sales wherever they were shown. In 1929, the first year of sound-film exhibition in Europe, audiences in London, Paris, Berlin, and other European capitals waited in long lines at a small number of first-run theatres to buy tickets for screenings that ran throughout the day and evening. Regardless of the high admission prices—and, by some accounts, the mixed quality of the films and the projection—sound movies generated extraordinary profits for the few theatres able and willing to pay for equipment licensing fees and other conversion costs. As with the early, turn-of-the-century *actualités,* with their revelatory views of everyday life, or the magical transformations of the trick film à la Georges Méliès, the appeal of sound films was inseparable from the sheer novelty of the technology's effects. In the case of the sound films of the late 1920s, effects associated with innovations in electronics were especially noteworthy. The sound cinema's impression of radio-broadcast liveness was revelatory; even newsreels drew a sensational audience response.

One effect of the initial flood of box-office profits was the perception that cinema, supported by rapid growth in the gramophone and radio industries, was irreversibly "moving forward" during the early sound years. In the United States, film attendance is estimated to have nearly doubled between 1926 and 1930, and to have reached a level during the 1930s of one visit per week for each American.[9] Dramatic attendance increases were also reported in other countries.[10] In Paris during 1930, a 33 percent rise in box-office receipts was attributed solely to the screening of sound films in the city's several dozen sound-equipped theatres; concerning the top twelve theatres, the first six months of 1930 marked an astonishing leap in revenue from 59 to 77 percent over the first half of 1929.[11] The disproportionate income from the tiny number of sound theatres demonstrated recorded sound's inevitability for the future of the national film industry, whatever the aesthetic gains and losses.

The extent to which this future required conceptualization in global terms became evident in the film trade-press, where sound conversion was often discussed in a comparative manner, with the American film industry providing the standard for measuring developments elsewhere, industrially and aesthetically. For many countries, films from the United States were often key to the idea of sound cinema. The United States, the world's first major sound-film producer, had a two- to four-year lead on Europe's major national film industries, which began experimenting with producing sound films commercially only in 1929—three years after the first Vitaphone productions. By then, the American film industry, which was already close to monopolizing distribution in parts of Europe, exported a backlog of dozens of sound features to countries with sound-equipped theatres. In Europe, where such theatres were often inaugurated with exclusive showings of American films, sound cinema was commonly regarded as a product of the American film industry.[12] As novelist Paul Morand said, "A Frenchman invented the cinema but the Americans have invented the talking cinema."[13]

The circulation of American talkies across the globe ensured that audiences outside the United States came to understand the artistic potential of sound cinema with reference to a relatively limited corpus of "A-picture" exports from the United States. If this circumstance can be regarded as necessary for the cinema's sound-era homogenization, was it sufficient? That is, did the playing of the same American films in sound-equipped theatres around the world necessarily mean that the cinema, including the culture of moviegoing, was becoming more homogenous internationally? To answer yes would seem to presuppose that American films meant the same thing from place to place. But as with the film-industrial adaptation of sound technology, such uniformity seems unlikely. Not only did film-cultural conditions vary from one country to the next—in some cases, quite substantially—but the American films in question were designed for export and thus required effacement of certain American particularities so as to invite interpretation in local terms. In a study of Hollywood's export market during the interwar years, Ruth Vasey discusses how American films were made to enable appropriation according to local tastes and cultural traditions; thus, these films tended to minimize the amount of dialogue, instead conveying their narratives through a style emphasizing editing and visual action.[14] With respect to film production outside the United States, national differences evident in popular remakes of Hollywood films suggest the extent to which local traditions of art and entertainment shaped the ways in which American films were understood. *The Jazz Singer* (dir. Alan Crosland, 1927) is said to have inspired both the Japanese-made *Furusato* (*Hometown,* dir. Kenji Mizoguchi, 1931) and the French-made *La route est belle* (dir. Robert Florey, 1929); but the Japanese film's modernist style differs considerably from the French film's classical theatricality.

As with issues concerning sound-film technology, inquiry into how the diffusion of sound films across national borders affected film styles requires an analysis sensitive to the place-contingent manner in which the films were understood. Regarding countries where languages other than English were dominant, the emulation effort could entail significant ambivalence. In France, for instance, where demand for native French-language productions was extremely high in the early 1930s, and remained consistently strong throughout the decade, the French film industry attempted to appropriate Hollywood's film style, but in ways conditioned by the project of producing films that could count as national alternatives to Hollywood films. Unlike the major export-oriented film companies in the United States and Germany, French producers typically set their sights exclusively on the domestic market. Thus, Pathé-Natan, the largest French production company of the early 1930s, produced few foreign-language versions, and dubbed none of its films for foreign release; the demand in France for French-language films was sufficiently strong to require only success in the home market for the company to reap massive profits. Likewise, Pierre Braunberger and Roger Richebé, upon opening their Western Electric–equipped studio in June 1930, stated their intent to supply the home market exclusively: they would not produce foreign-language versions of their films nor did they plan to modify their films for international distribution.[15] The strategy of producing films for domestic consumption carried important implications for film style. Filmmakers in France were relieved from the need to limit dialogue, to minimize national cultural references, and to ensure that a comedy or drama would be intelligible to viewers unfamiliar with the films' sources in popular French theatre. In the French film-production context, departures from Hollywood style, or parodic invocations of it, could serve to distinguish French films favorably for French audiences. (See Figure 1.1.)

## The Trend toward Media Amalgamation

Basic changes in the structure of the world's film industries added to the perception that national film-style differences were flattened during the 1930s. Most fundamental was the trend toward media-industrial concentration, whereby single companies, financed by large bank loans, assumed ownership of media businesses that hitherto had functioned independently, massing them together to form vast media-industrial combines. Exemplary in this regard was the emulation in numerous countries' film industries of the "vertical integration" characteristic of

Fig. 1.1. The emulation in Europe's film industries of American film practice during the early sound years, when the translation of Hollywood conventions into national entertainment idioms became widespread, entailed an ambivalence that sometimes exhibited an ironic aspect, as is suggested by this brief scene in the Braunberger-Richebé romantic comedy *Je serai seule d'après minuit* (Jacques de Baroncelli, 1931), in which the film's farcical "battle of the sexes" shows up in a parody of a wild-west shoot out.

Hollywood's studio system. In such a system, production companies distributed their films to their own theatre chains, thereby effectively controlling the entire chain of production, distribution, and exhibition, which helped guarantee the large, regular income needed to pay the loan installments and other conversion costs. In many countries, the expansion of film companies through vertical restructuring defined film-industrial change during the sound years. In Great Britain, for instance, Associated British Pictures and Gaumont-British—vertical combines with large theatre holdings—were created in 1928 and 1929, respectively.[16] In Germany, the Ufa company had been vertically integrated since the late teens, providing an institutional basis for further film-industrial concentration in Europe during conversion.[17] Most notably, in March 1929, the Dutch company Tobis (Tonbild Syndicat) merged with

German Klangfilm to create the new Tobis-Klangfilm, which dominated the sound-film-technology market in Northern and Central Europe during the 1930s—from Scandinavia through the Balkans.[18] In France, two new combines, Pathé-Natan (1929) and Gaumont-Franco-Film-Aubert (1930), established a degree of vertical integration in French filmmaking that had not been seen since the years before World War I.

But if the push toward industrial concentration appears universal, questions remain concerning the particularities of its impact on film style. Film-industrial concentration occurred in multiple forms. In addition to vertically integrating production with exhibition, film-industrial concentration also typically entailed the "horizontal" linkage of film companies with other entertainment businesses, including radio, phonograph recording, illustrated magazines, sheet-music publishing, and the popular stage. As conversion unfolded, film companies entered into agreements with stage producers, founding or purchasing radio stations, recording studios, music publishing houses, phonograph companies, and fan magazines. (See Figure 1.2.)

The conversion-era cinema's interconnectedness with other entertainment media powerfully conditioned the notion, widely shared among film critics, that synchronous sound had undermined the art of film. Many critical judgments against early sound film cite the cinema's evident links to the popular stage and also to the new electronic media of radio and the electric phonograph. Like the early filmed photoplays of the 1900s, sound cinema—with its many reproductions of stage, radio, and gramophone acts—often looked like a rough, unfinished composite of other media rather than a self-sufficient art form. To borrow a term from early cinema studies, sound cinema exhibited a high degree of "intermediality"—a formal hybridity evident in the clash of aesthetic and technical norms associated both with cinema and with multiple, extra-cinematic media.[19] While cinema had evolved relative to other entertainment forms since its fairground beginnings, conversion-era cinema was notable for the extent to which the cinema's unresolved relations with other media became manifest in the films themselves. Featuring stars, styles, and program formats culled from other media, and sometimes—as in the case of "revues" such as *Paramount on Parade* (dir. Charles de Rochefort, 1930)—employing variety-show shifts in genre and style from scene to scene, the new sound films often seemed far less unified aesthetically, and hence "cinematic," when compared to films of

Fig. 1.2. *A nous la liberté* (René Clair, 1931), with its rags-to-riches story of a vagabond turned phonograph-industry magnate, is the most famous of the many conversion-era films alluding to the cinema's new links with the cognate sound-entertainment media of the electric gramophone and radio—both of which underwent rapid growth in France simultaneously with the sound-film boom.

the late silent years. In the judgment of many conversion-era critics, highly sensitive to differences between sound and silent cinema, the sound cinema's commercial interconnectedness with other media made sound films seem artistically derivative.

The cinema's sound-related integration into an entertainment system encompassing radio, theatre, and the phonograph industry occurred in countries around the world during the 1930s. In Theodor Adorno and Max Horkheimer's seminal analysis (1947) of this development, the sound-era amalgamation throughout North America and Western Europe of "movies, radio, jazz, and magazines" signaled a flattening of cultural difference that occurred worldwide, as if all media were converging into a single, totalizing "culture industry."[20] The general claim regarding the international trend toward media amalgamation draws attention to a film-historical development of inescapable importance. Essentially a corporate, big-business project, sound conversion had the effect of pushing to the margins artists unwilling or unable to adapt to the constraints of studio filmmaking. But did media amalgamation during the early sound years necessarily serve to homogenize film style? Given national variations in relations among the new sound media, answers to this question are anything but predictable. Consider, for instance, national differences in the use of recorded music on film soundtracks. In the case of the role of songs in American cinema, a linear pattern of development is evident. During the late 1920s, recorded songs were prevalent in the American sound films; but they had largely disappeared by 1931, at the culmination of Hollywood's conversion, when the American film industry curtailed the production of revue musicals and began standardizing the making of orchestral scores for films. By 1933, music no longer functioned as a special attraction à la the recorded pop song but instead became integrated into a film's overall formal design, via a romantic symphonic score, in a manner comparable to Hollywood feature films of the 1920s.[21] In other film-producing countries, however, such as France, recorded pop tunes remained essential to film soundtracks up through the mid-1930s. It is difficult to think of a French film of the 1930s that doesn't feature a popular song, just as it is difficult to think of a French film of the period with a contemporary setting that doesn't include a moment when a character places a needle on a spinning phonograph. (See Figure 1.3.) Links between the film and phonograph industries were strong in 1929, at the outset of the national cinema's conversion, when the recorded-music industry, spurred by introduction of electric recording in 1925, had another year of record-breaking sales.[22] According to one analysis of music- and film-industry documentation, popular songs released on 78-rpm discs featured in more than half of the French films made between 1930 and 1933.[23] These recordings were often released in numerous versions by a wide variety of French and foreign labels—including Pathé, Gramophone, Parlophone, Polydor, Decca, Odéon, Columbia, and Perfectaphone, to name some prolific companies, in both vocal and instrumental versions. According to the author of the weekly "*disques et musiques*" column in *La cinématographie française*, the market during 1931 was saturated with nearly one thousand film-related recordings.[24] A limit case can be found in the hit musical film *Il est charmant* (*He Is Charming*, dir. Louis Mercanton, 1931), whose ten songs were released in a total of fifty-three recorded versions.[25]

In Paris, cinema and theatre competed directly for the same audi-

Fig. 1.3. Conversion-era films starring high-profile recording artists such as singer-actor Henri Garat were replete with references to the stars' profile in other media. An example is the Garat vehicle *Le prince de minuit* (René Guissart, 1934), a romantic comedy set in a record shop that includes among the its musical numbers this flight of fancy in which a routine day at work is broken by the lovers' waltz on a giant spinning gramophone disc.

ence, and the radio and phonograph industries evolved rapidly with the new sound-film industry.[26] The young audiences that increasingly preferred films over stage entertainment also listened to radio and purchased phonograph records. A significant number of the sound-film actors came from the music hall—including stars such as Josephine Baker, Jean Gabin, Arletty, Florelle, and Albert Préjean, who also performed on the radio and released film-related 78-rpm discs. (See Figure 1.3.) The sound cinema's intermediality registered in the materiality of sound and image, a mix of norms and techniques that suggested a kind of entertainment composite—"the union of cinema, music hall, and jazz," according to one Parisian critic.[27] (See Figure 1.4.)

The proliferation of recorded songs on French film soundtracks points to how sound-era industrial concentration made a distinctive film-

Fig. 1.4. Like many French film stars of the 1930s, singer-comic Georges Milton was known to his fans through his ongoing presence in other media, including radio—a circumstance alluded to in this production still from *Le roi du cirage* (Pière Colombier, 1932), a film ranked by French exhibitors as one of the most popular of the year.

stylistic impact in France. In the United States, conversion's occurrence years after the film industry's industrial integration enabled the domestication of sound technology in terms of established aesthetic and technical norms. By 1931, a film's theatrical, musical, and filmic elements became incorporated into the American cinema's established, editing-based interpretation of the norms of classical narration. In France, however, where film-industrial integration occurred relatively late, filmmaking, in significant respects, remained a cottage industry throughout the 1930s. As a consequence, old conversion-era practices endured, and recorded songs continued to permeate the mainstream cinema through the mid-1930s, featuring in operettas and other types of musicals but also in dramatic films, including the many melodramas featuring *chanteuses réalistes* ("realist singers") such as Damia, Frehel, and Line Noro.[28] It was late in the decade that French films came routinely to exhibit an integrated musical style comparable to the Hollywood cinema—after the film-industrial combines of the conversion years had collapsed, and

French film production had splintered into a multiplicity of small companies. In short, industrial concentration during the 1930s worked differently in France than in the United States, opening the cinema to apparently extra-cinematic norms, techniques, and genres, and thus making French film style additive rather than unified, still fragmented through the cinema's unfinished relations with other media.

## New Exhibition Practices

With respect to claims for the cinema's sound-era homogenization, film exhibition practices, which underwent an unprecedented and permanent standardization throughout the world during the 1930s, provide strong though ambivalent evidence. A key issue concerns the standardization of camera and projection speeds, which tightly locked sound to image in a way that transformed the latter's phenomenology—to the point of altering the very nature of the film experience. The standardization of camera and projection speeds during conversion is rightfully regarded as a major event in the history of film style, given the fundamental differences from silent practice.[29] During the silent era, hand-operated cameras and projectors had allowed films to be made and shown at a variety of speeds.[30] In some cases, significant national differences were evident. In France, for instance, films were reported to have been filmed and projected at slower speeds than in the United States, with the French maximum for the 1920s reaching twenty-one frames per second versus an American maximum of twenty-four.[31] In a 1931 article on differences between silent and sound film styles, director Marcel L'Herbier referred to a late twenties norm of eighteen frames per second; but different figures were reported by other sources, such as Marcel Carné, who cited a norm of sixteen.[32] Up through the 1920s, exhibitors in France relied mainly on hand-operated projection, which allowed projectionists to alter speeds during the course of the screening. Venue-to-venue variation appears to have been considerable, as if each of the country's many independent, family-owned theatres had been free to adopt their own approach, ungoverned by a national or company norm.[33] When the motive was not simply to shorten the program's duration for commercial reasons but to adjust a scene's tempo in light of the genre (e.g., fast for comedies) or the character of the dramatic event (e.g., slow for romantic scenes, fast for chase sequences), projectionists can be said to have functioned as interpreters or translators of a film, mediating between film and audience in a manner analogous to the musicians, lecturers, and other on-site accompanists of the silent era—attuned to audience response and responding to the demands of the moment, in circumstances singular to each screening.[34]

Over the course of sound conversion, conditions that had sustained place- and event-specific exhibition practices began disappearing, and technical and financial requirements served to restrict the number and variety of sound-capable exhibition venues. While a silent one-reel Chaplin comedy projected against a café wall might well offer the magic of cinema, sound-film projection of merely tolerable quality required a major technological and architectural investment. In France, conversion costs and licensing fees caused many of the country's small, family-owned theatres and venues, a large number of which screened films only on weekends, to postpone wiring for sound until mid-decade.[35] During 1929–1933, sound-film exhibition in France became dominated by a relatively limited number of large picture palaces, comprising from 1,000 to 6,000 seats, located in the centers of capital cities and designed specifically for sound-film projection. In Paris, certain of the new theatres, with their plush armchairs and furnishings, air conditioning, and exotic lighting effects, were more luxurious than the finest stage venues.[36] Owned mainly by the largest of the production companies, the luxury theatres effectively monopolized the showing of lucrative first-run French-language films during the early 1930s. Their entertainment-palace ambiance, with its strong live-performance component, helped define the new sound-film culture in France.

The situation differed in the United States, where sound-on-disc systems, which required careful attention from projectionists during the screening, began disappearing in 1929. By 1930, projection was fully mechanized, and the exhibitor's role in shaping the film experience had diminished greatly, as editorial control over the film experience shifted definitively toward film producers, who in effect worked to predetermine audience response through a film style in which sound was integrated into the panoply of established fiction-film techniques. In effect, in the United States the sound-era viewer's experience, in a crucial sense, became site-independent, defined by the space and time of a film's story-world rather than by the physical environment of the exhibition venue. While the top venues attracted viewers with their movie-palace amenities, once a screening began, the viewer became absorbed into the film's story-world and oblivious to the physical environment of the auditorium. In this event, film viewing can be said to have become a private rather than a collective activity, with exhibition circumstances, together with film style itself, disposing the viewer during the act of viewing to lose awareness of his/her co-presence with other viewers and to become absorbed perceptually into the film's story-world.[37] In sum, conditions in the United States worked to ensure that the simulated space of the film's story-world effaced the real-world place of the moviehouse.

But how uniform was this development internationally? At a time when so many films served as vehicles for stage-trained actors, the relation between film exhibition and theatricality became exceptionally complex, and, as the French situation suggests, varied significantly from one country to the next, just as the cinema's links to the theatre and popular music industries also varied internationally. In the United States, relatively clear, across-the-board differences between sound and silent exhibition suggest a definite direction in the American cinema's conversion, away from live entertainment. With the arrival of recorded sound, the large theatre chains phased out costly programs of "prologue presentations," featuring live entertainment.[38] In fact, the replacement of live with recorded entertainment—a cost-cutting measure estimated in the United States to have put up to 25 thousand film-theatre musicians out of their jobs—is often cited as an essential motive for the American cinema's conversion.[39] In France, however, the main film companies pursued a different course, undertaking efforts to enhance rather than reduce moviegoing's live-theatrical ambiance. While small and mid-sized moviehouses typically reduced expenses by substituting prerecorded music for live acts, the country's largest and most important film venues featured live shows to an extraordinary degree. In Paris, many of the major sound-era moviehouses were converted music halls, located on the same *grands boulevards* as the top stage venues. After wiring for sound, the converted music halls often maintained their capacity for live entertainment. Indicative here is the endurance in 1930s France of the institution of the movie-house orchestra. When Pathé-Natan built up its chain of dozens of upscale theatres during 1929–1931, it outfitted them with large orchestra pits.[40] Although these and other major sound-film theatres in France screened only sound films, they did so in the context of a significant capacity for live performance. At major venues like the Rex, the Olympia, and the Paramount, up to five full-scale stage shows occurred per day, with vaudeville stars, female dance troupes, musicians, jugglers, and acrobats, accompanied by orchestras of up to sixty pieces, performing during intermissions between screenings.[41] The orchestras sometimes provided supplemental musical accompaniment during the film screening, adding extra music to a synch-sound film.[42] In any case, at major Paris moviehouses, live, music-hall entertainment, backed by the house orchestra, remained a part of cinema programs through the mid-1930s.[43] Thus, relative to the American film-exhibition trend, the case of the French cinema of the 1930s appears paradoxical: although the decrease in the number and variety of sound-movie theatres suggests a homogenization of national film-exhibition practice, the film experience in France appears to have become more theatrical than in the United States—more rather than less defined by live entertainment à la the music-hall and vaudeville.

A consideration of the live-entertainment ambiance of French film exhibition can be helpful in making sense of the style of the many stage-derived comedies and farces that the national film industry produced during this time. According to one trade-press report, of the 384 feature-length sound films made in France during 1929–1933, nearly half were adaptations of popular stage plays, the majority of them comedies, and featuring performances by actors familiar to the theatre-going, radio-listening, and disc-buying public.[44] The distinctiveness of these national popular films is evident in the sort of viewer that they imply. One way to characterize this viewer is in terms of the relation between narrative space, the imaginary space of the film's diegesis or story-world, and auditorium space, the physical environment of the moviehouse. If the American cinema invited viewers to become absorbed in a film's narrative, an absorption contingent on the viewer's obliviousness to the theatre auditorium, the French cinema, with its simulation of theatrical liveness, evolved in a different direction, working to dissolve differences between film and theatre spaces so as to suggest a co-presence between viewers and actor. Describing people exiting a movie theatre after seeing a *film parlant,* René Clair noted that "they talked and laughed, and hummed the tunes they had just heard," and thus acted as if they "might have been leaving a music hall."[45] Clair's comment points to basic national differences in the sound-film experience: whereas in Hollywood synchronous sound ultimately served to encourage the viewer's narrative absorption, in France it stimulated the viewer's recognition of himself or herself as part of a group, gathered in a stage venue to see a show.

## The Emulation of the American Film Industry in Other Countries

The worldwide emulation of American film practice during conversion raises a central issue regarding Hollywood's position in world cinema: the extent to which other film industries worked deliberately to adapt Hollywood's industrial methods, and to emulate the style of Hollywood films, rather than maintain or develop alternative systems and styles of their own. As other film-producing countries converted to sound, American production methods were adopted, and "new Hollywoods" were created in countries across the globe. In France, for example, Pathé-Natan remade the Cinéromans studio at Joinville into what the press labeled "*le Hollywood français*." [46] In the Soviet Union, the principal center for counter–Hollywood filmmaking during the 1920s, attempts were made to refashion the film industry along Hollywood lines, as with Film Commissar Boris Shumyatsky's ambitious plans for the construction of a "Hollywood on the Crimea." [47] In light of the seemingly universal tendency toward film-industrial emulation, world cinema is said to have become "Americanized" during the 1930s, with film studios everywhere working to imitate Hollywood's methods of serial manufacture. In inspiring this sort of emulation, Hollywood could be said to have exercised power through hegemony during the conversion years. [48]

The emulation often rested on firsthand experience with Hollywood's studio system, whose exemplary significance became manifest through Hollywood's status during the 1930s as a pilgrimage site for filmmakers. "The Mecca of cinema," as writer Blaise Cendrars labeled it, Hollywood drew visits from entourages of international producers, directors, financial backers, and other film personnel who toured the studios to observe the latest film-production methods firsthand—as did the Pathé group in the summer of 1929. [49] As Europe's film industries began converting, MGM experimented with the production of foreign-language films in Los Angeles, where "colonies" of expatriate film artists took form. [50] The French community in Hollywood included actors Françoise

Rosay, Charles Boyer, and André Luguet; playwrights such as Yves Miran-
des; and directors Jacques Feyder, Robert Florey, and Claude Autant-
Lara. All of them ultimately repatriated themselves during the early
sound years, bringing Hollywood expertise back home to the national
film industry.

With regard to industrial practice, sound filmmaking, with its sky-
high costs and exceptional technical demands, seemed to offer few
choices beyond an industrialized, Hollywood-inspired approach to film-
production practice. Within the French film community, it was widely
accepted—at least in principle—that the national cinema's fragmented,
artisanal system should be modernized along Hollywood lines.[51] It is important, however, to distinguish between what film-industry reformers
publicly aimed for—the stated hopes and ambitions for productivity and
quality—and the reality of what happened in specific film-production
contexts. Given its rapidity and ultimate universality, the worldwide
changeover to sound lends itself to portrayal as a kind of industrial-
technological juggernaut that ran roughshod over local film-cultural
institutions. Certainly, all film industries ultimately converted and the
film experience changed forever with conversion. But as historians of
film technology have observed, a major technological change such as
sound conversion tends to occur only when established forces are capable
of containing the disruption. One way or another, new technologies become domesticated in terms of established, place-particular practices
and commitments, brought into alignment with local work routines,
personnel hierarchies, and aesthetic and technical norms. With diverse
parties working in myriad ways, and sometimes at cross-purposes, to ensure that technological changes happened on their own terms, in light
of their interests and activities, modernization efforts inevitably encountered formidable inertia in the face of local cultures of film practice,
which often proved surprisingly resilient in the face of modernization-
related change.

In this regard France provides a strong example, with much of the national film industry's decentralized, artisanal "mode of production"—its
patchwork of small and mid-sized companies, craftlike methods, ad
hoc contractual arrangements, and silent-era physical infrastructure—
enduring well into the 1930s. Filmmaking in 1930s Hollywood, with its
oligopoly of studios producing some 500 feature films per year, was
compared to automobile manufacturing; whereas filmmaking in France,

whose scattered film companies produced an average of 130 films per year throughout the 1930s, was likened to the making of stained glass windows, a traditional, craft-based activity rather than a modern, advanced-industrial process. The endurance in the French film industry of established, silent-era institutions, and the piecemeal rather than systematic approach to film-industrial modernization that it facilitated, was a focus of critical commentary in the film trade-press. A typical assessment of the native industry appeared in the following 1934 survey of French film practice:

> Our cinema (production in particular) is in a state of anarchy. There exist nearly as many companies as there are films produced. Each film is an ad hoc endeavor [*un affaire à part*]. Each member of the crew is hired as needed, by the week, day, or hour. These collaborators often have not worked together before, and in order better to command them (to hector them is a more accurate description), a self-appointed leader puts them to work by pitting them against one another.[52]

As such remarks suggest, French film production remained largely an independent, one-off endeavor well into the sound years. With each production often a transient effort, directors frequently retained editorial control over films to an extent unheard of in Hollywood. Moreover, practices of scripting and preproduction planning remained minimal in French filmmaking throughout the 1930s. Thus, in marked contrast to the situation in the United States—and also in certain other important film-producing countries, such as Germany and Great Britain—filmmaking in France, to a large extent, rested on the making of key creative decisions during the shooting phase of a film's production, not during scripting. The emphasis on shooting over scripting proved crucial in distinguishing French film style from the contemporaneous national styles of the United States and of Germany, as will be detailed in later chapters. The point to be made in the meantime is that the impact in France of Hollywood's hegemonic role during the early sound years produced contradictory effects. On the one hand, attempts were made in France to emulate Hollywood's highly industrialized, producer-dominated system, which made the anarchic, low-tech French film industry look like a holdover from an earlier time. On the other hand, the endurance of old local practices, personnel hierarchies, work routines, and physical structures ensured that the new technologies were understood and used differently in the French film industry than in Hollywood, and in ways that produced singular effects at the level of film style. The artistic benefits of artisanal production methods were recognized in 1930s France, notwithstanding concerns for the national film industry's primitive plant and equipment.[53]

## The Homogenization of Film Style

In the view of mainstream film historiography, conversion's most significant effect was a standardization of film style throughout the film-producing world during the 1930s. Recognition of this standardization occurred simultaneously with the beginning of Europe's conversion, when celebrated filmmakers such as René Clair, Charlie Chaplin, and Sergei Eisenstein decried the film industry's limited understanding of sound's artistic potential, evident in the proliferation of theatre-inspired talkies. The claim for homogenization became commonplace in film historiography in the years after World War II, when American film style appeared exemplary for virtually all of the world's film industries. Writing in 1945, Roger Leenhardt claimed that "the formation on the screen of a sort of international style took place only after the cinema began to speak. The triumph of the talkies gave us a Hollywood-style film fabricated in series in Paris, Berlin, and even Moscow."[54] According to André Bazin, "From 1930 to 1940 there seems to have grown up in the world, originating largely in the United States, a common form of cinematic language."[55] The notion that world film style had become standardized during the 1930s became further established in book-length surveys of cinema history published in numerous languages in the decades after World War II. For example, according to Arthur Knight in *The Liveliest Art* (1957): "The techniques of sound rapidly became standardized throughout the world. The stylistic differences that distinguished a French or Russian film from a Hollywood film during the silent era virtually disappeared."[56] Although film-historical scholarship has evolved considerably in the half-century since Knight wrote his survey, few film historians today would dispute his claim regarding world cinema's post-conversion sameness.

But how much is actually known of conversion-era film style? One fundamental obstacle to meaningful generalization is the highly restricted nature of the corpus of films available for study. Very few films of the period have survived, and much of world cinema during this period remains undocumented, to the point that "the first decade after sound outside Europe and Hollywood" can be dubbed "a forgotten era of cinema history," in the words of film historian Robert Sklar.[57] With regard to the world's second- and third-largest film-producing countries of the 1930s—Japan and India, respectively—only a minuscule percentage of the films of the time are reported still to exist.[58] Of all the major national cinemas of the time, the French cinema is among the most accessible and best documented, thanks to the restoration efforts of the Centre National de la Cinématographie and also to the release during the past decades of dozens of titles on home video and DVD. Nonetheless, it must not be forgotten that the available titles represent only a small fraction of the French film industry's total output of some 1,300 films for the 1930s. The situation concerning the French films of 1929–1934—the period emphasized in this book—is particularly severe, with, in Colin Crisp's estimate, only 10 percent of the national output of the time currently available to researchers, versus some 30 to 40 percent available from the latter half of the decade.[59]

Besides the difficulty of locating films, a further obstacle to the study of conversion-era cinema has been historiographical prejudice. Given film history's traditional film-as-art orientation, in which privilege is accorded to international auteur films, national film companies that supplied the domestic film market, mainly with stage-derived comedies, have rarely attracted film-historical interest. In the case of French film history, for instance, the conversion years have long been associated with an undifferentiated mass of low quality *films d'alimentation*—low-quality commercial entertainment, made to trade on its cultural specificity, and intended strictly for the home market.[60] Exceptions that prove the rule are the rare masterworks of Clair, Vigo, Renoir, and Grémillon, which are admired precisely for their alleged singularity relative to the mainstream of the contemporaneous national cinema. The denigration of the popular cinema was common during the conversion years, when, for many critics, the sound-era cinema's interconnectedness with popular theatre, and also with the new electronic media of radio and the electric phonograph, undermined the hard-won aesthetic autonomy brilliantly evident in the auteur films of the 1920s directed by Dulac, Gance,

Epstein, and others. With nearly half of the theatrical sources for the French film industry's numerous stage adaptations of the early sound years dating from the period before World War I, France's sound cinema, notwithstanding the irreducible novelty of the electric amplification and tight lip-synch, looked decidedly retrograde.[61] Writing in 1934, critic Emile Vuillermoz summed up the situation as follows:

> The main grievance against the sound cinema's invention was the fear of seeing the filmic art transformed into a sort of inferior theatre, at the moment when the principle of its independence, of its own technique, seemed to triumph over the cinema's detractors. Twenty years of struggle to make the cinema into something more than a succession of mimed scenes, captured in animated photography, risked being lost under the assault of a technique that was still imperfect.[62]

But while the new sound cinema's supposed aesthetic backwardness was often disparaged, it wasn't equated with the contemporaneous Hollywood film. Indeed, France's filmed theatre, with its strong live-performance aspect, clearly differed from the contemporaneous Hollywood film, and film-industry observers were keenly aware of the technical and aesthetic departures. But film historians have only recently tried to grasp the distinctiveness of the national popular cinemas of countries such as France, which resist analysis in terms of the familiar film-historical understanding of European cinema as international art cinema. Neither international art nor Hollywood imitation, France's entertainment cinema of the early sound years comes up as a historiographical anomaly.[63]

A final obstacle to a proper assessment of conversion-era film style concerns a historiographical prejudice more fundamental than the bias against popular cinema: the enduring neglect in film studies of sound in favor of the image. The claim that film style became homogenized during the 1930s may rest on the familiar assumption that film is essentially a visual art. In studies of film style, editing and cinematography are often examined entirely apart from their sound accompaniment. When concerned with 1930s cinema, such studies invite the conclusion that sound had brought about a reduction in the cinema's stylistic range. But to assess stylistic changes during the 1930s, it is necessary to examine not only image techniques but also how the latter became transformed through recorded-sound accompaniment. As theorists such as Eisenstein and Rudolf Arnheim had recognized, synchronous sound did more than add something extra to the image; instead, it altered the phenomenology of cinema in ways that forever affected image-editing and cinematography.[64] Moreover, these alterations took multiple forms. An image whose sound is dubbed may, in phenomenological terms, differ radically from one whose sound has been direct-recorded, just as the same shot sequence might well take on a transformed stylistic identity through a change in the nature of the sound accompaniment. An awareness of this mutability was implicit in much of the film criticism in conversion-era France. As will be discussed in chapter 3, French films were typically categorized by sound technique, in recognition that the viewer's experience of a film might vary considerably in light of whether the sound was direct-recorded, dubbed, or manipulated via some multi-track combination of both techniques. One possibility raised by this circumstance, and explored in this book's subsequent pages, is that while image practices may have become standardized by the late 1930s, the sound accompaniment may well vary substantially from one national cinema to the next to thus condition national approaches to mise-en-scène, cinematography, and editing. In this context, the notion that conversion had produced a homogenization of film style appears to be the effect of an overly restricted, solely image-based understanding of what constitutes film style.

The objective of this chapter has been to show that an assessment of the notion that sound conversion had produced a homogenization of cinema worldwide will benefit from a differentiated understanding of how conversion occurred. When technologies, techniques, and films are examined relative to the place-specific ways in which they were used, the conversion-era trend toward film-industrial and stylistic sameness can be seen to have enabled significant place-specific divergence from what is generally regarded as film history's overall pattern of development during the 1930s. The aim in the remaining chapters is to show what can be learned of sound's diffusion globally from an examination of how conversion touched ground, so to speak, in a particular national film industry. As detailed in subsequent chapters, the decentralized, fragmented French film industry of the 1930s provided conditions for approaches to sound filmmaking whose stylistic results sometimes diverged radically from Hollywood's norms—notwithstanding the use of American technologies and techniques in French filmmaking and, in some cases, the emulation of American films. Such divergence is especially evident in the area of sound technique, where the French cinema's distinctiveness relative to the Hollywood cinema was quite substantial—and, in important respects, remains so today.

# 2 Film History after Recorded Sound: From Crisis to Continuity

This chapter frames the book's comparative approach to the French cinema's conversion to sound through a critical overview of the film-historical literature. This overview of the history of writings on the changeover to sound cinema reveals significant discontinuities, suggesting that history is continually rewritten in terms of a discipline's evolving interests and activities. Nonetheless, behind the changes in conceptualization, archives, and methods, not to mention varieties of research funding and institutional support, certain continuities in the film-historical literature are also evident. When viewed in terms of historian Fernand Braudel's notion of a multitemporal historiography, in which a history of sudden, disruptive *events* interacts with a history of relatively long-lived, stable *structures*, the continuities imply an overall pattern of development. In rough outline, the pattern can be summarized as follows: whereas initially sound conversion was defined exclusively in terms of dramatic crisis, in the most important work of recent years the focus has shifted almost entirely toward entrenched conditions, that is, structures, or stable material formations, both industrial and aesthetic, which remained relatively constant across the silent and sound eras.

The case for historical continuity has evolved in the context of studies of Hollywood's sound conversion. Given the uniquely integrated character of the American film industry, and the apparently unidirectional character of its conversion, a study concerned with sound-film production in countries other than the United States cannot assume the relevance of recent film historiography's emphasis on long-term continuities. With respect to the cinema histories of many other countries, as in France and elsewhere, where the film industries typically functioned in a far less coordinated, systematic, and preplanned manner, aesthetic and industrial differences between practices in the sound and silent eras have received far more attention from film historians than have similarities.

Concerning France specifically, where the major modernist and avant-garde styles of the 1920s quickly faded in prominence during conversion, the early sound years have long been understood as a radical break from the national cinema's past.

In light of a change in how a national cinema is conceptualized, however, the French case can appear differently. The traditional, exclusive manner of defining the French cinema is in terms of the internationally celebrated *film d'auteur* (auteur film). But if the French cinema is defined inclusively, to encompass both auteur films *and* the mainstream popular cinema, then similarities between French silent and sound practices come to the fore. A film history sensitive to such similarities views the period from 1929–1934 differently from how the period saw itself, and also from how it is seen in much subsequent historiography, which has remained grounded in the crisis emphasis of the film-critical writing of the conversion years.

In this chapter's concluding section, the possibilities of an inclusive approach to conversion-era cinema are explored through a consideration of two key continuities for the French film industry's conversion: (1) the long-take style familiar to French cinema since the 1900s, which became newly prominent in the many "filmed theatre" productions of the conversion years; and (2) the practice among French film producers of producing films mainly for the domestic rather than the international film market—a practice that began at the major French companies in the 1910s and continued, under altered industrial conditions, through the 1930s, until certain auteur films, notably those associated with what would become known as "poetic realism," gave the French cinema an international profile for the sound era. In this chapter, the key question concerns the historiographical implications of an inquiry into how these aesthetic and industrial continuities conditioned the French cinema's adaptation of sound-film technology and technique—an inquiry pursued in detail in subsequent chapters.

## Scholarship on Sound Conversion: A Periodization

The transition from silent to sound cinema has attracted a vast amount of discussion and study, manifest in a wide variety of publications. Written commentaries examined for this book encompass primary and secondary sources, including trade-press articles, filmmakers' interviews and memoirs, government reports on the film industry, journalistic accounts of sound-era filmmaking, and academic monographs on national cinema. This voluminous literature might be organized and categorized in a diversity of ways, depending on critical purposes. The aim in the following brief overview is not to encompass the literature's full range but to identify basic assumptions informing broad trends in the historiography of sound film.

One fundamental assumption, common throughout the history of film-historical study, is that the world's film industries had begun moving forward en bloc, in a common direction, technically and aesthetically, during the sound era. As noted in chapter 1, characterizations of sound conversion in terms of an increasing standardization of filmmaking practice define virtually all accounts of the period. Such characterizations find empirical support in important developments in world cinema during the 1930s. A majority of film-producing countries had converted by mid-decade, and sound-film technologies and techniques first introduced in Hollywood were adapted in other national film industries. Avant-garde and modernist styles became marginalized, as films made in diverse countries came increasingly to display similar, "classical" conventions of narration and style. In contrast to the variety of film styles that had coexisted during the 1920s, cinema during the sound era seemed to exhibit a single style, evident in films made in places across the globe.

But while sound's homogenizing impact has been a constant theme in film historiography, the conceptualization of this impact has evolved considerably since the 1930s. In recent decades the orientation of film-historical study has changed radically, to the point that research today is oriented according to priorities that look like the inverse of those dominant prior to the 1980s. Essential to this shift has been the extraordinary expansion of film historiography's variety of archives and research methods. This expansion has coincided with the formulation of explanations of film-historical change of extraordinary precision and complexity.[1] In the following brief survey, the history of sound-film study is examined in terms of a basic change in how the cinema's past has been conceptualized as an object of historical study. At issue is an evolution away from the traditional stress on crisis and toward the current emphasis on underlying, long-term continuities.

## Conversion as Crisis: Film Historiography in the 1930s

The first major trend in sound-film historiography took form during conversion, when sound's introduction into cinema was widely seen as effecting a radical break from the cinema's past. The sense of rupture is evident in the partisan quality of early responses to sound film, in which critics, filmmakers, and film-industry executives self-consciously declared themselves either for or against recorded sound's introduction into cinema. Sound's opponents included many prominent filmmakers and theorists, for whom sound-related technical limitations threatened to erase decades of hard-won aesthetic progress. Typical in this regard was Charlie Chaplin's description of sound's impact as "a complete and destructive revolution" that threatened to devastate the art of film, or Eisenstein's warnings concerning the talking film's capacity to destroy the "culture of montage."[2] Taking what amounted to an opposing stance, film-industry leaders and publicists, thrilled by the talkies' popularity, celebrated sound cinema as one of modernity's great technological triumphs—a leap forward from what had just recently become known as silent (or "speechless") cinema.[3] Here, too, synchronous sound's introduction was seen as an across-the-board break from the cinema's past, as in the claim by French studio head Bernard Natan that "the discovery of the sound film has reduced everything to zero. The formulas based on twenty years of experience have been annulled."[4]

In reflecting the experience of those who lived through the period, characterizations of sound conversion in terms of crisis exemplify a genre of historical writing whose popularity traces back to national histories of the nineteenth century. Characterizing this genre as a "history of the event," Fernand Braudel emphasized its temporal outlook, manifest in a tendency to privilege the world-altering impact of the exceptional military victory, decisive act of diplomacy, bold artistic masterpiece, or great scientific discovery. Unfolding according to the rhythms of history's human agents, defined relative to "the dimensions of their anger, their dreams, and their illusions," the past depicted in event-oriented histories "still simmers with the passions of the contemporaries who felt it, described it, lived it."[5]

The sort of crisis emphasis that Braudel refers to pervades writings on sound conversion, and perhaps especially writings on conversion in

France, where the local film culture's exceptional sensitivity to questions of film aesthetics ensured the salience of differences between sound and silent cinema. In Paris during the 1920s, film-cultural institutions such as ciné-clubs, film journals, and specialized art-house movie theatres fostered an unprecedented intellectual interest in film; in no other city had film been taken so seriously as art.[6] When French-language sound films began to be produced regularly in 1930, the transformation of film practice was dramatically evident to those whose sensibilities had been shaped in the vibrant national film culture of the previous decade.[7] Celebrated modernist styles of the late 1920s proved resistant to sound-era industrialization, and thus, ironically, appeared no longer truly modern. The most prominent tendency in sound-era filmmaking—the recording of stage plays featuring celebrated theatre actors—looked decidedly retrograde, as if cinema had somehow regressed back to the national film style of 1907. Whether seen as a technological step forward, or an aesthetic step backward, or both at the same time, sound cinema looked, and sounded, like a new entertainment form, technically and phenomenologically distinct from the silent cinema, and with no possible use for much of modernist film technique.

## Film Historiography after World War II

The crisis emphasis of the early literature on sound conversion remains highly relevant today, as it continues to inform accounts of the period.[8] By the end of the Second World War, however, a powerful alternative conceptualization of sound-film history had emerged, as a new generation of critics and cinéphiles in France reassessed synchronous sound's significance with regards to current trends in world cinema. Approaching the conversion-era past in light of the sound-defined present, the new generation of critics no longer saw sound film solely against a silent-cinema background. As one observer noted in 1946, commenting on the many young people frequenting movie theatres and the increasingly numerous ciné-clubs, "young people today know only the talking cinema"; thus they approached sound cinema from a perspective of detachment unavailable to conversion's contemporaries.[9]

Further shaping the postwar outlook was the large and varied body of sound films produced during the preceding twenty years. For critic and theorist André Bazin, who played a pivotal role in orienting the young generation of critics, the "neorealist" depiction of contemporary social conditions in Italian films by Roberto Rossellini, Vittorio De Sica, and others demonstrated the ongoing vitality of a film-realist tendency whose history traced back to the cinema's turn-of-the-century beginnings. Also significant was Hollywood's recent adoption of widescreen and color for feature films, which highlighted sound as one phase in a process of technological and artistic evolution extending into the postwar present.[10] In the face of what increasingly looked like a long and ongoing aesthetic and technological process, the old conception of synchronous sound as a total break in film history came under direct criticism. For instance, Georges Charensol, claiming that it is "an error to separate totally the sound cinema from the silent," argued that conversion was best understood in terms of an interaction between two relatively independent histories of film, as art and as technical practice: "If the talking film seemed, between 1927 and 1931, to mark in the cinema's evolution a clear break in continuity, this was because of the trouble it caused for certain individuals and work methods rather than any challenge it posed for the basic principles of the seventh art."[11] Similarly, Bazin posed the question as to whether "the technical revolution created by the sound track was in any sense an aesthetic revolution."[12] In Bazin's view, the case for continuity was especially strong for filmmaking in the United States, where practices of continuity editing, with scenes planned, filmed, and assembled in terms of the drama's psychology, had remained essentially unchanged since the 1920s.

## Academic Historiography: From Short-Term Event to Long-Term Structure

The repudiation of the notion of sound-as-crisis in the work of Bazin, Charensol, and other postwar critics counts as a major historiographical innovation. It invites comparison to the new historiography advocated contemporaneously by Braudel, and henceforth associated with the prestigious Annales School of historical study, which entailed a self-conscious effort to redirect the field of historical study away from its traditional concern with dramatic, crisis-like events and toward the subliminal effects of long-term structure.[13] It also points ahead, as it were, with the postwar critics opening the path for the academic historians of recent decades, whose historiographical interventions entailed a further push in the direction of the postwar notion, advanced by Bazin and others, of a multi-temporal historiography, in which the novelty of recorded sound's impact on cinema appears against the background of unnoticed long-term trends.[14] The key difference between the academic writers and the postwar critics rests on the diversity of the archives examined by the academics and of the research methods employed. A basic issue here concerns the expansion in the type of films examined. Largely indifferent to questions of aesthetic judgment, recent scholarship's corpus of films extends well beyond the familiar canon of film masterpieces to include virtually the entirety of the film industry's output during the period studied. A vast number of ordinary rather than exceptional films have become incorporated into the field of research—from commercial features of all genres to fiction shorts, cartoons, documentaries, newsreels, and other types of film besides conventional feature-length movies. An important related development was experimentation with new research methods, such as statistical analysis of film editing and cinematography, which enabled unprecedented precision in the study of broad trends in film style.[15]

Coinciding with recent scholarship's inclusiveness in its coverage of films has been recourse to a wide range of research materials, including—in addition to films themselves—film-industry trade publications, government reports on the film industry, records relating to trade diplomacy, and diverse traces pertaining to film exhibition and reception. Beyond unearthing important new facts, academic historians asked fundamentally new sorts of questions, and thereby radically transformed the early sound period as a field of film-historical study. The contrast with the established historiography of crisis could not have been more sharp. Instead of analyzing outstanding events—breakthrough films, first-time uses of a technique, career failures, and overnight successes—the focus of historical analysis has become broad patterns: aesthetic norms, industrial routines, and standard rather than exceptional uses of techniques. The new film historiography has effectively transformed the study of Hollywood's conversion, to the point where, as Donald Crafton observes, "it is difficult to think of a more profound discrepancy between popular and academic discourse on a subject than that which currently exists with regard to movie sound."[16]

One way to characterize the discrepancy is in terms of the historian's stance vis-à-vis the period's self-understanding. Unlike popular accounts of the introduction of sound, which attempt to immerse the reader in the "sound revolution" as it was experienced by those living during the period, academic studies adopt a perspective of scientific detachment, so as to position the reader outside the passions of the time. Exemplary here has been the work of Douglas Gomery, who has examined the "logical and systematic" manner in which the American film industry's various sectors worked together to coordinate the American cinema's massive, yet relatively rapid and smooth, changeover to sound. Gomery's account can be contrasted to that of Alexander Walker in his fine study, *The Shattered Silents* (1978), in which the cinema's transformation during 1926–1929 is said to have been decided "[n]ot in any cool-headed, rational fashion: but amidst unbelievable confusion, stupidity, accident, ambition and greed."[17] Offering a radically divergent assessment, Gomery documents how MGM, Paramount, and other major Hollywood studios, heavily indebted to banks, colluded to manage the legalities, logistics, and finances of sound conversion so as to avoid a costly patents war. Rather than pushing the industry into chaos, conversion enabled powerful economic forces in the United States to expand and become further entrenched. According to this long-term view, sound conversion appears to be not the cataclysmic overturning of the cinema's status quo but rather a consolidation of the major and minor studios that would define the next thirty years of Hollywood's studio system.

Another academic contribution to film-historical research with major implications for sound-film historiography was David Bordwell, Janet Staiger, and Kristin Thompson's *The Classical Hollywood Cinema* (1985).[18] Like Gomery, these authors examine the oligopolistic manner in which the main sectors of the American film industry worked together to normalize sound-film production within a brief five years. But instead of exclusively focusing on film-industry economics, Bordwell, Staiger, and Thompson undertake a detailed examination of relations between stylistic and industrial trends, via the art-historical concept of "group style." The result is an account of sound conversion whose understanding of the art/industry relation is far less agonistic than virtually any preceding study. Unlike earlier histories, which described the panic surrounding conversion, as well as despair over the "death" of silent-film art, *The Classical Hollywood Cinema* presents the evolution of American sound-film style as a process of normalization in which the conversion years register as a brief and temporary disruption against a decades-long background of industrial and aesthetic stability. Refuting the traditional notion of sound as a break from the cinema's past, the authors describe the style of Hollywood films as essentially continuous throughout the history of Hollywood's studio system, from 1917 up through the late 1950s. From this standpoint, Hollywood's post-conversion style circa 1931 looks like a restoration of the "classical" style of the 1920s rather than a new artistic beginning.[19] As in Bazin, a key technical issue surrounding the claim for continuity concerns methods of film editing. Notable here is Bordwell, Staiger, and Thompson's intriguing claim that the temporary adoption during conversion of the costly technique of multiple-camera shooting allowed Hollywood-style classicism to endure in spite of the technical upset of synchronous sound.

Academic alternatives to film historiography's traditional concern with crisis have proven highly rewarding in revealing important aspects of Hollywood's conversion that had escaped the awareness of conversion's contemporary critics. In disclosing the subliminal impact of long-term trends, and in highlighting developments that at the time had been invisible, because taken for granted, academic historiography, with its formidable powers of hindsight, understands the conversion period better than the period understood itself. For the same reason, however, the new film historiography exhibits its own blind spot, insofar as the emphasis on continuity occludes the technical and aesthetic diversity of the early sound years. Most fundamentally, occurrences and trends that defined the period but that fail to anticipate subsequent developments may fall outside of the historian's field of vision. In the case of American film history, conversion-era aesthetic developments risk becoming of interest only when they appear congruent with Hollywood's classicism. An example is the historiography of film comedy, which traditionally has favored plot-oriented romantic comedy over vaudeville-derived "comedian comedy."[20] This sort of danger, in a different form, looms large in the history of French film, in which the conversion years often are approached in a highly selective manner, insofar as they seem either to mark the end of the silent-era avant-garde or to anticipate the poetic realism of the late 1930s. What might it mean to define conversion-era cinema in positive terms, that is, in terms of what it was rather than what it wasn't?

## The Relevance of Long-Term Structure to
## Sound Filmmaking Outside the United States

With respect to the topic of sound conversion's impact on cinema globally, the question that must be asked today, as historians increasingly take up issues of Hollywood's international impact, concerns the relevance of long-term structure to the study of sound conversion in countries other than the United States. In Europe, for instance, where continuities across the silent and sound eras seem nonexistent, the arrival of synchronous sound has been widely regarded as radically remaking the cinema, sending it onto a new and unforeseen path of development, both aesthetically and economically. Typical in this regard was critic Jan Mukařovský's judgment (1936) that "the rapid tempo of innovation in talking motion pictures . . . in very brief time destroyed the bases for artistic development established by the silent film."[21] Regarding the French cinema, this characterization of sound cinema as an across-the-board break would seem to apply thoroughly. The national film industry underwent a radical structural change with the formation of the vertically integrated combines Pathé-Natan and Gaumont-Franco-Film-Aubert, and also a major aesthetic crisis had occurred, evident in the sudden and permanent marginalization of the modernist and avant-garde currents of the 1920s. Still today, the notion that the French cinema's conversion amounted to a break from the national cinema's past remains widely accepted among film historians.

But as the preceding discussion of film historiography suggests, France's sound conversion can appear differently through a shift in the construction of national cinemas as objects of film-historical study. More precisely, if the French cinema is understood inclusively, to encompass the entirety of the national film output, the conversion years show up in a new context of industrial and aesthetic continuities across the silent and sound eras. In the French case, such an understanding requires expanding the corpus of films beyond the familiar canon of internationally recognized auteur films—many of which were recognized as important only retrospectively, years after the French film industry's conversion ran its course—to include the many entertainment productions intended strictly for domestic consumption. The project in this chapter's remaining section is to show how such a shift brings to the fore important aesthetic and industrial continuities between France's sound-era cinema and its silent-era past, with an emphasis on two continuities particularly relevant to the national film style: the aesthetic practice of conceiving a scene as if it were a theatrical performance, staged for camera and microphone, and the industrial practice of producing films mainly for the domestic film market. In France, both practices pre-dated the sound era by a decade or more. As will be detailed in later chapters, these practices served as crucial conditions for the national cinema's distinctive stylistic evolution during the 1930s—particularly with regard to the American cinema, France's main source of film imports. When these continuities are taken into account, certain aspects of the French cinema's conversion that have puzzled historians—most notably, the decisive turn away from modernist and avant-garde approaches to film style in favor of "filmed theatre"—no longer seems so anomalous, congruent as they are with long-term currents in national film practice.

## Aesthetic Continuity: The Scene as Theatrical Performance

A clue to the relevance of long-term structure to the French cinema's conversion can be found in observations regarding the anachronistic style of the early sound films, which were pervasive in the critical writing on French film at the time. However novel from a technological standpoint, the new sound cinema exhibited aesthetic tendencies that seemed notably old-fashioned, as if recorded sound opened the way for an industrywide retrieval of the national cinema's premodernist past. As director Léon Poirier stated, in an observation typical of the time, "The invention is new, but the use of it is a copy of the old."[22] The key factor here was the obvious theatricality of sound films, manifest, for instance, in the showcase-like presentation of performances by stage-trained actors and singers. Often characterized as an "actor's cinema," the many French films of the 1930s based on popular plays are said to have been staged, filmed, and edited so as to facilitate actors' relations with their public. Referring to French films of the 1930s, film scholar Dudley Andrew notes that "[p]lot, dialogue, and décor were designed to prepare for those moments when the actor could play himself and remind the audience of the special relation they enjoyed."[23] A crucial point regarding this relation between actor and audience is that typically

Figure 2.1: One of the country's most popular actors, Jules Raimu—shown here in a promotional still for the Pathé-Natan production *Théodore et cie.* (Pière Colombier, 1933)—claimed to play his roles in film in the same manner in which he performed them on stage.

it had been formed prior to sound conversion, not in film but in live entertainment—such as boulevard theatre, the music hall, the circus, and the café-concert. As film producer Pierre Braunberger had noted, by the time major film actors such as Raimu and Fernandel began their film careers, "they had practically ten years of music hall or theatre behind them. For this reason, their personalities as actors were already wholly constituted, and barely evolved in the course of their film careers."[24] According to Raimu, one of the most popular French actors of the 1930s, "For my part, I use exactly the same dramatic or comic means in the cinema and in the theatre."[25] (See Figure 2.1.)

In France, where Paris served as the capital for both film and theatre, stage employment remained important to actors even after their entry into the cinema, with the majority of film actors continuing to perform in theatrical entertainment—in some cases, filming scenes in the studio during the day while appearing on stage in the evening.[26] Actors appearing in films had, in many instances, already played the same roles on stage, and film scripts were often written by playwrights and dialogue specialists adept at creating roles for the same actors (or actor "types") currently performing on stage and on radio.[27] According to a 1932 report, film producers often offered contracts to actors before deciding on scenarios, which would be written later so as to match the actors' personae.[28] In some cases, actors simultaneously played the same roles in both media, and entire casts carried over from theatre to film, as in the celebrated case of the film version of Marcel Pagnol's *Marius* (dir. Alexander Korda, 1931), which featured the same troupe that had performed in the hit stage version for over a year prior to the making of the film.[29] Performers such as comedian Georges Milton sang the same songs in films and on stage, and used their stage appearances as a means of promoting their forthcoming films.[30]

The extensive film-radio-theatre crossover, with the same performers starring in all media, powerfully affected the style of the films, as critics and filmmakers were keenly aware. Referring to the top French actors, Jean Renoir, writing in 1935, noted that "their films must be conceived strictly to showcase their personalities, otherwise one risks failing to respond to the wishes of their public."[31] Rather than incarnate fictional characters, actors displayed public personas that had been cultivated outside the cinema, on the popular stage and also increasingly on radio and on 78-rpm disc. Thus they could be said to "play themselves," via an exhibitionistic yet subtle interplay between the actor (as understood by the public) and the role played, with the latter always already mediated through the former. According to Michèle Lagny, Marie-Claire Ropars, and Pierre Sorlin in an extended analysis of the popular French cinema of the 1930s, "one discovers that the actors play not characters so much as they play themselves, in the full social, narrative, and fictional senses of the term. Under the mask of the character, the mask of the comedian interposes itself between spectator and film."[32] This sense that the film actor presented himself or herself to a group of fans, gathered in a theatre auditorium, was facilitated by the manner in which the films were made. As will be discussed in later chapters, the prominence of stage actors in French films, with their unique skills and public appeal, proved highly consequential technically. In the context of the French cinema's recording-oriented conception of film acting, the scene was thought of less as an assemblage of shots than as the recording of an extra-filmic performance; as a consequence, sound-film style in France

Fig. 2.2. At a time when the American film industry had integrated sound technique into its established approach to film narration, the French cinema produced numerous films conceived as recordings of stage plays. This basic difference in national film practice carried important implications for the film-viewing experience, as is suggested by the credits sequence of Pathé-Natan's "*opérette filmée*" *Chacun sa chance* (Hans Steinhof and René Pujol, 1931). The latter's curtained backdrop alludes not to a filmic storyworld but to the communal space of a stage venue. Enhancing the theatrical simulation is the absence of synchronous sound during the credits; instead, musical accompaniment had been provided on site, by the orchestras that were standard in theatres comprising the Pathé-Natan chain. Thus, in the manner of a stage show or a silent-film screening, *Chacun sa chance* opened with a performance that occurred less on the screen itself than in the space between screen and audience.

diverged from that in the United States and in Germany, where a conception of the scene as a construction rather than a recording held sway during the 1930s. (See Figs. 2.2, 2.3, and 2.4.)

### Industrial Continuity: Films for Domestic Consumption

Supporting the recording-based film style was an important industrial continuity: the practice on the part of French film producers of making films strictly for domestic rather than international consump-

Fig. 2.3. Immediately following the credit sequence of *Chacun sa chance* is an explicitly theatrical prologue, in which actor André Urban, playing the role of emcee, invites the film's principal players out from behind the curtain to be introduced to an implied gathering of spectators. As in the Vitaphone shorts of 1926–1928, in which orchestra conductors and other personalities bow to the left, right, and centre, as if facing a live audience, Urban's broad gestures and histrionic demeanor seem directed less toward an idealized film spectator than to an auditorium of fans.

tion. This practice took form in the years after World War I, when Hollywood emerged as the world's major production center, and the French film industry became oriented toward supplying the home market exclusively. This commitment to the domestic market intensified during the boom years of the early sound cinema, when the shortage of French-language sound films facilitated the dominance of filmed adaptations of popular plays. As Erich Pommer, Ufa's top producer, had observed, the technical conditions of synch-sound filmmaking required that producers decide prior to a film's production whether a film was to be made for export or for the home market.[33] In France, virtually the entire film industry was geared to serving the domestic market exclusively, a circumstance that powerfully conditioned the sort of sound films made there.

The frequent characterization of the *film parlant* as a return to the

Fig. 2.4. In this singing performance in *Chacun sa chance* (Hans Steinhoff and René Pujol, 1931), Jean Gabin, in an early film role, addresses the camera as if facing a room full of fans. At one point during the performance, Gabin lowers his voice and momentarily turns from the camera to glance stage right, as if privileging a particular section of the (imagined) auditorium of viewers. Reminiscent of the Vitaphone shorts of 1926–1928, in which orchestra conductors and other entertainers, bowing left and right, likewise pretended to address a collectivity of theatre-goers, this sort of performance style had a long life in the French film industry's "théâtre filmé," where, in contrast to the contemporaneous Hollywood cinema, it remained common throughout the 1930s.

national film style of earlier decades had a basis in the training of the personnel who shaped the French film industry's conversion. Many of the directors, for instance, had backgrounds not only in silent cinema but also in cinema prior to the film modernism of the 1920s. Directors with film backgrounds tracing back to the teens played important roles in conversion-era French film production, among them Henri Diamant-Berger, Léonce Perret, Camille de Morlhon, Louis Gasnier, Henri Fescourt, Léon Poirier, Jean de Limur, Louis Mercanton, Bernard Deschamps, and Maurice Tourneur. Already formed in what might be called the premodern school of cinema, these directors sometimes came with notable experience directing stage adaptations. Louis Mercanton, director of the Paramount-Paris production *Il est charmant* (*He Is Charming*, 1931) and other hits of the early 1930s, had directed Sarah Bernhardt in *La reine Elisabeth* (*Queen Elizabeth*, 1912) and other films prior to World War I. When making films ten to twenty years later during conversion, these directors, in some cases, remade films from their silent-era past, as did Tourneur, whose 1932 *Les gaîtés de l'escadron* (*The Squadron's Frivolities*) was based on a stage play already adapted for film in 1913, in a version directed by Tourneur himself. Director Léonce Perret, whose career likewise began in the early 1910s and who worked under contract at Pathé-Natan during the early sound years, referred to the Pathé-Natan production *Enlevez-moi!* (*Lift Me Up!* dir. Léonce Perret, 1932) as his three-hundred-eighty-sixth film![34] It is not surprising that film historian Jean Mitry and others characterized France's conversion-era cinema as a retreat to the stage-identified style of *L'assassinat du duc de Guise* (*The Assassination of the Duke of Guise*, dir. Charles Le Bargy and André Calmettes, 1908): the French cinema's *films parlants* had been directed by a remarkable number of silent-era veterans, including some with backgrounds in the cinema of the prewar years.[35]

In France, the centrality of "filmed theatre" began to erode in the mid-1930s, as French films won international awards and new ambitions arose within the French film community for producing films with export potential. In this context, the reliance on "the terrible formula of photographed theatre" hindered the French cinema's exportability and hence its economic health.[36] A key concern was the French-language film market's small size. During the early 1930s, this market, including North Africa and francophone countries other than France (e.g., Belgium, Switzerland, and the Canadian province of Québec), was estimated to comprise some 75 million spectators and 5,000 theatres, making it two-thirds smaller than the Anglophone market of 225 million people and 30,000 theatres.[37] Also, the French market was smaller than the numbers suggested. In 1932, of the supposed 4,000 theatres in metropolitan France, over one-half were not yet wired for sound-film projection.[38] In addition, the frequency of movie attendance in France was relatively low, with only 7 to 10 percent of the populace estimated to attend films regularly during the 1930s, versus 40 percent in the United States during the same period.[39] Finally, roughly half of the French populace lived in rural areas, where the majority of the exhibition venues screened films only on weekends, and where a significant part of the populace—up to 30 percent—was estimated to lie outside the reach of commercial film distribution.[40] In any case, many French movie theatres, particularly in the provinces, had signed exclusive block-booking agreements with American distributors, and thus, for contractual reasons, did not screen films made by French companies.[41] The small market size was sufficient for absorbing the low output of French-language sound films during the first years of the national film industry's conversion. But by 1932, national production increased to well over one hundred films per year, and theatre receipts, undercut by economic depression, began falling. Under the economic pressure, limitations of the French film market's size became a focus of concern within the film community. By the mid-1930s, it was commonly said that France's survival as a film-producing country would depend on the production of films with some potential for export.[42]

During the 1930s, market-related concerns were central to the deliberations of various government-sponsored committees for film-industry reform. For example, in the wake of the financial collapse of the major conversion-era film companies, the Renaitour Commission of 1937 brought together film-industry representatives and politicians to ponder government intervention in the film industry. Besides matters of industrial structure, financial and accounting practices, credit terms, tax policy, and censorship, the discussion encompassed questions of film genre and style. Anticipating the *cinéma de qualité* (quality cinema) of the 1940s and 1950s, the Renaitour Commission's deliberations concerning a feasible alternative genre for the French cinema centered on big-budget historical films based on prestigious French literary sources. The consensus was that the French film industry should curtail its reliance on stage adaptations: "It is incontestable that as long as French film actors perform for us in the cinema as if performing in a stage play [*une pièce de théâtre*], the French cinema will not have the expansion that one would hope for," as one commission member said.[43] In this context, at the inauguration of the *cinéma de qualité* that would define France's national cinema for the next two decades, the commercial potential of the filmed-theatre style of the early 1930s appeared decidedly proscribed. Although filmed theatre would remain perennially popular, and hence a mainstay of the French film industry, it was no longer central to the way in which the film industry sought to define itself. The aim instead was to remake the French cinema's identity through the production of international art films.

When direct-sound techniques characteristic of conversion-era filmed theatre resurfaced in French filmmaking during the 1950s and 1960s, it was in the context of the work of innovative auteur directors, often working with magnetic rather than optical sound, whose films drew an international critical reception. As discussed in this book's conclusion, the context changed from the strictly national to the international and from commercial entertainment to auteur cinema. These changes were crucial to the appropriation of 1930s mainstream production methods by ambitious and singular filmmakers, who effectively redefined the sound practices of the 1930s as art-cinema techniques. In sum, while certain techniques associated with conversion had resurfaced during the decades after World War II, they did so in the context of significant changes in aesthetic function.

Major advances today in the study of sound-film history have often rested on a self-conscious abandonment of the traditional emphasis on sound as crisis or revolution. This former emphasis has been supplanted by an unprecedented analysis of industrial and aesthetic continuities across the silent and sound eras—continuities that traditionally had received little attention from film historians. In recent studies of Hollywood's conversion, the effects of the focus on continuity have been powerfully evident, offering a compelling alternative to the crisis emphasis of popular accounts. With regard to a study of conversion's international or global dimension, however, questions remain concerning the relevance of the continuity emphasis to conversion-era filmmaking in countries other than the United States. In the context of world cinema, aesthetic and industrial continuities comparable to those of the Hollywood cinema seem less evident, as in the case of the major film-producing countries of Europe—and perhaps France especially.

However, this circumstance can be seen as a function of the traditional definition of national cinemas in terms of art films that receive an international reception. A different, less crisis-dominated view of sound conversion becomes possible if the French national cinema is understood inclusively, to include art films together with the numerous French films made solely for domestic consumption. In the event, the *film parlant* shows up differently. Its performance-based concept of the scene appears continuous with French film industry practices that date back to the 1900s, decades prior to the emergence of either Hollywood's classicism in the late teens or film modernism in the 1920s. In this context, conversion-era filmed theatre looks like a technologically mediated return to the national cinema's very beginnings, a return to first principles, as it were, rather than a break from the national film past. In the next chapter, the project of examining conversion-era film culture inclusively is furthered through a study of the reception of sound films in conversion-era Paris. How were imported sound films understood in the French film community, and what does this understanding reveal of the singular manner in which sound-film technologies and techniques, many of which were imported, were adapted within the French film industry?

# 3  The Talkies in France:
## Imported Films as Exemplars

The study of film history has long been organized according to national categories. One of the most fundamental assumptions of film historiography has been that national cinemas are comprised of films produced by and within particular nation states. In other words, as Andrew Higson has observed, national cinemas are traditionally defined in terms of production rather than reception, that is, in terms of films made in a particular country rather than films shown there.[1] This book's analysis of national sound-film practice shares the film-production emphasis of traditional histories of national cinemas. Nonetheless, in attempting to illuminate the singular ways in which sound technologies and techniques were understood in the French national cinema, the examination in this chapter situates French films within the range of films distributed there. The latter includes films imported from other countries —especially from the United States and Germany, which at the time were the two countries oriented toward making sound films for export, specifically French-language films. As this chapter's analysis reveals, films imported from the United States and Germany served as crucial points of orientation for the French film community's understanding of the challenge of creating a French-language sound cinema.

Although film imports had long been a crucial, if not defining, component of a majority of the world's national film cultures, the centrality of imports was inevitable during conversion, when, in many national film markets, foreign films far exceeded domestic productions. During 1929, for example, as Europe's film industries began converting and sound films drew keen interest from the public and from film-industry professionals, the majority of the sound films shown on the Continent came from the United States, which had been producing sound films commercially since 1926. According to a September 1929 report in the French film trade-press, of the 110 "*films sonores et parlants*" (sound films and talking films) available on the French film market, 104 were

American, whereas 4 were French and 2 were German.[2] In this context, at the beginning of the French film industry's conversion, American sound films served as exemplars for putting the new technologies to artistic purposes. They were concrete examples of what the cinema's future might amount to, and they functioned, in one respect or another, as reference points for virtually anyone making a sound film during this time. Certain films—such as *The Jazz Singer* (dir. Alan Crosland, 1927)— served as a focus of discussion for national film communities throughout the world. To study the reception of these films is to study the conceptual commitments and the interpretive outlooks of the communities that formed around the films.

With respect to the historiographical issues outlined in the preceding chapters, certain questions arise. Did the global distribution of American films serve to homogenize world-film practice? Must an affirmative answer assume that the world's filmmakers, critics, and audiences— scattered throughout many countries, and acculturated in diverse entertainment traditions—understood American films in the same ways? As the following analysis of film reception in France shows, Hollywood films, and their implications for the future of sound cinema, were sometimes understood in ways that were local in nature, in response to current circumstance, and hence were unpredictable relative to Hollywood precedent. In this chapter, the French film community's understanding of sound film is approached through a study of the critical reception of a few key imported films in conversion-era Paris.

In France sound films were categorized according to production methods, with the recognition that audiences generally preferred the *film parlant* (or talkie), which featured direct-recorded sound, over the *film sonore* (sound film), whose sound had been post-synchronized. A consideration of the *parlant/sonore* distinction's relevance to French film practice illuminates a familiar question of national film history: the centrality in French cinema of the "theatrical" *film parlant* in the face of the modernist and avant-garde preference for the "cinematic" *film sonore*. In other words, however evidently "theatrical," an indigenized form of the live-performance style exemplified by Al Jolson in *The Jazz Singer* quickly came to define sound-era French cinema. In contrast, the alternative, "cinematic" style of *Le chemin du paradis* (dir. Wilhelm von Thiele and Max de Vaucorbeil, 1930) and the early sound films of René Clair inspired relatively minimal emulation in France, notwithstanding the style's commercial potential and its fervent support from the film community's modernist wing. As is sometimes the case with the history of film technology, the historian confronts the challenge of explaining the failure of an anticipated development to occur. Why didn't the style associated with Ufa's operettas and with the early sound films of René Clair, which attracted both audiences and critical praise in France, become important, if not central, to French film practice during the 1930s? Possible answers to this question, examined in detail in later chapters, require looking beyond film reception to consider film-industrial practices—particularly with regard to scripting and planning. In contrast to the situation in the United States and in Germany, scripting and planning remained minimal in the French film industry throughout the decade of the 1930s, powerfully affecting French film style.

This chapter's analysis of the French film community's reception of certain of the major films of the time will open the path conceptually for an investigation into the singularity of French film style, revealing the unique logic governing local understandings of sound-film technique. In what follows, the objective is to examine how imported films were interpreted within a national film community, thus illuminating the logic of the community's understanding of the filmmaking potential of the new sound technologies.

### The Jazz Singer as film parlant

It is difficult to begin a study of the early sound period without mentioning *The Jazz Singer,* even when the inquiry concerns conversion in a country other than the United States. Recent historical study has done much to clarify circumstances of the film's reception by documenting the degree to which its legendary impact was a function of media hype, deriving from the film industry's links to Broadway, rather than spontaneous audience response.[3] In the domain of film reception, however, hype can be highly consequential, ensuring that certain films remain in the forefront of the film community's attention, where they become a focus of discussion and analysis. In the case of a comparative investigation of the sort undertaken here, reception study can reveal the structure of a particular community's outlook. A basic question concerns the place-specific character of how the film community's understanding of exemplary sound films evolved in one national film industry relative to others.

One can begin by noting broad similarities between the reception of *The Jazz Singer* in France and how the film was received in other world capitals. For example, in London, in September 1928, some four months earlier, the film had likewise drawn considerable critical and popular interest. In Paris, as in London and major North American cities, *The Jazz Singer* was a commercial hit. During its eleven-month exclusive run at the Aubert-Palace, one of the city's first sound-equipped theatres, *The Jazz Singer* reportedly drew over half-a-million spectators and earned box-office revenues totaling a record-breaking eight-and-a-half million francs.[4] The impressive box-office performance led to revised expectations for sound's relevance to the national cinema's future.[5] According to an editorialist for *La cinématographie française*, the leading film journal, "when *The Jazz Singer* first appeared in Paris, no one, or almost no one, was planning to make talking films in France"; within a few weeks, however, "the revolution was underway," and the national film industry's conversion appeared inevitable.[6]

Concerning the film itself, especially notable was the brief, purportedly ad-libbed moment when Al Jolson, in a rush of nervous energy, chats rapidly to his mother while riffing on the family piano, promising to shower her with gifts that will impress the "Ginsbergs, the Guttenbergs, and the Goldbergs" ("Oh, a whole lotta Bergs; I don't know 'em all"). This brief section of the film proved sensational for its amplified clarity and sense of liveness which, phenomenologically, seemed more characteristic of a radio broadcast than a film screening. The lip synchronization was not flawless during the film's exclusive run at the Aubert-Palace, where the scene played in the original American version, accompanied by a second screen projecting a written French translation of Jolson's speech. Reminiscent of earlier attempts to link sound and moving image—as in the pre–World War I sound systems devised by Edison, Gaumont, and the German Oscar Messter—lip synchronization in *The Jazz Singer,* with the inherent flaws of sound-on-disc projection, was not always tight enough so that during the few lip-synched minutes in the film, Jolson's electrically amplified voice seemed to come from the actor who appeared in the image rather than from a phonograph player's loudspeaker or another off-screen source in the auditorium. But unlike earlier acoustic attempts to synchronize motion-picture image and recorded sound, Jolson's electronically magnified performance impressed critics in France as a major, world-shattering advance, promising "a cinematographic revolution," "a total overthrow of cinegraphic laws," "an absolutely new orientation for the cinema," and so on.[7]

Phrases such as these, which were also used to characterize the film in other cities, referred to aspects of sound-film practice that had a somewhat unique meaning in the context of the film's Paris release, which occurred fifteen months after the original premiere in New York in October 1927. At that point, dozens of American sound films made after *The Jazz Singer* had begun circulating in Europe. With both old and new films distributed together, American sound films often appeared in a manner unrelated to the chronological order of their production. Thus, as discussed below, *The Jazz Singer* was frequently contrasted to *Ombres blanches* (*White Shadows*, dir. W. S. Van Dyke, 1928), an MGM film made over a year later than *The Jazz Singer*, but released in France three months before. In the face of the sudden proliferation of sound films, critics in France who commented on *The Jazz Singer* did so in the context of the entire field of sound-film practice. Even short reviews published in daily newspapers situated *The Jazz Singer* within rapid surveys that linked specific films to specific film techniques and audience tastes. At issue was less the film's intrinsic quality than its significance relative to the cinema's overall development. The implicit question for the critics seems to have been: What does this film relative to other sound films tell us about the cinema's future?

### Film Parlant and Film Sonore

An intriguing aspect of French critical writing on early sound cinema was its attention to technique, which served as the principal basis for distinguishing among types of sound film. Most fundamental was the often-invoked distinction between the *film sonore* and the *film parlant*. The distinction was basically technical, although it carried aesthetic implications: a *film parlant* was a synch-sound film whose dialogue had been recorded simultaneously with the image, whereas a *film sonore* had been shot silent and then supplemented with a separately recorded soundtrack.[8] The *parlant/sonore* distinction was omnipresent in French film criticism during the early sound years, when it served as the essential conceptual tool, the basic category distinction, for classifying conversion-era films. The *parlant/sonore* dualism could be said to have marked the fault line in conversion-era aesthetics for the French film community.

In 1929 and 1930, the term *"film sonore"* referred to what in Hollywood was called a "scored feature": a film made silent and then upgraded with a post-synchronized music-and-effects track.[9] Scored features dated from 1926, the first year of sound film production in the United States, when Warner Bros. added a music-and-effects track to *Don Juan* (dir. Alan Crosland, 1926), the pioneering Vitaphone production starring John Barrymore. In 1927, Warner Bros. followed with other such films, as did Fox, Warner Bros.' chief sound-film rival at the time. Sound films began proliferating in 1928, as Paramount and MGM competed with Warner Bros. and Fox by retrofitting their silent catalogue, adding soundtracks to films that had been conceived and shot silent. Throughout 1929 and 1930, these and other sound-adapted silent films became the most common sort of sound film playing in Europe.[10] Also around this time, European *films sonores* began appearing. Examples include experiments such as Marcel Vandal and Charles Delac's *L'eau du Nil* (1928); certain of the few French-language films of 1929, such as *La route est belle* (dir. Robert Florey, 1929) and *Le collier de la reine* (dir. Gaston Revel and Tony Lekain, 1929); as well as numerous films of 1930, such as *Prix de beauté* (dir. Augusto Genina, 1930), starring Louise Brooks.

Like their American counterparts, these French *films sonores* often impressed conversion-era observers as being similar to the type of silent film to which audiences during the 1920s had become accustomed. The *films sonores* often looked the same as silent films; in fact, in many cases, they had been conceived as silent productions and "sonorized" as an afterthought. Moreover, in important respects, they could be said to have sounded the same, too. With the post-synchronized sound often only imprecisely matching the image, *films sonores* preserved some of the two-dimensionality and elastic temporality characteristic of silent-era cinematography. Also, the *film sonore's* recorded sounds were not necessarily naturalistically faithful to an original, but were often produced by the same stage-derived means as in silent-film exhibition.[11] Examples include the spectacular storm sequences common in the American *films sonores*, whose noises were simulated by musical instruments, Wurlitzer organs, and sound-effects devices familiar to stage entertainment. Recall, for instance, the French horn's simulation of a foghorn in F. W. Murnau's *Sunrise* (1927), an early Fox-Movietone production. The sounds for such scenes were sometimes recorded during a screening of a fully edited version of the film, with musicians and sound-effects technicians gathered around microphones to capture all sounds in a single take, in a studio designed for music recording. In this setting, it was difficult to record dialogue intelligibly; thus, *films sonores* featured minimal, if any, spoken language, and instead presented dialogue through intertitles. In much of the film-critical writing in France in 1929, the *film sonore*'s stylistic similarities to silent cinema made it deficient as a form of sound cinema—more a holdover from the silent era than a true, modern-day synch-sound film. "A limited compromise," in director G. W. Pabst's words, the *film sonore* looked like a stopgap measure that could be dropped once Europe's film industries were able to overcome the technical obstacles associated with synchronous dialogue recording.[12] According to Jacques Feyder, fresh from several years working on sound films in Hollywood, the *film sonore* amounted to "a weak, hybrid genre, a transitional genre with no future."[13]

In 1930, the *film sonore* underwent a rehabilitation of sorts as Eisenstein and other avant-gardists celebrated the formal flexibility made possible by the *film sonore*'s freedom from synchronous dialogue.[14] In championing the *film sonore* over the *film parlant*, Eisenstein—with the support of Clair, Gance, and others—engaged in a familiar avant-garde rhetorical strategy, inverting the mainstream critical hierarchy by embracing what had been a term of denigration. But despite the efforts of authoritative film-cultural figures, the majority of viewers and critics in France craved the technical novelty of films featuring synchronous speech, especially in French.[15] In fact, the *film sonore* enabled the persistence of avant-garde film-image techniques that were criticized in the mainstream film press as inappropriately ornate. For example, one critic pejoratively characterized avant-gardist practice in terms of "weird images [*images hazardeuses*], photographed from audacious angles, and curiously illuminated."[16] Sound cinema seemed most effective, and most true to its inherent representational potential, when approached in a relatively straightforward, realistic manner, as in the direct-recorded *film parlant*.

The *sonore/parlant* distinction carried important economic implications in France, where exhibitors earned significantly more revenue from *films parlants* than from *films sonores*. In 1930, a *film sonore* was expected to bring in a box-office intake of some 60,000 francs—three times as much as a silent film ("*film muet*"); but an "entirely French talking film" was the most lucrative, bringing in ticket sales of 100,000 francs or more.[17] Trade-press editorialists pushed for enforcement of the *parlant/ sonore* distinction, in response to what was seen as fraudulent advertising by exhibitors, who indiscriminately claimed to screen a *film parlant* but instead showed a *film sonore* or worse (e.g., a jerry-built travesty such as a silent film accompanied at random by a succession of phonograph recordings). Exhibitors were exhorted to advertise in ways that distinguished accurately among types of sound films, so as to avoid killing public interest in the *film parlant*—"this merchandise still too rare."[18]

The *parlant/sonore* distinction surfaces in the many reviews in which *The Jazz Singer* was contrasted to *Ombres blanches* (dir. W. S. Van Dyke, 1928), the French version of *White Shadows of the South Seas* (dir. W. S. Van Dyke, 1928). An MGM production that had been shot silent and then upgraded with a post-synchronized Fox-Movietone soundtrack, *Ombres blanches* premiered in France in November 1928 at the Aubert-Palace, one of the first Parisian moviehouses to wire for sound. A curious feature of comparisons of the two films is the routine identification of *The Jazz Singer* as the more modern work. Although made more than a year after *The Jazz Singer*, *Ombres blanches* seemed somehow earlier in stylistic terms, as if exemplifying an older form of cinema. With its exotic location footage from the Marquesas Islands, some of it shot by Robert Flaherty, *Ombres blanches* could be described as more cinematic than the studio-bound and openly theatrical *The Jazz Singer*; but its qualities were gauged according to a conception of cinema that, in light of *The Jazz Singer*, now seemed passé technically. Most fundamentally, the cinematographic style of *Ombres blanches* was possible only when the sound accompaniment was post-synchronized rather than direct-recorded—a technique most blatant in the film's dialogue scenes, which relied on intertitles, in customary *film-sonore* fashion. As one critic put it, *Ombres blanches*, whatever its artistic merits as an MGM "A-picture," differed from *The Jazz Singer* in exhibiting "purely cinematographic methods, in the old sense of the word."[19]

What made *The Jazz Singer* seem novel in comparison to *Ombres blanches* was the electrically amplified immediacy of Al Jolson's performance in a few direct-recorded scenes.[20] Rather than being a conventional film melodrama, *The Jazz Singer* had the "documentary" impact of a radio broadcast, with Jolson offering the sort of high-voltage earnestness that fans of the famed entertainer's stage and radio appearances had come to expect.[21] Instead of incarnating a fictional character, Jolson was said to have played himself: "It is a question not of characters but of actors," as one critic characterized the film's performances.[22] *The Jazz Singer* offered an experience that differed fundamentally from what French film audiences in 1929 had become accustomed to, implying a different entertainment form altogether, akin more to the vaudeville stage than to cinema. According to one critic's description of the experience of the film, "Briskly, one forgets one is in the cinema, to instead assume the mentality that one brings to the music hall or to a concert."[23] (See Figure 3.1.) With Jolson's presence in the film appearing to constitute a theatrical "intrusion" into the domain of cinema, *The Jazz Singer* recalled the films of the years prior to World War I, when films were likewise constructed to foreground the virtuosity of stage-identified stars.[24] From this perspective, *The Jazz Singer* looked like a descendant of the hundreds of Gaumont Chronophone films of 1902–1913 that likewise featured the performances of famous singers.[25] In the context of this prehistory of sound-film practice, Jolson's performance in *The Jazz Singer* struck critics as oddly familiar, even old-fashioned, and yet, by virtue of the electric amplification's astonishing expansion of the frequency range, as absolutely new at the same time.

## An Alternative, "Cinematic" Style: *Le chemin du paradis*

The sensational box-office performance of *The Jazz Singer* opened the way in France for the making of French-language imitations such as *La route est belle* (dir. Robert Florey, 1929), another film about a young singer struggling to balance family obligations with career success. The film's popularity was said to lie in singer André Baugé's performance rather than in the cinematic quality of the realization. Producers Pierre Braunberger and Roger Richebé were reportedly so disappointed in the quality of *La route est belle* that they debated not releasing it; but they did, and the film turned out to be astonishingly popular—with a box-office take lucrative enough to help finance construction of the Braunberger-Richebé studios.[26] Many similar productions, made by a variety of French

Fig. 3.1. A promotional still featuring Al Jolson in *The Jazz Singer*—a film celebrated in France for its astonishingly effective simulation of a stage star's "live" performance.

and foreign companies, followed in 1930. Within a year or two, filmed theatre in one form or another became the dominant tendency in the French cinema, and would remain so throughout much of the decade. Until 1931, however, when multiple models for sound cinema proliferated, a consensus on the national cinema's future had not yet taken form. According to one trade-press commentator, concerning the situation in mid-1930, "Since the appearance in France of the first talkie, we have seen the formation of schools and sects, which immediately, through their tendencies, plans, and goals, formulated in definitive terms their opinions on the new art."[27] At this point, *The Jazz Singer* by no means represented the only promising path for the national cinema's future. Among rival conceptions of sound cinema, most imposing was a sophisticated version of the *film sonore*, in which the relation between actor and viewer also seemed novel, but in a manner that differed radically from *The Jazz Singer*.

A key exemplar for the rival conception was *Le chemin du paradis* (dir.

Wilhelm von Thiele and Max de Vaucorbeil, 1930), the French-language remake of *Die Drei von de Tankstelle* (*Three from the Filling Station*, dir. Wilhelm von Thiele, 1930), one of the first of the highly successful film operettas produced by the German company Ufa during 1930–1932. (See Figure 3.2.) *Le chemin du paradis* premiered in Paris in November 1930, some twenty-one months after *The Jazz Singer*. Like *The Jazz Singer*, *Le chemin du paradis* was taken to mark a new stage in the sound cinema's evolution—and, in fact, a definitive advance beyond the earlier film. Typical in this regard was publisher Jean Fayard's assertion that *Le chemin du paradis* "will open a new epoch for the talking cinema."[28] Likewise, Emile Vuillermoz claimed that *Le chemin du paradis* "merits close study by anyone interested in the future of the talking screen."[29] The film's most illustrious champion was director René Clair, star director for Tobis Films Sonores, who claimed that he had revised the scenario of his innovative operetta *Le million* (dir. René Clair, 1931) in light of technical possibilities suggested by *Le chemin du paradis*.[30]

More than an extrapolation from the style of *The Jazz Singer*, *Le chemin du paradis* was an exemplar for a different style altogether: whereas *The Jazz Singer* simulated the experience of an appearance by the great Jolson, as encountered on stage or on radio, *Le chemin du paradis* thoroughly integrated actors' performances into the film's overall formal design, so as to offer a viewing experience that seemed distinctly cinematic. The stage operetta's popularity dated from the nineteenth century, and while *Le chemin du paradis* invoked this past, its updated setting—a contemporary world of high-spirited young men, flirtatious bosses' daughters, sports cars, petrol stations, nightclubs, and bachelor pads—seemed wholly modern, "pure style 1930." As one reviewer stated, referring to the film's stage-operetta source, "If the inspiration has been found outside the cinema, the cinema has used this inspiration without subjugating itself to it"; in short, rather than reproduce a theatrical performance, *Le chemin du paradis* disclosed sound technology's capacity to render theatre cinematic, and thus could draw acclaim as "the first film operetta that is truly cinematic."[31] Crucial here was a film-music technique far more sophisticated and technically challenging than the old "scored feature" method of adding a music-and-effects track to a film that had been shot silent. Music-defined from the start, *Le chemin du paradis* was scripted, rehearsed, filmed, and edited as a function of its musical performances. Especially notable was the film's novel incorporation of pre-

Fig. 3.2: The many German films of 1930–1932 made in both French- and German-language versions are estimated to have comprised some one third of Germany's total national film production of the time. In the case of the popular Ufa operettas, German and French versions were made essentially simultaneously, with both German and French casts in the studio on the same day, when they rotated through the sets, one shot set-up at a time. This promotional photo features the crew and casts for the Ufa-made operetta *Die Drei von der Tankstelle* and *Le chemin du paradis*. Appearing on left are German co-stars Heinz Rühmann, Oscar Karlweiss, and Willy Fritsch, while flanking them on the right are their French counterparts Henri Garat, Jacques Maury, and René Lefèvre; in the center is the multi-lingual star Lilian Harvey, who appeared in both versions, and director Wilhelm Thiele; behind are actor Jean Boyer and Max de Vaucorbeil, director/dialogue coach for the French-language version.

recorded popular songs. As noted in chapter 1, recorded songs were featured in many French films of the early 1930s—up to half of the national film output, according to one estimate.[32] Typically grafted on to a film's soundtrack in the late stage of post-production, the presence of such songs made the style of conversion-era films often seem merely additive —as if several distinct media had been opportunistically stuck together, in a manner reflecting strictly commercial rather than artistic motives. A notorious example here is *La chaland qui passe* (*The Barge Passing By*, dir. Jean Vigo, 1934), the distributor-edited version of *L'Atalante*; today celebrated as one of the masterpiece films of the 1930s, *L'Atalante* had been recut against Vigo's wishes, and renamed after the hit pop song that had been spliced into the film's soundtrack.

Like many other films circulating in France in 1930, *Le chemin du paradis* served as a vehicle for popular recorded songs, and thus exemplified the commercial media culture that Vigo's film was made to conform to. In fact, some thirty different companies released 78-rpm recordings of songs from *Le chemin du paradis,* with two of the songs—"Avoir un bon copain" ("To Have a Good Pal") and "Tout est permis quand on rêve" ("Anything Goes When One Dreams")—becoming major hits, selling in the millions, both in France and in other European countries.[33] But in the context of the typical practice of simply splicing a singing performance into a film's soundtrack, *Le chemin du paradis* looked like a major aesthetic advance. Instead of the film's musical performances seeming autonomous relative to the narrative sequences—as if cut into the film after the fact, with no foresight—*Le chemin du paradis,* with its seamless transformations from naturalistic acting to full-blown song and dance, exemplified in an integrated approach to the film musical, in which musical performances were carefully woven into the film's overall formal texture.

This synthetic approach to musical performance contributed powerfully to the cartoon-like lightness that distinguished *Le chemin du paradis* from the more naturalistic filmed theatre. In contrast to the latter, with its documentary-style recording of the performances of stage-associated actors, the fantastic *Le chemin du paradis* invited comparison to the sound cartoons of Walt Disney and the Fleischer Brothers, celebrated at the time for their inventive matching of image to music.[34] Indicative in this regard was the early, gravity-defying scene in the apartment of the three friends, in which the heroes watch helplessly as their repossessed furniture flies magically across the room and into the waiting moving van. Also remarkable was the use of a single song to meld together scenes into larger narrative units or syntagma. According to Emile Vuillermoz, prior to *Le chemin du paradis,* the film musical had been limited to "unity of place," characteristic of musical performance on stage, where voices were anchored to specific, flesh-and-blood human bodies; henceforth, however, in light of the "passed-along-song" sequences of *Le chemin du paradis,* a liberation was possible: "An operatic couplet begun outdoors can continue in a salon, carry over to an automobile, and conclude in a factory. A musical refrain can simultaneously galvanize the most diverse characters, passing from one to another with prodigious rapidity, while tossing a dash of gaiety into the most varied milieux, and yet preserving temporal unity."[35]

As with *The Jazz Singer*, reviewers commented on the nature of their experience of *Le chemin du paradis*, although in terms that contrasted sharply to those used for the earlier film: "It is a filmed operetta, but we have—for the first time regarding a film of this genre—the impression of being always in the cinema," reported one critic.[36] Whereas *The Jazz Singer* simulated the music-hall experience with astonishing immediacy, to the point of making the viewer aware of his/her membership in an audience of fans, gathered in a theatre auditorium to enjoy a show, *Le chemin du paradis* lifted the viewer out of the theatre milieu altogether and into a sort of imaginary world unique to cinema. The difference can be located at the level of the sort of viewer implied by the films. Whereas filmed-theatre productions à la synch-sound scenes in *The Jazz Singer* imply a viewer who recognizes himself/herself as part of a public gathering, co-present with other audience members as well as the film's performer(s), operettas such as *Le chemin du paradis* suggest a viewer who loses awareness of his/her presence in the auditorium space so as to become absorbed into the film's flow of images and sounds. Like the music-inspired, art-house films of the late silent era, *Le chemin du paradis* offered a singularly cinematic experience, distinct from the experience of a stage show.

### The Path Not Taken: René Clair and the German Operetta

Attracting both commercial success and critical acclaim in France and also in other countries, *Le chemin du paradis* exemplified a powerful, economically viable European alternative to the Hollywood talkie.[37] By some accounts, the film's commercial and aesthetic achievements seemed likely to mark the end of the prosaic *film parlant*. As one critic predicted, "The public that sees and hears the characters of this film will no longer tolerate the animated photographs of the music hall and the stage that have been shown so far, under the pretext of making the screen talk."[38] Such predictions, though in tune with the desire of many critics and eminent filmmakers, proved false. As *films parlants* proliferated, and film attendance numbers increased, the mainstream French cinema continued to evolve away from the German operetta and toward what one critic in 1933 referred to as the "triumph of photographed theatre."[39]

Symptomatic here are revised expectations regarding the impact on

French filmmaking of the work of René Clair, the gifted French director who cited the German operetta, and *Le chemin du paradis* specifically, as key exemplars for his own practice. It is difficult to overstate Clair's importance during conversion, when the astonishing international success of *Sous les toits de Paris* (*Under the Roofs of Paris*, 1930), *Le million* (1931), and *A nous la liberté* (*Liberty for Us*, 1931) made him "arguably the most celebrated film artist in the world during these transitional years," according to film scholar Dudley Andrew.[40] For many observers, Clair's highly successful films seemed to set the likely path for the French cinema's stylistic development. As with *Le chemin du paradis*, it was difficult to see the integrated approach to sound-image relations in Clair's films as anything but a definitive advance beyond the filmed theatre of the time.

By 1933, however, it was clear that Clair's films, whatever their international fame and intrinsic artistic merit, were attracting minimal emulation in the French film industry. Commenting on the film season of that year, Georges Charensol noted that "the films of René Clair are remarkable, but represent only himself."[41] By then, Clair seemed to be experimenting with altering his style in a direction compatible with the filmed-theatre mainstream. With regard to the production of *Quatorze juillet* (*July Fourteenth*, 1932), the last of the films he would direct at Tobis Films Sonores, Clair claimed that "I have renounced, for now, the sort of fantasy that I had constructed for *Le million*."[42] In contrast to the art-deco brightness of *Le million* or *A nous la liberté*, the working-class neighborhood setting of *Quatorze juillet* is visually darker. Cartoonlike moments familiar to Clair's earlier sound films still occur, but in the context of an overall approach to mise-en-scène compatible with the gritty naturalism common in sound-era French cinema. Moreover, in contrast to *Le million*, *Quatorze juillet* features considerable dialogue—some of which had been improvised by the actors. Although moments of pantomime familiar to Clair's earlier films still occur, they now alternate with the sort of dialogue sequences common in the contemporaneous French cinema but relatively rare in Clair's earlier work. Although Clair remained critical of the sound cinema's drift toward talkie realism, his work in 1932 on *Quatorze juillet* implicitly acknowledged the latter's centrality to the contemporaneous national cinema.[43]

The case of René Clair raises a question regarding the French film industry's adoption of the filmed-theatre style rather than the "cinematic" style of the German operetta. One way of framing the question is attempted in subsequent chapters, which move beyond questions of film reception to undertake an investigation into national differences in film-industry practice. With respect to the latter, the basic point to be made is that conditions in France were far more conducive to the production of filmed theatre than to the sort of operetta associated with Ufa and with René Clair. One key issue concerns the degree of preproduction planning required by the operetta. If *films parlants* captured the spontaneity of an actor's "live" performance, and thus exhibit a certain excess, with the immediacy of the actors' improvised performances sometimes outweighing the scene's narrative significance, German operettas such as *Le chemin du paradis* "waste nothing": each shot, each sound effect, carefully planned in advance, had been calculated to contribute to the narration's unfolding.[44] To create the proper effects, myriad details of the actors' performances were carefully scripted and rehearsed. In an account of the shooting at Ufa's Neubabelsberg studios of *Mélodie du coeur* (*Melody of the Heart*, dir. Hans Schwarz, 1930), a French-language version of one of Ufa's operettas, producer Erich Pommer reported that actors' performances in the film had been carefully segmented, broken into separate sections, and timed with a stopwatch.[45] The length of each shot was determined in advance. Actors rehearsed with a metronome, so that physical motions and bits of speech would perfectly match the music that would be added to the images during editing. Given such methods, actors' performances in the German operettas conform to the films' overall formal design, in contrast to the relatively over-the-top performances in many contemporaneous French films, whose style seems cut to the measure of the actors rather than the other way around.

The making of Clair's films involved the same sort of painstaking methods of planning, scripting, and rehearsal as in the making of the German operettas. For instance, in rehearsing actors for *Le million*, Clair used a metronome to time actors' movements, thereby rendering them formally compatible with the rhythm of the film's preconceived music track.[46] As the scripts for Clair's work at Tobis Films Sonores reveal, the films were planned in excruciating detail—far more so than was the norm in national film production at the time. In contrast to the many French films recorded in an improvised fashion, Clair's films were based on detailed scripts, which included shot breakdowns for each scene, the order in which the shots were to be filmed, notation regarding dissolves and fades, and precise indications regarding sound recording and post-production technique. For instance, the script for *Vive la liberté*—the working title for *A nous la liberté*—identifies six different types of shots, according to sound technique: "shots with direct sound," "shots whose sounds were recorded for another shot," "shots with both direct and post-synchronized sound," "post-synchronized shots," "shots whose action has been timed [*réglée*] for music," and "silence."[47] Each type of shot was identified by a color-coded, blue-and-red scheme, thus providing a visual mapping of an entire film's needs with respect to sound-image technique.[48] Clair's employment at Tobis Films Sonores, the Paris-based production subsidiary of the Dutch-German sound-film company, greatly facilitated the thorough predesign of the films' sound design, as did the collaboration of sound engineer Hermann Storr and other Tobis Films Sonores technicians, many of whom had trained in Germany.

The planning-intensive approach at Tobis Films Sonores was relatively unique in France, where, as detailed in the book's remaining chapters, the film-industrial conditions necessary for a predesigned approach to shooting ordinarily didn't exist. Moreover, as the critical reception of *The Jazz Singer* suggests, the "filmed theatre" style, especially when drawing on the talent of French actors, was sufficiently attractive to French viewers to obviate the need for adoption of the costly preplanned methods of the German operetta or of the films directed by Clair. In short, the filmed-theatre productions proved just as viable commercially, often raking in box-office receipts up to six times the films' production costs, while costing much less to make than a Clair-style operetta. Moreover, as discussed in the next chapters, filmed theatre also suited the skills of the actors, and proved compatible with established personnel hierarchies and work routines within the French film community. In sum, the operetta à la Clair required that filmmakers in France work against the grain of established national film-industry practice, quite in contrast to filmed theatre's technical path of least resistance.

This chapter's analysis of film reception in conversion-era Paris has attempted to reconstruct the distinctive logic according to which sound-film technique was understood in a particular country during conversion's beginnings. The key finding concerns the importance of the fundamental distinction between direct-recorded and post-synchronized speech, which served within the French film community as the principal technical and aesthetic distinction among types of sound films. Moreover, as suggested in the preceding consideration of the work of René Clair, the *parlant/sonore* distinction also proved highly relevant at the level of national film-production practice, with the French film industry proving far more conducive to the *film parlant*'s improvised, direct-sound methods. Whatever the apparent aesthetic drawbacks, the *film parlant* offered important advantages in France, such as the considerable improvisation afforded during shooting, when actors and production personnel, with minimal preparation, could assemble on the set, quickly work out the details of a scene, and then film an entire scene, sometimes in a single take. When made in such a fashion, a feature film could be shot in a mere two to three weeks, which minimized the costs of studio rental and actors' salaries. In short, filmed theatre was highly viable economically, and in the case of the most popular productions, astoundingly profitable.

In the analysis of French filmmaking in the remaining chapters, the focus is on the role of sound technique relative to the national cinema's improvised methods of film production. The analysis discloses conditions that enabled stylistic tendencies associated with the national cinema's old guard to return to the fore during conversion. This sort of return of the past is familiar to the historiography of film technology, in which fundamental technological change tends to occur only as established capitalist interests are prepared, insofar as can be seen, to limit the technologies' disruptive potential. As the case of the filmed theatre of the 1930s suggests, major technological changes may well seem aesthetically regressive, as if the technological advance had necessitated an aesthetic retreat. A question raised by this phenomenon for a study of sound conversion outside the United States concerns the variety of place-specific forms the relevant business and labor interests can assume, and their myriad effects on film practice and style. If all film industries attempted to convert to sound in a fundamentally conservative manner, so as to contain, as much as possible, the potential economic disruption, such conservatism—by virtue of fundamental national differences in film and entertainment media practices—also often exhibited a profoundly local character, and thus differed substantially from one national cinema to the next.

# 4 Sound-Era Film Editing: International Norms, Local Commitments

The preceding chapter's inquiry into film reception in conversion-era Paris brought to light film-cultural conditions that had shaped the French film community's understanding of sound-film technique. In this chapter, the investigation turns toward the relevance of these conditions to national filmmaking practice. In terms of historical method, a similar principle applies: just as a film must be examined relative to how it was understood by critics in particular places and times, film technologies and techniques must be seen according to the context-dependent ways in which they were put to use. As the case of French cinema suggests, filmmakers in countries other than the United States sometimes adopted Hollywood-identified techniques in ways that departed radically from Hollywood precedent. Regarding the conversion years, examples of such departure are evident in practices of film editing—notwithstanding the familiar notion that editing methods became standardized during this time.

Given editing's traditional status as the most inherently "cinematic" of film techniques, an inquiry into sound-era editing necessarily raises central questions of film history and theory. "The development of film technique . . . has been primarily the development of editing," wrote Ernest Lindgren, founder of Britain's National Film Archive.[1] Film history during the silent era is often presented as a chronicle of editing achievements. The 1920s have been particularly important in this regard, with many of the masterpiece films of the time famous for their innovative editing. Characterizations of editing as the essential film technique—the cinema-specific method that formally differentiated film from the other arts, especially theatre—pervaded the film theory of the 1920s.[2] During conversion, synchronous sound's unexpected transfor-

Table 1. Statistics on National Film-Style Trends during the 1930s

| country/ region | source | dates | #films in sample | natl. mean ASL | natl. median ASL | ASL range | ASL std. dev. |
|---|---|---|---|---|---|---|---|
| France | O'Brien | 1930–1933 | 54 | 11.2 | 10.7 | 3.8 to 30.5 | 5.5 |
| U.S. | B. Salt | 1928–1933 | 136 | 10.8 | 11 | 5 to 25 | 3.4 |
| France | B. Salt | 1934–1939 | 64 | 13 | 11 | 5 to 22 | 4.2 |
| U.S. | B. Salt | 1934–1939 | 184 | 8.6 | 8 | 4 to 18 | 2.3 |

mation of the phenomenology of the film image produced vexing technical problems, and much accepted editing theory came to seem irrelevant. Unforeseen difficulties were especially imposing for films whose sound was recorded simultaneously with the image: with the mise-en-scène of each shot indelibly inscribed with the time and place of its recording, direct-recorded shots did not join together in the familiar diversity of ways. The order of shots in dialogue scenes became relatively inflexible, the capacity to reshape a film's narrative during editing was vastly restricted, and film narration became more linear and naturalistic and less potentially figurative and associational in form.[3] The sense of constraint was particularly strong with respect to the commercial talkies and *films parlants,* whose characteristic liveness rested on their status as electric recordings of staged performances. In their famous sound-film manifesto of 1928, Sergei Eisenstein, V. I. Pudovkin, and G. V. Alexandrov warned that the proliferation of "talking films" threatened to "destroy the culture of montage."[4]

The investigation that follows is framed in terms of editing's contradictory role in the cinema's alleged sound-era homogenization. On the one hand, editing techniques associated with Hollywood cinema became widespread by the late 1930s, practiced in film-producing countries throughout the world, including France. On the other hand, French films had a look and sound that differed from Hollywood films. Concerning editing specifically, continuity rules proved far less determinant than in Hollywood. Montage techniques characteristic of the modernist and avant-garde cinema of the late silent era endured in post-synchronized form. Editing was used not only to delineate character psychology but also to express a scene's dramatic or comedic character. Scenes were often filmed in long takes, with multiple cameras, and thus captured "live," as it were, in real time, rather than constructed, according to scripted design, out of separately recorded shots.

The following examination of the French cinema's editing-related peculiarities relative to the Hollywood cinema evolves via a consideration of three topics: first, the effects on national film style of the diffusion of Hollywood's editing methods during the 1930s; second, the findings of statistical analyses of national differences in editing practices; and third, the effect on French editing practices when conversion-era French filmmaking reverted to the silent-era conception of a scene as the recording of a staged performance. In the chapter's concluding section, attention shifts to how the French cinema's distinctiveness might be explained, particularly with respect to the familiar film-historical problem of technological determinism. While certain peculiarities of French film editing (i.e., the relatively long average shot length of the French films of the late 1930s) can be attributed to the particular technologies used—or not used—in the national film studios, strict technological causes in this context, while an important and necessary causal factor, cannot by themselves explain the stylistic changes in question. As demonstrated also in chapter 5, what is required is attention to how particular film-production contexts inflected the technology's use.

## Film Editing after Recorded Sound

The case for the cinema's stylistic homogenization in the sound era appears imposing with regard to broad, international trends in film editing. By the end of the 1930s, editing practice in virtually all of the world's film-producing countries is said to have come to resemble the continuity approach practiced in the United States. "From 1930 to 1940 there seems to have grown up in the world, originating largely in the United States, a common form of cinematic language," as André Bazin wrote.[5] Barry Salt, who has compiled statistics on editing in hundreds of films of the 1930s, characterizes the latter part of the decade as "the cinema's most restricted and restrictive period"; by then, a broad, international consensus had emerged in favor of techniques associated with

Hollywood cinema, "with very little indeed going on at the innovative extremes."[6] Concerning the French cinema, Colin Crisp argues that French editing practice, beginning in the mid-1930s and continuing through the late 1940s, came increasingly to resemble contemporaneous American practice—a circumstance implicit in a gradual increase in the pace of French cutting during this time.[7]

The emulation of American editing in Europe's film industries was not novel to the sound era but appears to have predated Europe's conversion by some five years. Citing European developments such as a boost in the average cutting rate and a new prevalence of cutting within individual scenes, Salt claims that during the mid-1920s, filmmakers in Great Britain, France, and Germany engaged in a "conscious attempt . . . to follow the earlier developments in American film style."[8] What was new during the sound years were industrial and technical requirements at odds with the artisanal methods that had sustained the alternative, art-cinema movements of the 1920s, such as French impressionism and Soviet montage. During the 1930s, as adoption of Hollywood's industrialized production methods occurred in film industries worldwide, editing styles that might have counted as alternatives to Hollywood practice could survive only on the film-industrial margins.

The decline during the 1930s of the major avant-garde and modernist movements, whose conditions of possibility had been undermined by the sound cinema's economic and technical requirements, is often taken to indicate the homogenization of editing practice during the 1930s. But it should not be assumed that the many filmmakers who had moved away from film modernism necessarily did so by embracing Hollywood's classicism. The relation between film modernism's marginalization and the stylistic homogenization of the 1930s can appear far less linear, depending on how the relation between European film style and Hollywood's classicism is understood. The familiar link between the avant-garde's marginalization and the Americanization of film style presupposes a traditional conception of national cinema, whereby the major European cinemas are defined mainly in terms of art-house films with an international reception.[9] This export-defined form of national cinema invites characterization as a self-conscious alternative to the Hollywood cinema.[10] At the same time, during the 1920s, the European art cinema's oppositional relation to Hollywood sometimes exhibited a strongly ambivalent aspect, insofar as the project of competing with Hollywood pushed export-oriented European filmmakers toward an approach to film narration and style that might be characterized as "Hollywood-like." Thus, by 1929, European-made "international films," featuring multinational casts and story material presumably accessible to a broad, international viewership, were labeled by producer Erich Pommer as "poor imitations of American films."[11] Likewise, as Kristin Thompson proposes, referring to film-community rhetoric regarding Europe's international art cinema of the late 1920s, "perhaps internationalism simply meant copying Hollywood as well as possible."[12]

An indication of the complexity of the European cinema's relation with the Hollywood cinema can be found in the many instances in which film modernists defined themselves through a rejection, not of the Hollywood cinema, but of the national popular cinemas of Europe. In fact, with regard to editing, certain prominent modernists cited Hollywood as an inspiration for their struggle against the dominant European style, whose ongoing reliance on techniques of mise-en-scène over those of editing, was deemed excessively theatrical. Pudovkin, for instance, admired D. W. Griffith's *Intolerance* (1915) over the supposedly stage-bound cinema of Czarist Russia, which, like European popular cinema generally, relied on techniques characteristic of a putatively theatrical mise-en-scène, such as long takes and deep staging.[13] It was this theatre-identified style that Pudovkin and other montage filmmakers had explicitly rejected, rather than the editing-based Hollywood style; in fact, the latter, when approached selectively, and from within a film-theoretical perspective was a well of inspiration. From the standpoint of film modernism, including its renegade surrealist wing, the basic obstacle to aesthetic progress was less the Hollywood cinema than the older, pre-Hollywood, national cinemas of Europe.[14] As Richard Dyer and Ginette Vincendeau note, this "popular entertainment cinema made by Europeans for Europeans" has remained "stubbornly unacknowledged in film-historical study."[15] The lack of acknowledgment is particularly unfortunate with regard to the study of the cinema's "sound revolution," when the popular cinema's old long-take style, in a technologically updated sound-era form, suddenly returned to prominence, and, in what looks like a counterrevolutionary turn, quickly displaced the avant-garde and modernist styles of the 1920s. To understand the historical forces behind this multi-temporal dynamic will require examination of the impact upon the cinema of conversion-era Europe of established, popular national film practice.

Regarding film editing specifically, the singularity of the popular European cinema can be characterized by an alternative conception of the scene, the basic unit of classical narrative. Whereas avant-gardists and modernists of the 1920s pioneered a conception of the scene as an assemblage of shots—a construction whose phenomenological whole exceeded the sum of its material parts—Europe's national, popular cinemas were based on an understanding of the scene as a performance staged for recording. These differences remained operative until the 1920s, when new, editing-based approaches to film scenography, both classical and modernist, rose to prominence, and the old recording-oriented approach faded in importance. Then during conversion a kind of reversal in film history's direction seemed to occur; as commercial demands favored the showcasing of stage-identified singers and actors, and the technical demands of sound-on-disc recording necessitated the staging and filming of scenes in single takes, the performance-based approach resurfaced as a major film-style option.

An indication of the relevance to sound-era French cinema of the conception of the scene as a performance staged for recording can be seen in the extent to which critics in France recognized strong similarities between the *films parlants* of the early 1930s and the French films of the 1910s, prior to the emergence of the filmic avant-garde. When referring to conversion-era cinema as aesthetically regressive, critics cited the familiar practice of the recording of actors' performances that had defined popular European cinema since the 1900s. Thus, the possibility arises that the performance-based conception of the scene prominent in the *films parlants* of the 1930s is best understood not as a capitulation to Hollywood practice but instead as the vestige of an approach to staging and cutting older than both the Hollywood style and the major modernist styles. This approach can be traced back as early as 1907, when long-take methods of staging began to distinguish French from American film styles, and variations in editing technique became a function of differences in national practice rather than genre.[16] In this light, sound conversion's leap into the future looks less like a break from the national film past than a retrieval of that past's primal film-aesthetic practices—a circumstance also alluded to in the popularity in conversion-era France of the multi-temporal notion that the new synch-sound films amounted both to a technological advance and an aesthetic retreat.

### National Differences in Editing Practices:
### Average Shot Length

An indication of the ongoing relevance to conversion-era cinema of the national popular film style of an earlier time can be found in broad differences between French and American editing practices. One place to begin analysis is with statistics on the average shot lengths of films from various countries, compiled by Barry Salt, Colin Crisp, and myself, which provide an empirical basis for comparing broad stylistic trends for certain of the major national cinemas of the 1930s.[17] In offering a view of conversion-era film practice unavailable to observers at the time, the statistical analysis of film editing exemplifies the attention to unnoticed trends typical of the academic film historiography discussed in chapter 2. Whereas traditional film histories—with their emphasis on pathbreaking films, first-time uses of a technique, sudden ups and downs in personal fortune—mirror the period's self-understanding, editing statistics provide concrete evidence concerning national trends in film style that may well have escaped the awareness of conversion's contemporaries. For the historian, such statistics often have a healthy though disconcerting capacity to defy expectations, and thus, in undermining accepted hypotheses, stimulate historical explanation and revision.

With regard to sound's impact on broad stylistic trends, analysis can commence with the "average shot lengths" for films comprising a national film industry's output for a specific period. A film's average shot length, or ASL, can be computed by dividing its total running time by its total number of shots. Once individual ASLs for films comprising a national sample have been generated, they can be averaged to produce a national mean, which can then be compared and contrasted with means for other national samples.[18] According to Salt's analysis, based on a sample of several hundred American and European films, sound conversion coincided with an increase in the mean ASL in both Europe and the United States, with sound-era technical conditions reducing the amount of cutting on both continents. Although the American film industry remained committed to an editing-based narration, the number of cuts per film during the early sound years dropped as the American ASL more than doubled, climbing from a norm of 4.8 seconds for 1924–1929 to 10.8 for 1928–1933. The number of cuts for European films also fell significantly, as reflected in an increase from the European mean ASL of 6.6 seconds for 1924–1929 to roughly 12 seconds during 1928–1933.

During the 1930s, however, a divergence in the direction of change is evident. Whereas Salt's figures show that the ASL for Hollywood films gradually dropped during 1934–1939, to reach a low of 8.7 seconds late in the decade, the figure for European films during the same period went up slightly, to yield a norm of 12 seconds; among the European countries during the latter half of the decade, France featured the slowest cutting of all, with a mean ASL of 13 seconds.[19] With respect to French films of 1930–1933, my own statistics, based on a sample of fifty-four films, yield a figure of 11.2; the latter, when juxtaposed against Salt's figure of 13 for 1934–1939, indicates that French shot duration increased, on average, by nearly two seconds in the course of the decade.[20] (See Figure 4.1.) At issue appears to be a significant national difference in the direction of change, with the cutting pace for French films moving in an opposing direction to that for the contemporaneous Hollywood cinema: whereas Hollywood films of the latter half of the decade were cut with increasing rapidity, editing in French films, on the average, slowed down—and at a rate slightly greater than that for European films as a whole.

Just as telling as national differences in the average ASLs are differences in the ranges of dispersal of the data. In the French case, the data range is exceptionally wide, particularly for the early 1930s. Concerning the films of 1930–1933, my analysis records a low of 3.8 and a high of 30.5, which yields a range of nearly 27.[21] Salt's findings for American films of the same period entail a range of 20, roughly 25 percent less than for the French films that comprise my sample. Moreover, as a closer look at the sample reveals, the relatively wide range for the French films transcends differences in genre, with even those films falling within the category of commercial film theatre exhibiting a broad spectrum—ASLs for some films registered at double the mean national figure, while those for others fell far below it. For instance, *On purge bébé* (dir. Jean Renoir, 1930), a boulevard-play adaptation, yields an ASL of 26 seconds—an exceptionally high figure, more than double the contemporaneous national norm for the early 1930s of 11.2. At the opposite end of the spectrum are films such as *Le roi du cirage* (dir. Pière Colombier, 1932) and *Le chien qui rapporte* (dir. Jean Choux, 1931), both of which also feature performances by stage-identified actors as well as ASLs well under half the national average (3.8 and 4.3, respectively).

A great variety of sound-film techniques were employed in France, and technical choices sometimes strongly conditioned a film's editing pace. One 1934 account attributed wide variations in a film's total number of shots to specific sound-film production methods: a post-synchronized "film resting on 'cinematic' technique" might comprise up to 900 shots; "a film of medium length" (in which each shot was filmed separately, in silent-era fashion) commonly encompassed 600 shots; and a direct-recorded "filmed vaudeville" might include 400 shots or less.[22] At a general level, this sort of technical breakdown among types of French sound films can be helpful. It seems generally true, for instance, that high shot counts are likely in films made by directors with modernist backgrounds, disposed perhaps to practice "'cinematic' technique." For instance, *Le parfum de la dame en noir* (*The Perfume of the Lady in Black,* 1931), directed by Marcel L'Herbier, has 844 shots, some 300 more than the national feature-film norm of 547 for 1930–1933.[23] *Le fin du monde* (*The End of the World,* 1930), directed by Abel Gance, another illustrious film-modernist, likewise features an unusually high number of shots, as do the first three films that Clair directed at Tobis—all of which feature ASLs under 9 seconds. One can also cite films such as *Fantômas* (dir. Jean Tarride, 1932), *Le chien qui rapporte* (*The Barking Dog,* dir. Jean Choux, 1931), and *Le triangle de feu* (*The Triangle of Fire,* dir. Edmond Gréville, 1932), all with exceptionally low ASLs (i.e., 4 to 7 seconds), and which feature cutting patterns reminiscent of silent-era modernist montage.

A significant national difference in stylistic range becomes evident when the French figures are plotted on a graph. Salt's figures for American editing norms during 1934–1939 show a pattern that conforms closely to the curve for a normal distribution. The latter, as Salt suggests, implies predictability, and may indicate the existence in Hollywood of an implicit industrywide norm for editing pace, with "filmmakers unconsciously aiming at a standard cutting rate, and failing to hit it due to a variety of disturbing factors." Analogous figures for French films for the early 1930s invite different conclusions. When arranged on a graph, the French figures yield an irregular curve, with extra, non-normal peaks and valleys, as if to imply the force of multiple and perhaps contradictory norms, unchecked by any single standard for cutting pace. (See Figure 4.2.) In addition, the skew of the French figures toward the fast end of the scale, which produces a median (the number marking the middle value in the data set) lower than the arithmetic mean, suggests the probability that the ASL for a randomly chosen French film will be lower than the national norm of 11.2. In short, French films of the early 1930s were, on average, cut relatively rapidly—nearly as fast as American and more rapidly than French films at mid-decade.[24]

Finally, an additional finding regarding ASL suggests that the sort of diversity that obtains across the French cinema as a whole may exist also at the level of individual films. The key point here is that French films sometimes exhibit significant differences in the cutting rate from one part of the film to another. An indication can be found in differences between the ASL for the first thirty minutes of a film and the ASL for the remaining running time. In the computations performed by Barry Salt, ASLs were derived from an examination of only the films' opening thirty minutes, on the grounds that a thirty-minute sample is sufficiently indicative of a film's overall editing style.[25] To produce findings commensurate with Salt's, and thus enable methodologically sound comparisons between French and American films, my ASL figures initially were likewise based on the films' first thirty minutes.[26] But to confirm that these figures were indeed characteristic of the cutting rates for the films as a whole, I compared them to additional ASL computations based on the entire running times of half of the films comprising my national corpus.[27] What I found was surprising: in many cases, the ASLs for a film's entire running time were significantly higher or lower than the ASL for the first thirty minutes. In some cases, the variation was extreme. For instance, the ASL for the opening thirty minutes of *Le chemin du paradis* is 8.8, whereas the ASL for the remaining running time of the same film is 20.3—more than double! Comparable cases include *Marius* (dir. Alexander Korda, 1931), *Poil de carotte* (*Carrot Top,* dir. Julien Duvivier, 1932), and *Faubourg Montmartre* (dir. Raymond Bernard, 1931), all of which feature ASLs for the first thirty seconds over four seconds shorter than the ASLs for the remaining running times. Moreover, the direction of change appears unpredictable: that is, in some films, the editing pace slows down notably, whereas in others it speeds up. The most dramatic examples of the latter include certain films directed by Jean Renoir, whose cutting paces decline radically after the films' opening thirty minutes. For instance, the ASL for *On purge bébé* (*Purging Baby,*

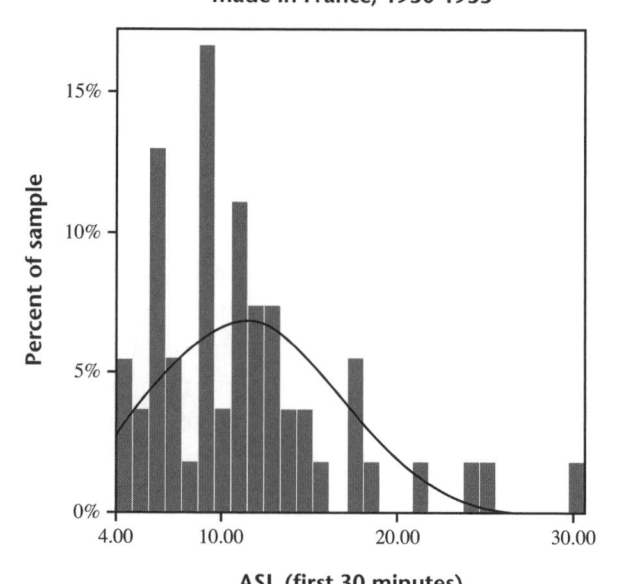

**ASL distribution for films made in France, 1930-1933**

ASL (first 30 minutes)

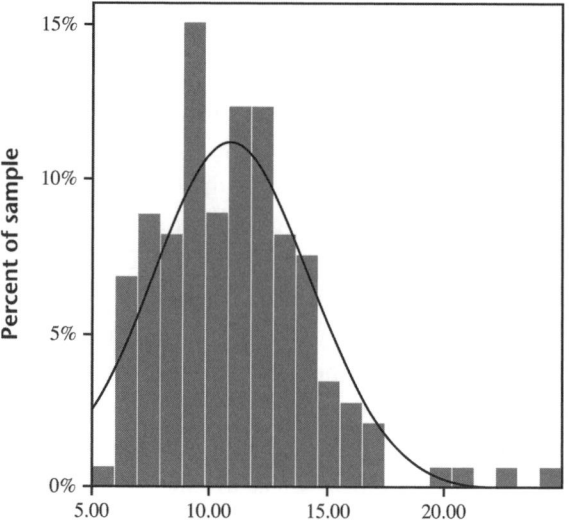

**ASL distribution for films made in U.S., 1928-1933**

ASL (first 30 minutes)

Figs. 4.1 and 4.2: These graphs display visually the statistical results for French and American films of the early 1930s reported in Table 1.

1930) drops from 26 seconds to 17.5, while that for *Chotard et cie.* (1933) falls from 25 to 18.2. At issue here may be a film-historical version of the familiar statistical phenomenon known as the "regression to the mean," whereby over the course of a film's total running time, an ASL that is extremely low or high will gradually tend to approach the statistical norm for the national sample. All the same, examples indicating an increasing distance from the norm in the course of a film's running time can be found. For instance, the ASL for the first thirty minutes of *Le sang d'un poète* (*The Blood of a Poet*, dir. Jean Cocteau, 1930) is 11.2, which is precisely the mean figure for French films of the early 1930s; but for the remainder of the film's running time the ASL shoots up to 19.3.

The wide range of figures and patterns of change—evident at the level both of the national cinema as a whole and of individual films—suggests that, even in light of the homogenization that allegedly occurred during the 1930s, French filmmaking exhibited multiple styles, especially during the early part of the decade. It is tempting to attribute this diversity to the survival in French filmmaking during this time of Gance, Clair, and L'Herbier, together with many other less famous directors, whose backgrounds in silent-era modernism may account for the rapid cutting, as Salt suggests. At the same time, exceptions to this general pattern are readily available. For instance, the German-made *Le chemin du paradis* (dir. Wilhelm von Thiele and Max de Vaucorbeil, 1930) includes only 389 shots, and yields an ASL of 14.1 seconds, roughly three seconds slower than the French national average. Nonetheless, as discussed in chapter 3, *Le chemin du paradis*, with its fluent sound-image technique, was regarded in France as among the most "cinematic" of conversion-era films and an exemplar for an alternative to filmed theatre. Conversely, the direct-recorded vaudeville, *Le roi du cirage* (*The King of Shoeshine*), would seem to count as filmed theatre; but, thanks to its liberal use of multiple-camera shooting, it comprises an astonishing 1,389 shots—more than three times the alleged norm for a film of that genre.

## Sound's Effects on Editing

To assess editing's effect on the viewer's experience requires looking not only at cutting pace but also at the effects on editing of sound and other techniques. As conversion-era observers were aware, sound did not simply supplement the film image but transformed it perceptually, to powerfully affect editing possibilities. Given the relatively slow cutting in some French films, one might assume that these films impressed viewers as moving slowly. But as critical commentary on the films suggests, the situation regarding the spectator's experience of the films is complex. While the sound-era cinema's alleged servitude to theatre was often disparaged, conversion-era French films were not described as slowly paced. What has been stressed instead has been the films' formal openness and sense of chaotic spontaneity, grounded in the liveness of the actors' performances, and the films' sometimes pell-mell mix of genres, styles, and techniques. With sound-image techniques in French films sometimes varying from shot to shot, movement lost through slow cutting may well resurface in a different technical register—via acting, camera movement, unorthodox changes in camera position, volatile ambient sound, and/or ensemble compositions crowded with speaking actors. Especially important in defining the 1930s French cinema in subsequent historiography has been camera movement, whose possibilities were explored in France to an extraordinary degree during the 1930s. Even seemingly unambitious productions such as *Les gaîtés de l'escadron* (dir. Maurice Tourneur, 1932) and *Le rosier de Madame Husson* (*Madame Husson's Servant,* dir. Bernard Deschamps, 1932) feature, in certain scenes, stunningly elaborate long takes filmed with moving cameras. Even when a film's overall cutting pace is slow, with numerous scenes comprising only a single shot, a virtually constant mobility may nonetheless be generated through figure movement together with a tracking camera. For instance, *Chotard et cie.* features an ASL of 22 seconds, a figure close to double the national norm. Nonetheless, actors not only move frequently but do so in ways that appear spontaneous, forcing the camera operator to adjust to spur-of-the-moment contingencies, as when the camera begins tracking, and then—as if responding off-the-cuff to an actor's unexpected movement—reverses itself suddenly, pulling back instead of pushing forward.

French filmmakers appear to have been particularly concerned to restore "mouvement" or "mobilité" to the cinema, according to the axiom that "all that does not move is anti-cinéma."[28] It is not clear, however, that the movement in question is narrative movement in the sense associated with Hollywood cinema. When invoking the need for movement, French critics and filmmakers often seem concerned less to push the plot forward than to overcome the stasis associated with France's dialogue-heavy popular stage. In interviews, filmmakers, when discussing the technical challenge of conversion-era filmmaking, stated the need to "animate" the image, as director Julien Duvivier put it.[29] Likewise, scenarist René Pujol claimed to strive for "a form as visual as possible," and described his work as that of "'cinematographising' a text."[30] In an interview regarding his labor on *Le roi du cirage,* a breakneck-paced vaudeville film comprising nearly 1,400 shots, director Pière Colombier declared relentless "action" the antidote for the *film parlant*'s visual monotony: "I believe that the rhythm of a 'talkie' must be more rapid than that of the silent films. The action must not stop, not even for a second."[31] Such comments allude to editing's power to generate a sense of movement, while saying nothing about the need to employ editing in the service of a character-driven, cause-and-effect narrative—as if editing's main function had less to do with storytelling than with maintaining the viewer's interest perceptually via a sort of aesthetics of ceaseless stimulation. The implicit question appears to have been: How does one record the performances of stage actors, simultaneously with images, and, in as "cinematic" a manner as possible, overcome the stasis of a stage-bound mise-en-scène?

Attempts to answer this question pushed French filmmakers toward new variants of a conception of film editing that Colin Crisp refers to as "expressive editing," according to which editing choices are not determined by character psychology but are expressive of a scene's overall dramatic or comedic nature, with certain types of scenes requiring certain editing patterns.[32] In other words, in French films, cutting is often seen as a function of the nature of the scene's dramatic situation or genre, so that, for instance, scenes involving physical or emotional conflict will be cut more rapidly than scenes of narrative tranquility— irrespective of considerations of character psychology. This genre-founded approach to cutting was common during conversion, with vaudeville-style comedies such as *Le roi du cirage* featuring an extraordinary amount of cutting, far more than necessary for narrowly psychological purposes, but appropriate in light of the film's "crazy comedy" status. The preponderance of this a-psychological editing in French filmmaking was sometimes criticized by trade-press editorialists, who cautioned that French filmmakers lacked "a sense of 'continuity,'" employing camera angles unjustified "by the action or the direction of the story."[33]

In addition to the amount of cutting, consideration must also be directed to national differences in the manner in which shots were joined. In Hollywood, techniques that entailed carrying sounds across the shot change were crucial to the Hollywood cinema's trademark—the impression of forward narrative movement. An example is an off-screen sound that anticipates slightly an image that reveals the sound's source—as when a shot's final frames are accompanied by a sound whose putative source appears in the next shot's space. In other cases, on-screen sound may continue momentarily beyond an image to become off-screen sound, as when a line of dialogue endures slightly beyond the shot change. Sonic overlaps of this sort opened intriguing possibilities for rapid storytelling, as Alfred Hitchcock noted (1937) apropos of "reaction shots," in which the image of an actor's face is accompanied by the off-screen voice of another character: "This overrunning of one person's image with another person's voice is a method peculiar to the talkies; it is one of the devices which help the talkies to tell a story faster than a silent film could tell it, and faster than it could be told on the stage."[34]

Editing in conversion-era French films was less dependent on sound-image overlaps, so that the cutting within scenes sometimes seems episodic, with each shot standing on its own, as it were, formally autonomous relative to other shots. By some accounts, editing in French films of the early 1930s recalled the succession of tableaux images in the first multi-shot narrative films of the 1900s, insofar as scale-matched shots likewise showed up as self-contained units—quasi-autonomous tableaux, or separate performance events. Such shots functioned almost as scenes in themselves, as Jacques Kermabon notes, apropos of the many scenes in films made at Pathé-Natan in which close-ups and inserts, filmed separately, fail to integrate into the space of the scene's master shot.[35] One condition for the effect of discontinuity that Kermabon describes are "parallel cuts," in which the shot change coincides exactly with the change in sound accompaniment. In tending to draw attention to themselves, such cuts exposed the artifice of the film's manufacture and thus undermined the all-important illusion of a coherent, self-contained story-world. Thus, in film-technical manuals, parallel cuts are identified as a mistake or continuity flaw.[36] Nonetheless, they occur frequently in French films of the early 1930s. (See Figures 4.3 and 4.4.)

In contrast to sequences of images that serve to propel the viewer ahead—via a logic of cause and effect—editing in certain French films might best be characterized as additive rather than causal, as if shots had accumulated or piled up rather than succeeded one another in linear time.

In certain cases, the question arises as to whether the shot sequence implies successive or simultaneous actions. An example can be found in the opening scene of Renoir's *La chienne* (*The Bitch*, 1931), in which certain of the shots of a dinner-table celebration succeed one another in ways open to contradictory temporal interpretations. (See Figures 4.5 and 4.6.) A comment concerning the open-ended temporality of the cutting of *La chienne* can be found in a 1931 review of the film, which includes the observation that "one can reverse the order of scenes or even shots without effect."[37] In a recent analysis of *La chienne*, Michel Chion, making the same point, explains the peculiar cutting as the effect of a mismatch, so to speak, between Renoir's filmmaking skills—cultivated in the avant-garde milieu of the French cinema of the late silent years—and the unavoidable technical and aesthetic demands of sound-era editing. At issue is the sort of phenomenon prominent in the multi-temporal historiography discussed in chapter 2, in which advances in the technical domain unfold at a rate that outstrips the capacity of the filmmakers to adapt artistically to the altered film-technological reality. In the case of *La chienne*, Renoir, not yet thinking like a sound-era filmmaker, had not appreciated how synchronous sound inevitably "linearized" a shot, inscribing it with relentless directionality.[38] With many silent-era veterans directing films in conversion-era France, it is worth examining the notion that the peculiarities of conversion-era film editing derived from filmmakers still thinking in silent-era terms. What did it mean in the context of early sound film to continue thinking like a silent filmmaker? Given the cinema's wide range of editing practices during the 1920s, a fine-grained answer to this question may vary considerably from case to case. Nonetheless, certain generalizations seem possible in light of the central role in conversion-era cinema of stage-trained actors, whose distinctive, live-entertainment virtuosity imposed certain stylistic requirements on filmmakers. Most fundamental here was the renewed pertinence of the notion of the scene as the recording of a performance.

## The Case of Scale-Matching

Indicating the relevance of the performance-based notion of the scene to 1930s French cinema are certain cases in which French film-

Figs. 4.3 and 4.4: A shot sequence from the Braunberger-Richebé stage adaptation *Le blanc et le noir* (Robert Florey, 1930) illustrates how direct-sound practice can complicate an otherwise conventional diegesis. When examined independently of the sound accompaniment, the succession of images—with its eyeline match and the actors' call-and-response gestures—implies temporal and spatial wholeness. But when the sound accompaniment is taken into account, a radical discontinuity becomes evident: while the first image features no ambient noise, the second image coincides with the din of off-screen voices of adjacent partygoers. Thus, in contrast to the continuous image track, the sound pulls in a different direction perceptually, inscribing each shot within its own space and time and thus isolating the actors' performances in spaces that seem decidedly non-contiguous. Direct sound's tendency to contradict the coherence of the story-world is evident in many French films of the 1930s, and helps explain the endurance into the sound era of what Alan Williams refers to "the French tradition of respect for the shot."

Figs. 4.5 and 4.6. This two-shot sequence from *La chienne* (Jean Renoir, 1931) reveals how direct-sound practices can affect relations between shots in ways that complicate the temporality of a film's narration. The first of the two shots begins with a toast and concludes with cheers from the men assembled at the table; the subsequent shot, taken from a significantly different camera position, depicts a portion of an event that seems similar if not identical: a burst of applause and laughter from the group at the table. The sense that a single action has carried over from shot to shot is attenuated by the ninety-degree change in camera position, which introduces a space only partially contiguous with that of the preceding shot. Also disorienting is the fragmentary character of the second shot's action, in which the table's laughter is presented without the remark that presumably caused it. Thus, questions arise as to whether the shot sequence depicts a single, continuous narrative event, two discrete and successive events, or two versions of the same event. In light of such questions *La chienne* has been described as a film whose editing at times seems arbitrary, as if Renoir, still thinking like a silent filmmaker, had not yet come to terms with synchronous sound's capacity to wreak havoc with the temporality of shot relations.

makers followed Hollywood's rules more rigorously than Hollywood filmmakers themselves did. An intriguing, editing-related example concerns the rule of scale-matching, which referred to microphone placement during the recording of actors' voices. In essence, the rule required that a single microphone be placed at roughly the same distance from the actor(s) as the camera. For an actor appearing in extreme long shot, the microphone was positioned at an equivalent extreme distance, thus ensuring a match of the voice's reverberation to the image's visual expanse. Conversely, a close-up of a speaking actor required a close microphone, to capture minimal reflected sound and thus produce an intimate voice, appropriate to the magnified image scale. In any case, the objective was to position microphones so as to endow the recorded voice with spatial qualities compatible with the image.

The case for the scale-matching of voice and image was articulated in numerous articles published in film periodicals during the 1930s.[39] The basic principle extrapolated from the familiar notion of the film viewer as an "invisible witness," in which the camera's visual field was likened to that of a human observer of a staged drama. Drawing a compelling analogy, scale-matching's proponents compared the microphone to a listener's ear, claiming that scale-matched shots served to locate the film viewer as an invisible auditor. Such shots, it was alleged, captured the sound as a firsthand witness, situated on the sound-stage, would have heard it. Compatible with the emphasis on fidelity in the music-recording field, the analogy between microphone and camera, from a technical as well as theoretical standpoint, carried the implacable authority of common sense. But in the domain of fiction filmmaking it proved surprisingly difficult to put into practice given the eventual need to integrate separate shots into a spatially and temporally unified scene. Scale-matched shots, however naturalistic as representations of a performance event, sometimes proved impossible to edit together properly. In the case of shot breaks involving major changes in camera position, they stood out as self-contained fragments, or unique performance events, separate and discontinuous from adjacent shots.[40] The shot's degree of formal autonomy, its tendency to function almost as a scene in itself was sometimes justified by principles that defied the Hollywood practice of ensuring that actors' speech carried across the cut from shot to shot. For instance, to minimize the problem of aurally disjunctive shot changes, filmmakers were advised that "the recording of a shot for a sound film can be begun or ended only during a pause in the dialogue."[41] With many filmmakers acting on this advice, and cutting only once the actor had finished speaking, a film's editing could be said to have become a "prisoner of speech," that is, determined by the length of the dialogue rather than by the nature of the dramatic action, film-genre convention, or by the film's internal formal logic.[42] According to filmmaker and theorist Jean Epstein, "It seems that the talkie renders useless all constructions of editing [*découpage*], other than those, given in advance, by the give-and-take of the dialogue's phrases and replies."[43]

Filmmakers in Hollywood soon developed a solution to the editing problem posed by scale-matched shots. The solution, in essence, meant varying the image scale as usual, while keeping the vocal microphone's distance constant, regardless of camera distance. Beginning in 1931, a typical Hollywood film featured changes in image scale encompassing the familiar permutations of master shot, medium shot, and close-up; but the actors' voice scales remained fixed, in the medium-close range. In the event, the continuous vocal foreground served to compensate formally for the visual disjunction of the shot change, while also facilitating the story-world illusion. The problem of how to integrate synch-sound shots into a spatially and temporally unified scene was thus solved, but in a manner that completely disregarded the imperative to match scales, as Hollywood filmmakers were well aware: "We place the mike as close to the actor as the camera angle permits . . . and we hardly try to create an acoustic perspective corresponding to the scene's visual perspective," claimed sound engineer John G. Frayne, referring to recording practice in 1930s Hollywood.[44]

In effect, attempts to scale-match had forced awareness of a conflict between an allegedly inviolable technical norm and established aesthetic norms for scene construction. As the nature of the conflict became clear, sound technicians explicitly repudiated scale-matching as doctrine, theorists of scale-matching modified their claims, and scale-matched shots became restricted to special, narration-related purposes. Examples include establishing-shot beginnings and endings of scenes, and instances of so-called point-of-audition sound, in which—in a manner analogous to the point-of-view shot—a scale-matched voice suggests a character's subjective perception of a narrative event.[45] However, in a Hollywood film, outside such exceptional cases, the vocal scale tends to remain constant, whatever the shot scale. Here a national style difference is evident. In French films, considerable shot-to-shot variations in sound characteristics can often be heard, as scale-matching remained common practice in the French film industry throughout the 1930s. As a consequence, according to one critic, "The grave difficulty of the talking film is precisely the rupture of equilibrium experienced by the auditor at the moment when the sound no longer [matches] the image following a change of shot." In such cases, "The unity is broken through the images of close or distant shots in rapid succession, the speech unable to follow."[46] In effect, while French and American filmmakers both embraced scale-matching in principle, the French were far more likely to rigorously match voice and image scales in workaday practice. Thus, in French films of the 1930s, individual shots often exhibit unusual formal autonomy relative to adjacent shots.

## How Might National Style Differences be Explained?

In the face of the scant attention in film historiography both to national popular cinema and to conversion-era film technique, the objective of much of the preceding analysis has been to define differences between French and American editing practices. The descriptive project has served to identify basic, national style differences during a time when such differences were generally believed to have eroded. At this point, now that certain editing-related tendencies of the 1930s have been specified, it becomes possible to ask how the national differences might be explained. The beginnings of an explanation are implicit in the preceding pages, whose analyses situate editing practice in a film-industrial context, and in relation to other techniques and practices, showing what happened in a way that suggests how it happened. In this regard, considerations of technology and technique have been central, but in ways that differ significantly from established explanations. In the remaining section of the chapter, the focus is on major alternative approaches to explaining French editing practice.

In much film historiography, style changes are explained in terms of the work of individual directors (key names here include Porter, Griffith, and Eisenstein), or of specific movements, such as German expressionism, the French New Wave, Soviet montage, and so on. But with regard to the conversion years, when style seemed so obviously a function of technical constraints, explanations in terms of filmmakers' intentions seem applicable to only a small portion of the film industry's output. Thus, conversion-era film style is commonly explained with reference not to aesthetic but to economic and technological causes. For instance, Salt attributes the increase in Hollywood's editing pace during the 1930s to the introduction of mechanical editing tables and other devices made necessary by the technical requirements of editing both image and sound. In the case of optical sound, sound and image didn't pass through the projector in the same place, so in order to remain in synch, they had to be cut in staggered fashion. Facilitating the proper staggering were sound synchronizers like the Moviola, introduced into American film-editing rooms beginning in 1930. By 1931, as Hollywood began adopting multi-track recording and mixing, special synchronizers, designed to manipulate up to four separate sound tracks at once, became standard in editing rooms. Another crucial new editing device was the rubber-number machine, which served to stamp common numbers on sound and image tracks. According to Salt, as these machines were installed in Hollywood editing rooms, and filmmakers became adept at using them, the Hollywood cinema's mean ASL began to decline, dropping by more than 2 seconds—falling from 10.8 seconds for 1928–1933 to 8.6 seconds for 1934–1939.[47]

In conversion-era France, the situation was different. Filmmakers continued to employ editing technologies and methods that dated back to the silent era, when editing-related tools were limited mainly to scissors, glue, and reels for winding film.[48] In conversion-era France, the person cutting the film sometimes worked manually, in silent-era fashion—holding the positive print up to the light, eyeing the image, and then cutting with a scissors.[49] In contrast to the film industries of the United States or Germany, where editors consulted with laboratories on the quality of negatives and prints, in France the editor's task was generally limited to the activity of physically cutting the film. Two-track editing machines, such as the Moritone, remained standard in France until the mid-1940s. In some cases, the individual who did the actual cutting was someone without specialized, editing-related training.[50] As late as 1933, directors were said to enter the editing room to cut the image track themselves, ignorant of the implications for the film's sound.[51] In any case, by the time a film was ready for post-production, money and time were often too scarce to enable the sort of repair work that filmmakers hoped for. By and large, sound-film editing in 1930s France was a hurried, low-tech endeavor. According to one critic, "The work on a film after the shooting, known as the 'montage' and on which a film's quality largely depends, is thus reduced to the minimum, if not eliminated altogether." [52]

It seems that the distinctiveness of French film-editing technology and technique endured long after the 1930s. According to Colin Crisp, as late as 1949, rubber-numbering machines and multi-channel synchronizers remained unavailable in France: "It seems that the technology already available to American editors in 1932 was still not available in France 17 years later, where the equivalent work was still being done by hand." [53] Given editing-related technical demands during the sound era, when the image could no longer be cut without an awareness of its effect on the sound, the persistence of the old low-tech methods in French filmmaking is remarkable.

How is this persistence to be explained? Or, put another way, what accounts for the French film industry's slow and selective adoption of the new technologies? Insofar as the particularities of a national film style are attributed to the technology itself (or, conversely, its absence), historical explanations are open to criticism for exhibiting "technological determinism." [54] Technologically deterministic explanations of film style have a long history in accounts of French cinema. Examples were abundant during conversion, when trade-press editorialists in France frequently lamented the effects on the national film style of the French film industry's chronically rudimentary plant and equipment. But given that numbering machines were inexpensive, simple mechanical devices, economic causes appear indirectly relevant at best, and thus must be seen relative to other sorts of forces, such as traditions of local film practice. It may be, for instance, that rubber-numbering machines were not used in France because they wouldn't have facilitated the task of film editing as practiced there. In the case of scenes that had been direct-recorded, there was, in effect, no sound to edit. The editing, as it were, had occurred in advance, so to speak—on-the-spot, with microphone inputs fed straight into the sound camera or disc recorder. In this context, American-style editing tables, with their capacity for cutting together up to four separate sound tracks, "are less practical than similar French tables," as one veteran filmmaker put it; such devices were useful only when there were separate tracks to edit. [55]

During a technology-defined period such as sound conversion, when film style often looked like a function of technological constraint, technologically deterministic explanations refer to important conditions for film practice of the time. But they can be highly misleading insofar as they become mono-causal, suggesting that technologies somehow determined their own use. As a consideration of specific, editing-related cases of technological adaptation in sound-era France suggests, a less linear understanding of technology's impact on film style, attuned to the particularities of local film and media cultures, is needed. However conditioned by industrial-technological factors, film style also appears underdetermined by such factors, even during a technology-defined period such as sound conversion. As a consequence, the explanatory project can benefit from a case-oriented approach that situates technologies and techniques within the national film-cultural contexts, the web of practices and commitments, in which they became meaningful in specific places and times.

A key condition for the impression that sound conversion had flattened national film-style differences was the adoption of editing techniques associated with Hollywood in diverse national film industries during the 1930s. The emulation internationally of Hollywood practice stands as prima facie evidence for the sound-era homogenization of world film style, as does the awareness among filmmakers worldwide of the norms of Hollywood-style editing, evident in films made in diverse countries. But how is the sound-era diffusion of such norms to be understood? In traditional accounts, editing's standardization is understood as a byproduct of conversion, as if the introduction of recorded sound had necessitated adherence to certain editing norms, associated with Hollywood films. In this chapter, the project has been to reveal a different dimension to early sound cinema through a focus on national differences in how editing norms were interpreted.

In light of the shift in perspective, the possibility arises that while continuity techniques and rules may have become universalized during the 1930s, how they were put into practice was a function of current and local circumstance, with the same norms open to multiple and sometimes divergent interpretation. In the next chapter, the place-specific dimension of sound-era filmmaking is examined further through an analysis of practices of shooting and recording. At issue here is a film-technical domain where the effects of local circumstance proved uniquely powerful, with French recording methods differing substantially from Hollywood's methods throughout the 1930s—notwithstanding the shared emphasis in both film industries on a tight voice-image synch, and the selective adaptation in the French film industry of Hollywood's tools and techniques.

# 5 Shooting and Recording in Paris and Hollywood

The French cinema's stylistic distinctiveness relative to the Hollywood cinema is especially evident with respect to practices of shooting and film-sound recording. This distinction can be seen in comparing the fate of the phonographic imperative in the French and American film industries. According to the phonographic imperative, or fidelity principle, a recording should faithfully reproduce a sound as a witness to the performance can be presumed to have heard it. Foundational for key sound technologies of the late nineteenth century, such as Edison's phonograph (1878) and Berliner's gramophone (1887), the fidelity principle informed Hollywood's sound-film practice beginning in 1926, with the first Vitaphone and Fox-Movietone productions. By 1931, however, following a sustained trial-and-error effort to utilize sound technology in line with Hollywood's silent-era aesthetic and technical norms, the relevance of music-industry standards faded, and the emphasis throughout Hollywood's studio system shifted away from sound's fidelity to performance and toward its story-world intelligibility. Thus, in recent scholarship, the U.S. sound conversion has been analyzed as an industry-wide change from one basic conception of sound-film recording to another.[1]

In France, fidelity-based techniques had a similar overall history, but with a different chronology and a more protracted, less linear pattern of change. Fidelity-oriented filmmaking was introduced into the French film industry in 1930, at the beginning of industrial sound-film production in Paris, just as it was being phased out in Hollywood. Moreover, fidelity techniques remained central to French filmmaking throughout the 1930s, nearly a full decade later than in Hollywood. It wasn't until the 1940s, with the standardization of the multi-track "psychological realism" of quality cinema, that intelligibility considerations displaced the fidelity norm in France; and even then, the displacement was partial, with fidelity techniques remaining prevalent in French filmmaking. Referring to the French cinema's enduring preference for direct sound, sound engineer Willem Sivel, writing in 1948, claimed that French and American practices continued to exhibit alternative understandings of "a satisfactory use of sound."[2]

In this chapter, national differences in film-sound recording are examined through a comparative investigation into American and French aesthetic norms, techniques, work routines, and personnel hierarchies. First, fundamental national differences in aesthetic norms are examined in terms of a basic distinction between the French cinema's stage-performance style and the contemporaneous American cinema's editing-based narration. Next, the comparative inquiry is extended into differences in how these norms became concretized in specific sound-film recording methods. Topics discussed here include: "re-recording," a post-production technique much touted in the French film industry trade-press during the 1930s but rarely practiced in France until late in the decade; differences in voice-recording practice deriving from the American use of a single microphone versus the French preference for multiple microphones; differences in studio acoustics, with the French favoring the high reverberation characteristic of music recording in contrast to the American preference for the acoustic deadness appropriate for recording dialogue; and finally, the French cinema's unorthodox adaptation of the old American technique of multiple-camera shooting. In the chapter's concluding sections, an explanation of the French approach to shooting and recording in terms of film-industrial conditions focuses on the sound technicians' role in the French film industry relative to that in the United States.

## Hollywood's Emphasis on Sound's Intelligibility

A notable feature of Hollywood's adaptation of sound technology to classical story-construction norms is how quickly and uniformly it occurred. By early 1931, less than five years after the release of the first Vitaphone and Fox-Movietone films, the Hollywood community had substantially revised its approach to film sound. In a detailed study of Hollywood's year-by-year output during this time, Donald Crafton identifies the film season of 1930–1931 as the decisive turning point—the year when a new, post-conversion sound style coalesced. Instead of "overt theatrical presentations" à la the 1926 Vitaphone shorts featuring artists from the New York Philharmonic Orchestra to guitarist Roy Smeck ("Wizard of the Strings") or revue musicals such as *Paramount on Parade* (dir. Charles de Rochefort, 1929–1930), the films of 1930–1931 exemplified the narrative-defined style familiar to American feature films since the late 1910s.[3] Variety-show successions of stand-alone songs, dances, and skits gave way to the "integrated musical," with its seamless transitions between "real-world" narrative and utopian song-and-dance. By 1933 Hollywood films were routinely accompanied by orchestral scores, written by film-industry composers. Sound-film technique no longer served to foreground self-contained "acts" or performance events but instead to contribute to Hollywood's established storytelling project.

The new, narrative-defined soundtrack, with its intermittent orchestral accompaniment, did not evolve naturally from conversion-era precedent but instead was the product of a coordinated effort of technical research and experimentation. In a cooperative project sponsored by the major studios, filmmakers and technicians collaborated with technical-support companies to adapt sound technology in conformity to Hollywood's established approach to film narration. The challenge entailed the unexpected, counterintuitive revision of established, sound-related assumptions deriving from the music industry and other sound-technological domains, such as those relating to the telephone and other electronic communications. Film personnel confronted awkward problems deriving from the history of the sound technologies, which had been developed entirely outside the film industry, in the context of projects whose aim, in one regard or another, was to accurately reproduce an original sound signal. The history of such projects traced back to sound recording's beginnings in the mechanical telegraph of the late eighteenth century, and to more recent phenomena such as the wireless telegraph, long-distance telephone service, public address technology, and military and transport communications such as ship-to-shore radio—endeavors all informed by the goal of the accurate reproduction of a signal.[4]

The objectives informing the development of these communications technologies were far from congruent with the project of fiction filmmaking, whose basic technical goal was not to reproduce an original signal but to create the illusion of a coherent fictional world. In this context, considerations of fidelity were largely beside the point. As had been evident throughout the history of narrative cinema, a film's impression of story-world wholeness did not require the reproduction of an extra-filmic reality. In fact, more often than not, a film's diegetic world amounted to a construction whose impression of coherence rested on technical ruses of one sort or another, from the virtual geography of the eyeline match to showstopping *trucages* ("tricks") and special effects, as well as tried and true costcutting methods such as trompe l'oeil scenery and day-for-night shooting. In fact, representational accuracy, in some cases, could prove problematic. With respect to sound, for instance, attempts to capture reality sometimes undermined the story-world illusion, as when the physical presence of the actors, the recording environment, and/or the recording technology itself became overly emphatic. Recall that the evident "liveness" of Al Jolson's direct-recorded performances in *The Jazz Singer* allowed critics to claim that Jolson had "played himself" rather than incarnate a fictional character.[5]

Essential to Hollywood's abandonment of the fidelity emphasis were technological developments that freed filmmakers from the need to record sound and image simultaneously. As sound production split off from image production, synchronization's extraordinary capacity to suggest a causal link between what is seen and what is heard became subject to the filmmakers' control. When isolated onto separate tracks, a sound's phenomenal characteristics were no longer limited to what had happened on the set, at the instant of recording, but could be manipulated after the fact in diverse ways. These manipulations ranged from "filtering" (the use of electronics to cut out the high and/or low end of the frequency spectrum) to altering the speed of the recording, and included the addition of artificial reverberation, whereby the ratio of direct to reflected sound was augmented through electro-acoustic means. During the 1930s, electronically "tweaked" sounds, à la the post-synchronized honk of Harpo Marx's horn, became increasingly common on Hollywood soundtracks. Such sounds contributed powerfully to the Hollywood cinema's trademark sense of linearity by simplifying a shot's effect or meaning, pulling the viewer's attention toward a single aspect or feature of the image.

Most fundamentally, the isolation of sounds onto separate tracks made it possible, simply through volume control, to make sounds seem close or distant, and thus to generate a sense of story-world three-dimensionality. More than simply a modification of existing practice, the shaping of film sound in foreground-background terms signaled a basic shift in aesthetic priorities, whereby the construction of a story-world took absolute precedence, regardless of whether the result accurately reproduced a real-world original.[6] Adopted quickly throughout the studio system, multi-track methods quickly came to define Hollywood's approach to film sound. By the summer of 1932, even minor studios such as Universal had institutionalized them. In 1933, at Warner Bros.—a famously cost-conscious studio—"as many as sixteen separate sound tracks, each one carefully controlled as to level, perspective and quality, [were used] to make a pleasing composite soundtrack."[7] Since the 1930s and up through the present, a layered, multi-track approach to film sound has defined the Hollywood cinema relative to other national cinemas.

## The French Cinema's Fidelity-based Alternative

It is with regard to practices of sound-film recording that the French film industry's divergence from the American film industry is especially evident. Throughout the 1930s, direct sound (*son direct*), the simultaneous recording of sound and image, was described in the French film trade-press as inherently superior to sound that had been recorded separately and then added to the soundtrack during post-production.[8] By and large, significant movement away from direct recording occurred in France only in 1938 and 1939, when techniques of post-synchronization began to be used in the French studios not only for dubbing but also for purposes of ordinary scene construction.[9] In short, throughout the sound cinema's first decade, French recording practice could be said to have rested on the inverse of what Rick Altman has identified as the fundamental principle guiding the evolution of Hollywood's sound style: whereas technicians in 1930s Hollywood developed a battery of methods for separating sound production from image production, filmmakers in France privileged the "naturalism" that came from simultaneous sound-image recording.[10]

Indicative of the French cinema's naturalist priority is the extent to which fidelity-oriented methods were undertaken regardless of the technical problems. Examples include the numerous moving-camera shots in French films during which actors speak. With sound and camera personnel required to choreograph their movements so as to keep microphones, cords, and shadows outside the camera's visual field, such shots imposed a formidable physical challenge for production crews. For tracking shots made in the studios, microphones were often "planted" on the set rather than suspended from a mobile boom. Technicians ensured that the final track would reproduce only or primarily sounds whose sources appeared within the camera's view by "opening" or "closing" microphones as the camera moved through the set. In cases when the dialogue's volume and reverberation varied considerably in the course of a single shot, it proved difficult to edit the shots together.[11] Such "mobile shots" were "the great terror of the studios," according to Fritz Lang, commenting on his work on *Liliom,* a film he directed in Paris in 1934.[12]

Although technical difficulties might be assumed to have limited the incidence of direct-recorded camera movement in French films, the opposite is said to have been the case; according to a 1937 trade-press report, the use of traveling camera shots in which actors spoke while moving had become increasingly prevalent in French filmmaking, despite requiring "acrobatic" efforts from the production crew.[13] (See Figure 5.1.) The device of the direct-recorded moving camera was pushed to extremes in films such as *L'illustre Maurin* (*The Illustrious Maurin*, dir. André Hugon, 1933), whose tracking shots, recorded outdoors and featuring soliloquy-like monologues, required the laying of camera tracks of up to 375 meters in length.[14] Special difficulties arose from certain forms of location shooting that were unusually common in French sound films. Numerous French films of the 1930s feature scenes filmed in noisy, automobile-clogged public places. A striking example can be found in *Le roi du cirage* (dir. Pière Colombier, 1932), in which a direct-recorded conversation occurs on a Parisian *grande boulevard,* in the backseat of a moving car—a convertible with the top down. (See Figure 5.2.) Similar shots featuring direct-recorded conversations, recorded on streets in moving cars, appear in other films made in France during this time, such as *Le sexe faible* (*The Weak Sex,* dir. Robert Siodmak, 1933). Most remarkable of all, however, are the numerous dialogue scenes filmed in interior locations—commonly regarded by sound technicians as the most difficult of recording sites.[15] Besides *L'illustre Maurin,* examples occur in certain high-reverb interior scenes in *Le chien jaune* (*The Yellow Dog,* dir. Jean Tarride, 1931). (See Figure 5.3.)

These practices—which were virtually nonexistent in Hollywood filmmaking—endured in French filmmaking through the 1930s and into the next decade. As late as 1939, multi-track sound in the Hollywood sense remained a relatively new technique in the French film industry, where it was practiced only in an ad hoc, non-routinized manner,

Fig. 5.1. A production still of the making of a direct-recorded traveling camera shot for *La kermesse héroïque* (Jacques Feyder, 1935)—a type of shot frequent in the French cinema of the 1930s, despite the exceptional technical challenges it posed for production crews.

and in the context of an overall approach to film sound emphasizing direct sound.[16] Even after the modernization of film-industrial practice during the German occupation of France, direct sound remained an important option in French filmmaking. According to sound technician Willem Sivel, commenting on French cinema in the late 1940s: "A simple formula expresses the situation: we make our best sound while the camera operator makes the image."[17] In short, the sort of fidelity-based approach that had been decidedly marginalized in Hollywood by 1931 remained central to French filmmaking decades later.

### The Case of Re-Recording

Throughout the 1930s, the latest multi-track techniques were discussed in the French film trade-press, where they sometimes found strong advocates, but typically standardization of these techniques occurred only during the 1940s or even later. A telling example concerns

Fig. 5.2. Indicative of the experimental character of the mainstream French cinema's sound practices—regardless of potential technical problems—are scenes like this one in *Le roi du cirage* (Pière Colombier, 1932), in which a direct-recorded conversation occurs on a busy Parisian boulevard—in the wind-blown backseat of a speeding convertible!

the post-production technique of "re-recording," which involved re-cording the track(s) comprising a film's finished, positive-print sound-track a second time, so as to produce a new negative for the film's release prints.[18] When undertaken on a multi-track system, re-recording offered great advantages for leveling out moment-by-moment variations in loudness and for creating the proper hierarchy of dialogue, music, and ambient sound. When re-recorded, scenes comprising shots and sounds made in different times and places could be made to seem formally continuous in a film's final print.[19] In Hollywood, the practice of re-recording became widespread immediately following its introduction in 1931; by 1932, up to 50 percent of the average Hollywood film was said to have been re-recorded.[20] Re-recording's effects on the overall technical quality of Hollywood films were immediately evident in France, where

Fig. 5.3. A frame enlargement from one of several scenes in the Braunberger-Richebé production *Le chien jaune* (Jean Tarride, 1931) whose dialogue appears to have been recorded not on a sound-stage but in a real-world interior—the sort of space widely regarded by film-sound specialists as the most technically problematic of recording sites. In this scene, set in a cavernous, warehouse-like space, a direct-recorded conversation between actors Robert Le Vigan and Abel Tarride (barely visible among those standing to the left of the table) comes embedded in the ambient sound of the set's vast interior. Defining the latter is the reverberant voice of an off-screen auctioneer, which resounds in the room's hollow space throughout the scene's duration.

the "unity" and "homogeneity" of the Hollywood films of 1931 was attributed to the re-recorded soundtracks.[21]

The technique was of particular interest in France, where the domestic cinema's soundtracks often exhibited considerable random variation in volume from scene to scene, and even from shot to shot.[22] The problem was serious enough in 1932 that projectionists in theatres were advised to raise and lower projection volume accordingly during a film's screening, in a manner reminiscent of the early days of sound-on-disc projection.[23] With re-recording offering great promise for regularizing the technical quality of French soundtracks, editorialists in the French trade-press advocated the practice's adoption throughout the national film industry.[24] Regarding re-recording's impact on sound-film practice, "we are in the presence of a true revolution," predicted one commentator.[25] Nonetheless, as late as 1938, re-recording was still practiced only infrequently in the French studios.[26] Moreover, in one trade-press weekly, *Le cinéopse,* standardization of the practice was explicitly rejected, with the journal's editor characterizing re-recording as an option of last resort, to be used only when a film's original, direct-recorded soundtrack proved so problematic that there was no way to repair it.[27]

As is sometimes the case in the history of film technology, the historian is confronted by a pattern of evidence that imposes the challenge of explaining why something did *not* happen. Given recognition within the French film community of re-recording's "quality" advantage, why wasn't this technique practiced immediately and systematically in the French film industry? When approached from a film-cultural standpoint, the answer lies in the extent to which re-recording, as practiced in Hollywood, presupposed a multi-track system, which allowed adjustment of the dialogue's volume level separately from that of the other sounds. In France during the 1930s, however, all sounds were often recorded together, onto the same track. In this single-track context, Hollywood-style re-recording went against the grain of established film-industry practice and thus happened mainly through singular, ad hoc efforts. It was only later—during the German occupation of 1940–1944, when multi-track sound became prevalent in the French film industry—that re-recording became standardized in French filmmaking. Occupation-era commentators even went so far as to propose a ban on scenes that had *not* been re-recorded.[28] But as the proposal for a ban suggests, the use in France of re-recording and other multi-track techniques remained far less systematic than in Hollywood, and French films during the 1940s were still released "raw," as it were, with minimal modification of the soundtrack in post-production.

### Voices in Context: The Fidelity/Intelligibility Trade-Off

The basic national preference for direct sound carried crucial implications for French film style, especially with regard to the treatment of actors' voices. It is often said that Hollywood's soundtracks accord formal privilege to dialogue over other types of sound, privileging voices on the soundtrack in a manner analogous to the centrality of the human figure in the image.[29] Given the physiology of human audition, a voice-dominated viewing experience may be inevitable, so that, as Michel Chion proposes, "[I]n every audio mix, the presence of the human voice instantly sets up a hierarchy of perception."[30] What distinguished Hollywood films went beyond the anthropocentric stress on human speech to encompass an emphasis on dialogue's intelligibility: "For the Americans, a good sound is essentially the one that procures a clear comprehension of the dialogue," as Sivel had observed.[31] During conversion, the privilege accorded to speech can be characterized as literal, with the general rule being that voices and other sounds be accompanied by the visual depiction of their source. At Paramount's studio in Paris, for example, cinematographers were instructed to frame actors so that their faces remained visible while speaking: "We are in the business of selling voices and actors," studio head Robert Kane was said to have informed the company's production personnel.[32]

Like the Hollywood cinema, the "actor's cinema" of 1930s France privileged actors' performances, and voices were obviously crucial in this regard. Indeed, the "filmed theatre" of 1930s France was known for voluminous talking. Less centered on spectacular chase sequences and action-based physical gags than analogous forms of American film comedy, the comedies and farces of conversion-era France often featured ensemble performances and profuse repartée and banter, as was the case with boulevard comedy in particular, but also with other, "lower" forms, including vaudeville.[33] The French cinema's stage-derived scripts were dense with speech, and actors such as Jules Berry, Sacha Guitry, and Raimu, who also performed on radio, were known for their irrepressible volubility.

At the same time, given national differences in recording practice, voices in French films may invite a different type of interest from those in Hollywood films. In contrast to Hollywood's telephonic clarity, French films, with their direct-recorded soundtracks, capture the phenomenal characteristics of actors' speech—dimensions of voice quality and timbre—together with the spatial characteristics of the recording environment.[34] While vocal characteristics can be said to define recorded speech in American films as well—and indeed in sound films made virtually anywhere—in French films their salience, the way they compel the viewer's interest, may exceed the role of dialogue as the conduit for a film's plot development, to instead substantiate the materiality of the scene's setting. When René Clair remarked on his intent in modifying his style for *Quatorze juillet* (dir. René Clair, 1932) in light of the mainstream French cinema's "filmed theatre," it was exactly this aspect of speech, its potential as an index of place or milieu, that he stressed. Noting that *Quatorze juillet* had more dialogue than his earlier sound films, and that, in certain moments, the dialogue appears to have been improvised (one thinks, for instance, of the curbside argument between the taxi drivers), Clair agreed that in the new film "They speak all the time. . . . But it is the 'sound' of the words and not their meaning that counts here. The words of the rumbling crowd are a sort of accompaniment of the action, in the same manner as the music and the noises."[35]

In the case of *Quatorze juillet,* made at Tobis Films Sonores, the dialogue's embeddedness was achieved through multi-track methods comparable to those employed contemporaneously in the film industries of Germany and the United States. For the majority of films made in France, however, dialogue was recorded together with ambient sound, and thus the dialogue's intelligibility was sometimes compromised, as when "wild" ambient sounds recorded by chance—a creak in the floor, the clink of tableware, or an off-screen car horn—momentarily masked the actors' speech. An indication of the technical difficulties associated with this direct-sound approach can be found in "script reports," which describe the sound and image quality of a given day's rushes; for instance, one such report, prepared for *Feu!* (*Fire!* dir. Jacques de Baroncelli, 1937), a "quality" production, lists numerous takes whose dialogue by virtue of the direct recording had been obscured by concurrent ambient sounds, such as the clink of a glass on a tabletop, the slam of a car door, noise from a piece of machinery, and so on.[36]

In the context of narrative cinema, direct recording's tendency to emphasize the recording environment's physical characteristics sometimes posed a problem in itself. Through electronic amplification, the microphones captured not only the actors' voices but also the volume of air in the studio space where the recording had occurred.[37] Instead of ensuring the viewer's absorption into the film's story-world, the "room tone" of a direct-recorded film can disclose that world's material conditions, that is, the site of the recording, the bodies of the actors, and the technology itself. Far from enhancing realism, the attempt to meet the imperative of fidelity to an original sound can serve to foreground the scene's artifice, by revealing the technology's role in mediating the viewer's perception of the image. (See Figure 5.4.)

In Hollywood, technicians' attempts to limit potentially distracting side-effects of this sort involved the use of multi-track techniques that systematically stressed sound's intelligibility within a film's story-world over its fidelity as the reproduction of a performance. Coinciding with the intelligibility emphasis was an extensive use of prerecorded ambient sound. As Donald Crafton observes, Hollywood's soundtracks, beginning in 1930, featured diverse prerecorded sounds: ambient voices, desert wind, foghorns, creaking doors, footsteps, typewriter keys, gun shots, sirens, and so on.[38] Constructed so as to minimize phenomenal characteristics that might impede the viewer's comprehension of the story, such sounds were intended to refer to their putative source in the film's story-world rather than their actual source in the recording studio. As film-sound work in Hollywood became further mechanized and specialized during the 1930s, generic sounds of this sort became increasingly prominent on Hollywood soundtracks. According to one French observer, by the mid-1930s, Hollywood had effectively rendered ambient sound into a form of music—to the point of altogether replacing actual or simulated noises with the kind of musical sound effects common in sound-era cartoons.[39]

In contrast, the French cinema was developing a noise-tolerant, direct-sound alternative. According to one 1934 account, the same ambient sounds manufactured separately in Hollywood ("noises of clinking glassware and conversations in a café, the rumble of distant sounds") were recorded on the set in France, at the same time as the dialogue.[40] This direct-sound approach, and its distinctive stylistic effects, endured into the late 1940s, when the refusal on the part of French filmmakers to efface "the thousands of prosaic sonorities of real life" could still be contrasted to "the anonymous character, the absence of soul of American film sound."[41] (See Figures 5.5 and 5.6.) This doesn't mean that ambient sounds in French films are necessarily more audible than in Hollywood films. In fact, in many cases, direct-recorded French films do not feature the sort of sonic realism that a Hollywood-acculturated viewer expects. Consider, for instance, the countryside laundry scene in *Toni,* in which Toni protects Marie from attack by an invisible and unheard bee; in a contemporaneous American film, a comparable scene would surely have featured a post-synch bee noise.

Fig. 5.4. A frame enlargement from a direct-recorded scene in *Toni* (Jean Renoir, 1935) during which the cliff side can be seen collapsing a moment before the sound of the explosion is heard. The sound-image mismatch can be attributed to the placement of the microphone in the shot's foreground, near the actors, which required the blast's sound to travel across the shot's space before registering on the sound recorder. As this example suggests, far from enhancing the story-world's realism, attempts to meet the imperative of fidelity to an original sound can foreground a scene's material conditions—in this case, by drawing attention to the mediating role of the recording technology.

Differences between American and French sound-film practices suggest a trade-off familiar to fidelity-based filmmaking, whereby an increase in spatial fidelity implies a decrease in speech intelligibility, and vice versa. In other words, the need to ensure the dialogue's clarity required close miking and low reverb, whereas the demand to render accurately the space of the recording environment required distant miking and high reverb.[42] In the case of direct-recorded scenes, the sound crew faced the challenge of somehow "squaring the circle" by reconciling the contradictory demands of voice recording (intelligibility) with the proper restitution of the recording site (fidelity).[43] The challenge was inescapable in the French and American cinemas, which favored a tight,

Fig. 5.5. A production still of the making at Paramount's Paris studio of a multiple-camera scene from *Le monsieur de minuit* (Harry Lachmann, 1931), a Paramount film based on an original French-language script. Note the locations of the cameras, which imply the sort of shot/reverse shot pattern associated with American-style filmmaking. Filmmakers in France often adapted the multiple-camera technique in a notably free-wheeling manner—to the point of ignoring the 180-degree rule, the 30-degree rule, and other Hollywood conventions.

naturalistic synchronization of actors' voices and lips. One way to characterize the basic national difference is to say that French and American cinemas came down on opposite sides of the intelligibility/fidelity split. In French films, direct-recorded scenes can be said to be faithful in that they record the actors' performance as it might have been heard by a witness, located on the soundstage during filming. But these direct-recorded scenes may lack intelligibility, as when voices and other sounds overlap, reverberation causes discrete sounds to mass together perceptually, and the technology's mediating role is made evident.[44] The situation concerning Hollywood films looks something like the opposite. In Hollywood films, sounds were not necessarily faithful: they may have been artificially produced or otherwise electronically "tricked"; gunshots might have made by a cane striking a chair's leather cushion, or the rhythmic clop of horses' hooves produced by the clacking of halved

Fig. 5.6. The range of Renoir's experimentation in sound-film technique is evident even in relatively minor works in Renoir's oeuvre, as is suggested by these frame enlargements from *La nuit du carrefour* (Jean Renoir, 1932). During this scene, two separate conversations occur simultaneously, with no attempt made to establish a hierarchy between them; the viewer is thus faced with the cognitively impossible demand of comprehending two streams of speech at once.

coconut shells.[45] Nonetheless, the scenes are extraordinarily intelligible: all dialogue can be heard, voices overlap only in exceptional cases (e.g., at a scene's establishing-shot beginnings and endings), only a single sound important to narrative causality occurs at a time, and ambient sounds (ultimately) refer to an identifiable source. From the perspective of the American film industry's storytelling project, the French cinema's fidelity emphasis implied an alternative sound-film aesthetic, founded on opposed principles.

## How Many Microphones?

A fascinating aspect of national sound-film aesthetic and technical differences is how the two film industries coincidentally used many of the same technologies. Beginning in the fall of 1929 and continuing through the 1930s, the principal French studios contracted with American suppliers to purchase blimped Bell and Howell cameras, "noiseless" Western Electric and RCA multi-track recorders, ribbon microphones, and so on. The reliance on imported technologies continued in later decades; as late as 1954, half of the fifty sound-recording systems at use in the French film industry were estimated to have been imported, primarily from the United States.[46] All the same, any notion that the prevalence of imported technologies in French filmmaking entailed sound-era homogenization is contradicted by substantial style differences between French and American films. If the same technologies were sometimes employed by the two film industries, the manner in which they were used sometimes differed substantially.

With regard to sound technique specifically, an example can be found in French methods regarding a basic issue in sound-film practice: the number of microphones used to record a scene. The practice for early sound films, such as the Vitaphone productions of Warner Bros., was to record with multiple microphones, all functioning simultaneously to capture a performance staged for camera and sound. The multiple miking of numerous, simultaneous sound sources exemplified the American film industry's fidelity emphasis during the sound cinema's first years. By the late 1920s, however, sound-film technicians in the United States worked to limit the number of microphones during recording sessions so as to reduce the white-noise hiss associated with multiple miking. The key shift occurred in 1931, with industrywide deployment of the "single-microphone" method, which involved recording voices to the exclusion of other sounds, through use of a single, directional microphone, suspended from a mobile boom, and placed at a close, constant distance from the actors.

Although simple in principle, single-microphone recording entailed a radical overhaul of American sound-film practice, which included the development of new technologies and the transformation of sound-stage acoustics. The technologies included new, directional microphones, such as RCA's ribbon model (introduced in 1931), whose restriction of the aural field to a seventy-degree radius allowed voices to be recorded to the exclusion of ambient sound. During the scene's recording, this dialogue microphone was the only one needed; music and ambient sounds—footsteps, doors opening and closing, the clop-clop of horses' hooves, telephones ringing, typewriters clacking, and so forth—were now recorded separately, in special studios, and then, via multi-channel technology, mixed into the soundtrack during post-production. Copies of generic sounds of this sort were compiled in studio libraries or *phonothèques*, where they could be reused later, as the need arose. Another essential new device was the extendable/retractable microphone boom, which facilitated the microphone's placement at a constant distance from a speaking actor, including when the actor traversed the soundstage.

In ensuring dialogue's intelligibility, a lock-tight voice-image match, and great flexibility in creating a coherent, three-dimensional story-world, the single-microphone method met the need in Hollywood for an approach to dialogue recording compatible with the industry's established narrative-film project. Moreover, in isolating dialogue onto a separate track, the single-microphone approach also facilitated the dubbing of Hollywood films for the world market—a crucial consideration during the early 1930s, when Hollywood struggled, in the face of new, sound-era linguistic barriers, to maintain a foreign market estimated to bring in some 30 to 40 percent of its gross income. The main method for preparing sound films for export to foreign-language markets during 1930–1932, for both American and German producers, was the making of "multiple versions," that is, films featuring the same scenarios and sets but with different teams of actors.[47] But as multi-track sound became standardized throughout the studio system in 1931, the American film industry ceased producing multiple versions and instead began dubbing films for export. By 1932, the injunction to limit on-set recording to a single microphone became a technical norm in Hollywood, and then in other film industries throughout the world—including, ultimately, France.[48] In filmmaking manuals today, the single-microphone method is cited as a sine qua non for high-quality film sound.[49]

In France during the early 1930s, however, film sound was often recorded in a fundamentally different manner; instead of a single, directional microphone, three to five microphones, positioned to capture both dialogue and ambient sound, were commonly used.[50] As late as December 1938, scenes featuring dialogue continued to be recorded in the French studios with up to eight microphones.[51] In certain cases, up to twelve microphones were employed for a single scene.[52] The microphones often varied in type, and were placed at varying distances from the sound source(s) so as to capture the recording environment's spatial characteristics. For dialogue scenes, additional microphones were suspended from the soundstage rafters to ensure *relief sonore*—the requisite sense of three-dimensionality, which was contingent on an appropriate level of reflected sound. In France, reflected sound was typically a function of what happened on the set during filming, and thus depended on the judicious placement of multiple microphones.[53] Directional microphones were sometimes used, but in a manner that contradicted the rationale of their use in Hollywood.[54] At Pathé-Natan, for instance, the adoption in 1933 of the latest RCA directional mikes did not entail a coincident switch to the single-microphone method; instead, the new devices were incorporated into Joinville's existing multiple-microphone, multiple-camera system. Serving established national film-industry purposes, ribbon microphones at Pathé-Natan were supplemented with additional, omnidirectional microphones, so as to ensure as full a restitution of the recording environment as possible. Commentators in the French trade-press even argued against using a single microphone, on the grounds that the spatial characteristics of single-microphone scenes were insufficiently naturalistic.[55]

## Multiple-Camera Shooting

With the use of multiple microphones in France often coinciding with the technique of multiple-camera shooting, choices in sound-film technique sometimes powerfully affected a film's visual style. Examples include cases of French filmmakers adopting American technique in ways that differed fundamentally from American precedent. One factor skewing such adoptions concerns national differences in the timing of a technique's introduction. Multiple-camera shooting was introduced in Hollywood in 1926, with the production of the first Vitaphone shorts. At that time, technical conditions for sound-on-disc recording required that a scene's sound be captured in a single, unedited take.[56] With the sound recorded on a wax disc, sound editing was effectively impossible: to remove a sound required redoing the entire six- to ten-minute disc. In this context, the multiple-camera system offered the great advantage of ensuring that shots chosen for a film's final print would match the original, uneditable phonograph recording.[57]

Although facilitating sonic continuity across cuts from shot to shot, multiple-camera shooting had severe drawbacks. For one, it was expensive, requiring a large crew and, on average, the exposure of roughly three times more film stock than was needed for the film's final, edited print. It also imposed extraordinary demands on actors, musicians, and technicians, who were required to perform continuous takes, up to ten minutes long, in studio environments often poorly ventilated and stiflingly hot.[58] Only professional performers, with significant stage experience, could survive the rigors of this sort of work. Finally, multiple-camera shooting contributed to the pictorial blandness that critics found artistically retrograde about the talkies. With regard to cinematography, for instance, it was necessary that a scene's lights be positioned to illuminate actors' faces evenly from all camera positions. As cameras and lights increased in number, cinematography acquired a flat, high-key look that seemed aesthetically inferior to the refined, chiaroscuro effects of the silent era.[59] Technical limitations were also evident in a routinized, by-the-rules approach to staging and cutting. Prior to 1930 and the introduction of the camera blimp, cameras (and camera operators) were encased in soundproof booths, which greatly restricted camera mobility, lens choices, and other cinematographic options. In addition, the booths ordinarily were arranged in a fixed, semicircular curve around the actors, in a manner comparable to early television talk-shows, thus facilitating "a repetitive, even routine, method of cutting up the narrative space."[60]

With editing and cinematography subservient to the rhythm of the performance staged for the camera and microphone, extreme close-ups, rapid cutting, point-of-view shots, and other devices prominent in silent-era films were largely ruled out. The formulaic quality was evident in films made at the Paramount-Paris studio, according to cinematographer Michel Kelber, where technicians were instructed to shoot according to a pre-given pattern: "[L]ong shot, close-up, long shot, close-up . . . and we were always supposed to show the actors from the front—not in profile; not from the back—because the management wanted to show the public how the sound was perfectly synchronized with the lip movement."[61] (See Figure 5.7.)

In light of the material and aesthetic costs, the adoption of multiple-camera shooting in Hollywood is remarkable. The very occurrence of such adoption indicates the depth of Hollywood's commitment to an editing-based narration in the face of sound-era technical demands.[62] By 1931, however, the studios abandoned multiple-camera shooting. Multi-

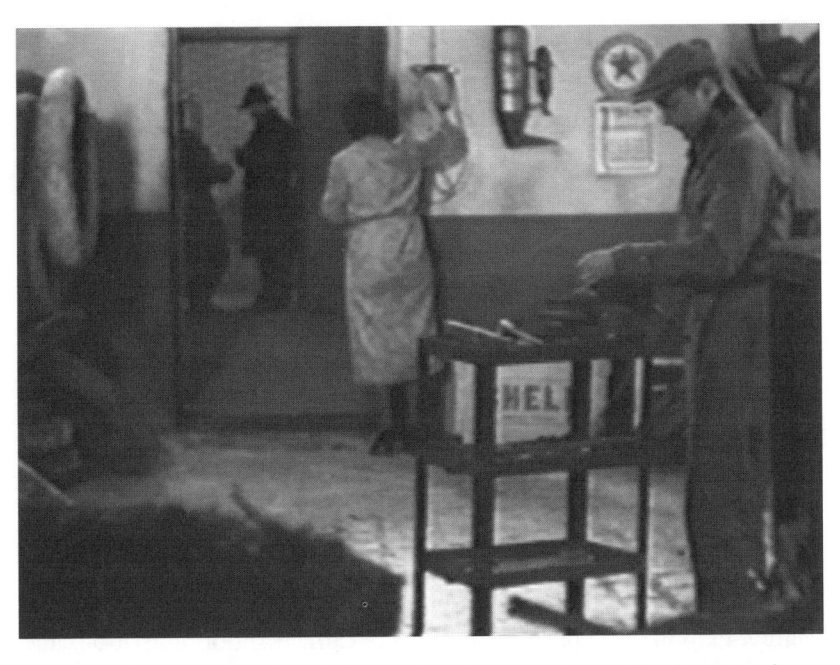

Fig. 5.7. In this scene from *La nuit du carrefour*, the three planes of the deep-staged action are established through a three-plane audio counterpart. Changes in sound accompaniment prompt the viewer to scan the image so as to shift attention from one plane to another, depending on which of three sounds dominates: the voices of the characters positioned at the very rear of the set, the ringing telephone on the wall in the shot's middle-ground, or the abrasive grind of the machine tool in the foreground.

track technologies enabled retrieval of a modified version of the old single-camera, multiple-take system of the silent era, whereby each of a scene's shots was filmed separately, its mise-en-scène organized solely for the vantage point of a single camera.[63] The effect on the look of the Hollywood films of 1930–1931 was immediately evident: while appearing stylistically unified, if not homogenous, the new films also featured a vast increase in the range of options for lighting, camera angles, lenses, set design, and so forth—including a variety of silent-era image techniques that had vanished in the face of the technical difficulties of sound-on-disc filmmaking.

In France, the history of multiple-camera shooting unfolded differently. The technique was adopted there in 1930, several years later than in Hollywood, and just as technical developments were allowing Hollywood's return to single-camera shooting. By then, certain constraints associated with multiple-camera shooting were no longer a factor. Most fundamentally, the introduction of the camera "blimp" in 1930 freed cameras from enclosure in massive, relatively immobile booths, thus allowing for increased camera movement. When multiple-camera shooting was adopted in France, it was with new soundproofed technologies, such as the six blimp-encased Bell and Howell cameras purchased by Pathé-Natan in March 1930 for use on the Joinville sound stages.[64] In addition, multiple-camera shooting was used in France throughout the 1930s, far later than in Hollywood, when scenes in French films continued to be filmed with up to four cameras, both in the studio and on location.[65]

Adapted under different technological and industrial circumstances, multiple-camera shooting in France sometimes functioned quite differently than in the United States. Certain films such as *Fanny* (dir. Marc Allegret, 1932), a filmed-theatre production based on a play by Marcel Pagnol, exhibit an approach to multiple-camera shooting that decades later would become common in television production, where it likewise served to record performances by actors with considerable live-entertainment experience.[66] But other French multiple-camera films, while still falling within the genre of filmed theatre, exhibit blends of styles than can only be characterized as experimental. Essential here was an approach to staging far less predictable than in multiple-camera films made in Hollywood. In contrast to the limited range of camera positions and predictable cutting patterns of multiple-camera Hollywood films, French films exhibit a remarkably open-ended approach to filmic space, defined, for instance, by frequent hops across a scene's axis of action. As discussed in chapter 6, continuity violations were so frequent in films made at Pathé-Natan's Joinville studios that it seems mistaken to refer to them as violations, as if an inappropriate standard of judgment were being applied. Concerning the wide range of multiple-camera films in France, a fascinating extreme can be found in *Le chien qui rapporte* (dir. Jean Choux, 1931). In this remarkable film, multiple-camera shooting allows stage performers such as Arletty (in her first film role), Paulette Dubost, and others to play their parts continuously, in a manner characteristic of filmed theatre, but the imagery nonetheless evokes—or even surpasses—the modernist cinematographic and editing styles of the 1920s. The cutting of *Le chien qui rapporte* is extraordinarily rapid, with an ASL of 4.2 seconds—one of the shortest in my sample of sixty-one films from 1930–1933. In addition, *Le chien qui rapporte* encompasses a technical range whose variety is dizzying: certain shots are speeded up while others are slowed down; others are modified via gels and filters placed on the camera lenses, while some are even projected upside-down.

## How Are National Differences in Film-Sound Recording to be Explained?

As discussed in chapter 4, early sound film style is commonly explained as an effect of technological constraint. In conversion-era France, for instance, the oddities of the national film style were routinely attributed to an outdated plant and equipment. Although pointing to crucial film-stylistic conditions, such explanations can be highly problematic insofar as they assume that technologies determine, rather than merely condition, particular stylistic outcomes. The project of this book has been to develop an alternative account, whereby technologies are understood as embedded within contexts of film-industry practice, and hence implicated in a web of relations involving other technologies. Thus, from the standpoint adopted here, the key questions concern less the technologies themselves than how those technologies made sense in local terms, in light of practices and commitments distinctive to the national film industry.

With regard to French filmmaking, one crucial technical and industrial factor was the emphasis on the shooting phase of a film's production. In contrast to the situation in Hollywood, and also in the German film industry, sound-film production in France entailed an extraordinary degree of improvisation during shooting. In important respects, the improvisatory approach amounted to a holdover from the silent era, when French films routinely went into production with minimal scripting, and directors were relatively free to improvise during shooting and also during editing. In 1929, Léon Moussinac, commenting on "the difficult problem of film construction," claimed that in French filmmaking, "[c]hance and intuition seem to take precedence over principle and system. . . . Today's filmmakers write their screenplays in haste; the most important thing for them is the filming, after which they grope along."[67] The pressure to regularize preproduction planning and scripting increased during conversion, in the face of the sound cinema's unprecedented costs and technical demands.[68] Nonetheless, throughout the 1930s and into later decades, conditions for an improvised approach to shooting endured, and films continued to enter into production prior to the script's completion. As late as 1949, one *directeur de production* reported that it was "not rare to see a film's production begin in the studio or on location prior to the completion of the shooting script."[69] Moreover, in contrast to the "continuity scripts" used in Hollywood, French film scripts (with the notable exception of René Clair's) often contained no indications concerning the number of shots per scene, camera placement, sound-recording methods, and other film-technical considerations —not to mention budgeting and other matters related to the logistics of production.[70]

Thus, while directors in Hollywood were required to adhere rigorously to the dictates of the so-called continuity script, which provided a detailed "blueprint" for shooting and editing, directors in France typically worked in a far more improvisatory fashion, often making decisions concerning camera placement and the number of shots per scene only once the crew had actually assembled on the set to shoot the scene. According to one trade-press survey of French filmmaking during 1931: "There exist directors who still work in the manner of the cinema of the 1900s and rely greatly on the gift of inspiration. They change the script on the set as needed, eliminating scenes that no longer please them, add new details, and allow themselves to be influenced by the mood of the actors, the day's weather, and any of a number of other contingencies."[71] As such reports suggest, dialogue rehearsal was relatively rare in French filmmaking, unless it happened on the set, while the crew waited and the studio clock ticked. According to director Marcel L'Herbier, writing in February 1931, films were typically shot in France in only three weeks with little or no time devoted to rehearsal, whereas in the theatre even actors with small parts rehearsed one month prior to a show's opening.[72] Actors were said to show up at the studios without knowing which role in the script they were to play; but since the actors often played the same character types from one production to the next, they were often capable of improvising their parts effectively.[73]

The rapid shooting schedules, and minimal planning, scripting, and rehearsal, imposed severe limits on the sound technicians' role in shaping a film's artistic quality.[74] Rather than encompassing each of the basic film-production phases of scripting, shooting, and editing, sound work in France was limited mainly to tasks performed during the shooting phase alone. In fact, in France, sound personnel were typically assigned to a film's production only immediately before shooting began, and only rarely were provided with a copy of the script.[75] According to a 1937 trade-press report, sound technicians and film directors approached the same tasks from the perspectives of different professional worlds: "The engineers serve a film's production, but only as borrowed wage-earners, most often on loan to a producer who the engineers can challenge only at the risk of antagonizing the film's director, who, in turn, often pursues an artistic vision which does not match the purely technical possibilities of concern to the engineers."[76] The commonplace notion that sound-film work was fundamentally technical rather than artistic in nature profoundly conditioned the sound crew's participation in the filmmaking process. Sound technicians were the most anonymous of film workers, and sometimes they went unlisted in the credits of French films. Studios were allegedly reluctant to identify sound technicians by name lest a competing firm hire them away.[77] Until 1938, film reviews in *La cinématographie française,* the main film industry trade-press publication, listed only the film's sound system (RCA, Philips, Tobis-Klangfilm, Marconi, etc.) rather than the names of the sound personnel who had actually worked on the film.

Further conditioning the sound personnel's marginalization were their backgrounds in fields unrelated to filmmaking. In many cases, sound technicians had learned methods of sound recording and reproduction in the technical domains of the radio, phonograph, and telephone industries. From the perspective of veteran filmmakers, the sound personnel, with their expertise in the prestigious science of electronics, came from a different professional world, defined by what looked like alien priorities. As Marcel Pagnol put it, regarding circumstances at Paramount-Paris's St. Maurice–Joinville studios in 1931 during the filming of *Marius:* "The technical services, and especially the sound men, still believe that actors and scenarists have no use other than to demonstrate the excellence of their technologies."[78]

In this respect, the situation in France invites comparison to that in the United States, where the great majority of sound technicians also came from non-film backgrounds, and where film-sound work was also initially understood as a technical rather than artistic task.[79] According to technician and sound-film theorist Carl Dreher, 80 percent of the approximately one thousand sound specialists working in Hollywood in 1930 had come from outside the film industry.[80] The principal difference between the French and American film industries lay in the speed and uniformity of the sound crew's integration into the film community. In Hollywood, a sustained, industrywide integration effort began as early as 1927, when the recently founded Academy of Motion Picture Arts and Sciences created dozens of committees to inform and educate the film community on film-sound matters.[81] Conferences convening sound technicians, cinematographers, and representatives from technology suppliers such as Electrical Research Products, Inc. (ERPI) (the film-industry division of Western Electric) and RCA facilitated important technical developments relating to silencing arc lamps and cameras and sound-proofing sets.[82] The awarding of Oscars for sound recording, beginning in 1930, helped establish the notion that sound-film work was an aesthetic as much as a technical practice. By 1934, with the founding of the Society of Motion Picture Sound Engineers, sound personnel were as integrated into Hollywood's massive corporate labor force as any other category of studio employee.[83]

In the institutionally fragmented French film industry, however, the sound crew's integration happened in a notably protracted and uneven fashion. One factor concerned the sound crew's conditions of employment, which differed from those of other members of the production team: whereas composers, directors, actors, and cinematographers typically worked from contract to contract, one film at a time, sound personnel were salaried workers, employed at particular studio facilities.[84] With synchronous dialogue recording, location filming, sound-effects production, and music recording and mixing usually performed at different facilities, sound-film personnel were dispersed across a multiplicity of independent companies and studio sites. According to a 1934 spokesperson for the "Syndicat des Ingénieurs du son" (Union of Sound Engineers), each facility tended to function independently of the others, with no single individual responsible for coordinating tasks related to a film's soundtrack as a whole.[85] An exception was the Dutch-German company Tobis Films Sonores, which designated a sound supervisor who coordinated sound-related tasks and who instructed the laboratory on development and printing.[86]

An additional constraint on the role of sound technicians related to the architecture of sound stages.[87] In Hollywood during the 1930s, the trend in sound-stage design was toward a sonically "dead," soundproofed environment appropriate strictly for dialogue recording. In the context of a sound-film approach defined by Hollywood's multi-track methods, which entailed the recording of music and sound effects independently from dialogue, in separate, specialized recording environments, the sort of reverberation appropriate for music recording was no longer desirable for the main soundstages. Thus, the soundstages were redesigned, according to new, dialogue-specific acoustic principles. In France during the 1930s, however, sound stages remained configured according to music-industry standards, and thus tended to emulate the high reverberation characteristic of the concert halls of the nineteenth century rather than the acoustic deadness proper for dialogue recording. At Pathé-Natan's Joinville facility, for instance, the sound stages were prepared with input from musicians, who worked to avoid the aesthetic limitations characteristic of what P. Thomas, the company's technical director, referred to as "an overly amortized studio."[88]

In this context, adoption of the sort of multi-track techniques employed in Hollywood could occur only at the considerable expense of refashioning the high-reverb sound stages. But fundamental change in studio architecture was rare in France. Indeed, the only film studio in France that had been designed, from the ground up, for sound-film production was the American-managed Paramount-Paris complex at St. Maurice-Joinville, where the old facilities were bulldozed and new ones constructed.[89] Otherwise, the French film industry's conversion entailed modernizing the old studios in an ad hoc manner, with new sound-related facilities inserted into the existing physical plant. This piecemeal approach to studio renovation facilitated the endurance in the French film industry of acoustic norms derived from the music industry, and hindered the efforts of film-industry reformers to reorient French practice away from a sound-film style based on fidelity. As late as 1945, French film studios were characterized as "too reverberant" for proper sound recording.[90] Further impeding the forces of modernization was the atomized French production sector, with its multitude of tiny companies—formed in some cases to produce only a single film. Each production was often a unique project, and each facility functioned largely independently of the others. Imported tools were often used in a locally contingent manner, and in the context of an improvised approach to film sound that differed fundamentally from Hollywood's emphasis on thorough planning and scripting. While the latest technologies and techniques from Hollywood were introduced into the French film industry, it was in a manner that brought them into the fold of the established, fidelity-oriented system, to become domesticated according to the same aesthetic norms that Hollywood had recently abandoned.

In the French film industry trade-press, the national reliance on an ad hoc, improvised approach to sound filmmaking was frequently cited as a major obstacle to the French cinema's technical and artistic progress. From another perspective, however, the same practices could be seen as essential conditions for the distinctive artistry of the French cinema of the 1930s. For instance, Hollywood film director Rouben Mamoulian, writing in the late 1930s, attributed the artistic quality of French films to "the fact that in France there are no large production companies": "French films are the product of small, individual groups. The director is free and not subjugated by the enormous, complicated machinery of a large industrial studio. The result is that each film has a profoundly individual, personal quality, which is the mark of any truly artistic work."[91] As comments such as Mamoulian's suggest, however disadvantageous from a strictly sound-technical perspective, the improvised approach to shooting offered certain advantages stylistically. Particularly important in the French context were actors' preferences. The stage-trained actors who defined French cinema during the 1930s preferred recording methods that captured their performances holistically, as an ensemble, in continuous, real-time duration. Besides shortening the shooting schedule, and thus reducing production costs, multiple-camera shooting allowed actors to play their scenes in a manner familiar to their stage performances, thus facilitating the actors' bond with their public. It also helped the actors preserve a degree of control over how they would appear in the finished film, ensuring that their performances would amount to recordings of what had actually happened on the studio set, instead of post hoc constructions undertaken in the editing room without consulting the actors. When scenes featuring stage-trained actors were shot in single takes, with multiple cameras, the filming could proceed rapidly, with only minimal preproduction planning and rehearsal required. Here a basic national difference in the technique's function is evident: whereas multiple-camera shooting in Hollywood had served to maintain the aesthetic norms characteristic of Hollywood's editing-based narration, in the French film industry, it supported work routines involving an unusual amount of on-the-set improvisation.

The preceding investigation into shooting and recording has emphasized the French cinema's divergence from what is generally seen as the dominant pattern of development in the history of sound-film technique. In Hollywood, sound-film practice quickly and uniformly evolved toward a regime defined by the separation of sound production from image production; but until the late 1930s, French filmmaking rested on the simultaneous recording of sound and image. Moreover, fundamental elements of the French cinema's direct-sound approach endured into subsequent decades. In fact, still at the beginning of the twenty-first century—over seventy years after cinema's conversion to sound—direct-sound techniques familiar to the national film practice of the 1930s continue to define French cinema relative to other national cinemas. Hence, contra the common notion that sound conversion had served to homogenize film style, this book uses its investigation into the French cinema to raise new questions regarding conversion's effects worldwide. As suggested by this chapter's analysis of national differences in practices of shooting and recording, filmmaking in France differed in important respects from filmmaking in Hollywood, notwithstanding the frequent use in the French studios of American technologies and techniques. Adopting imported tools and methods in a selective, piecemeal fashion, filmmakers in France emulated features of the Hollywood technique compatible with their outlook while ignoring what was irrelevant. An implication for historical method is that, in order to grasp sound technology's effects on film style, one must examine how the technologies were used in specific film-production contexts, where they sometimes ended up performing novel functions.

# 6 Hollywood Indigenized: Pathé-Natan and National Popular Cinema

In this chapter's study of Pathé-Natan, France's largest production firm of the conversion years, the investigation concerns how global trends in sound-film practice became manifest at the local level of an important production company. With regard to the cinema's conversion to sound, the national popular films made at companies such as Pathé-Natan—closely linked to the popular stage, radio, and the phonograph—would seem impossible to ignore, given their importance to world cinema during this time. But how are such films to be understood? In which context(s) are they to be situated? Owing little to modernist and avant-garde film cultures, yet exemplifying a style differing in important respects from that of the American cinema, national popular films escape film historiography's familiar distinction between Hollywood entertainment and European art. In historiographic terms, the consequence has been invisibility; in spite of their centrality to the contemporaneous film culture, Pathé-Natan's films rarely receive the film-historical scrutiny they deserve.

Besides the general neglect in film studies of national popular cinemas, the case of Pathé-Natan has been complicated by factors specific to the company's unique history. One such factor concerns Pathé-Natan's status as the sound-era French film company most resembling a major Hollywood studio.[1] Vertically integrated through ownership of a chain of luxury theatres, Pathé-Natan was also horizontally linked to diverse ancillary businesses related to film-equipment manufacture, laboratories for film developing and printing, and cognate media such as radio broadcasting, phonograph recording, and sheet-music publishing. The company's policy of signing actors, directors, composers, and other personnel to contracts, as well as its licensing agreement with RCA Photophone, have made Pathé-Natan look like the French national cinema's rejoinder to the major studios of Hollywood, and also typical of a sound-era trend toward an "Americanization" of European cinema. As a consequence of the Hollywood resemblance, it is often assumed that Pathé-Natan's films were stylistically derivative from Hollywood films—a case of "Hollywood in foreign dress." Yet as suggested in the preceding chapters on national differences in editing and shooting, an examination of Pathé-Natan from a stylistic perspective, in terms of how the films looked and sounded, yields a different assessment. In the following analysis, the significance to sound-film history of the national cinema exemplified by Pathé-Natan is explored through inquiries into four topics: (1) complications regarding Pathé-Natan's place in film history; (2) the effects on film style of Pathé-Natan's strategy of producing films strictly for the French-language film market; (3) the importance of Pathé-Natan's theatre chain in conditioning the style of its films; and (4) Pathé-Natan's apparent retrieval of the national film style of the 1900s—evident, for instance, in the unorthodox adaptation of multiple-camera shooting at the Joinville studio facility. An underlying aim throughout this chapter is to illuminate the distinctiveness of Pathé-Natan's approach to national popular cinema relative to the Hollywood cinema with which it is often conflated.

## Pathé-Natan in Film Historiography

A national film company like Pathé-Natan poses a challenge to the film historian in that it appears anomalous relative to film historiography's established conceptual frame, which tends to see national film history in terms of a contrast between European art and Hollywood entertainment. Most fundamentally, Pathé-Natan produced commercial films exclusively for the domestic film market, and thus it does not fit the traditional definition of European cinema as a cinema of international auteurs. A related issue concerns Pathé-Natan's industrialized production of French-language talkies, which has made the company appear atypical of the French film industry as a whole. During the 1930s, the national industry's production wing consisted mainly of small-scale teams or "families," working on a single film at a time, and using borrowed money to rent studio and laboratory services on an ad hoc basis. In this context, Pathé-Natan's vertically integrated effort in industrial filmmaking offers the anomaly of a French company committed to an industrialized (and hence, non-French?) approach to film production, and yet devoted to the making of "national" films intended solely for domestic consumption.

All the same, the sheer quantity of films made at the company's production facilities has made Pathé-Natan's importance to film history undeniable. By the summer of 1934, some sixty feature films had been released bearing Pathé-Natan's logo, at a rate totaling up to nineteen films per year. This record for sound-film production exceeded that of other French studios of the time—including the conglomerate Gaumont-Franco-Film-Aubert, Pathé-Natan's chief French rival.[2] Also during this period, independent producers rented out Pathé-Natan's studio facilities, laboratories, and technical services to produce some sixty additional feature films. These Joinville-made films comprised a significant chunk of the national cinema's mainstream during the early 1930s. Featuring celebrated French entertainers and scripts based on popular French stage comedies, these films made up the core of France's "cinéma du sam'di soir" ("Saturday night at the movies"), the entertainment cinema of the general French film audience. Routinely ranked among the most popular releases by French exhibitors, Pathé-Natan's films can be said to have constituted a popular, national alternative to the Hollywood cinema during a decisive, transitional phase in film history. Later in the decade, after the company's bankruptcy, the same films retained a centrality of sorts in the national film culture, but in a transformed context. At that point, as French films began winning international awards, and French filmmakers worked deliberately to revise the national sound-film style in ways that would define the "cinema of quality" of the 1940s and 1950s, the "filmed theatre" of Pathé-Natan was disparaged as unexportable and artistically low-grade. Although stage adaptations—including the sort of vaudeville and music-hall comedies associated with Pathé-Natan—remained a staple of French film production, the film industry was now shifting toward the production of prestige films that might redefine the French cinema internationally.

In the national film history of today, Pathé-Natan is often remembered less for its films than for the scandal of the company's bankruptcy. The bankruptcy became official in December 1935, at the end of a difficult year during which dividends to Pathé-Natan's shareholders went unpaid for the first time, and the company's financial troubles, going back to its tangled dealings with the failed bank Bauer and Marchal, became a topic of newspaper headlines. These developments occurred in the wake of the financial collapse of other French film companies—most notably, the rival combine Gaumont-Franco-Film-Aubert, which had undergone court-ordered restructuring following its bankruptcy in July 1934. With the unraveling of mergers and consolidations that were undertaken during conversion, observers of the French film industry declared a state of crisis. As the Confédération Générale du Travail, the national labor union, pressed for the nationalization of the film industry, government officials met with film-industry representatives to plan the industry's technocratic reorganization. Also during this time, media culture in France had become increasingly ideological and polemical, and Pathé-Natan's collapse became linked in the press with a plethora of recent financial and political scandals, some unrelated to the film industry. Most notable was *L'affaire Stavisky*, or the Stavisky Affair, which implicated high-level politicians, bankers, and businessmen in a web of loans and financial transactions, and whose obvious conflicts of interest bore a family resemblance to the scandals of Pathé-Natan and Gaumont-Franco-Film-Aubert. Riots in the streets of Paris in February 1934 between right-wing militants and police, which threatened to overturn the French Republic, were widely characterized as a reaction against the Stavisky Affair. In the popular press, Pathé-Natan and Stavisky were cited together as symptomatic of the alleged corruption, not just of the film industry but of the entirety of France's financial system and also of its parliamentary system of government.[3]

Associated with a financial loss amounting to roughly double that of the Stavisky Affair, the Pathé-Natan scandal became a focus of strongly negative journalistic coverage, which in turn has conditioned accounts of the company in later film history. In contrast to press coverage during the early 1930s, when Pathé-Natan led the national film industry, the company has been characterized in subsequent historiography as an obstacle to the French cinema's artistic evolution. For instance, in Roger Manvell's *Film*, a film history survey published in 1944, "the collapse [in France] of some of the major studios in 1935" is characterized as a "fortunate" event for French film art.[4] Referring to Pathé-Natan specifically, Georges Sadoul approvingly cited Manvell's claim that the ruin of the conversion-era conglomerates opened the way for independent producer-directors to create "the famous French school of poetic realist films," which "despite the fewness of their number," "made the reputation of French cinema in Britain and America."[5]

Pathé-Natan's demise can be seen as exemplifying a global trend; other film conglomerates formed during conversion had also failed by mid-decade, both in France and in other countries. Thus, Pathé-Natan's rise and fall would seem to lend itself to analysis in terms of large-scale, systemic economic conditions and forces. In the case of Pathé-Natan, however, the focus instead was on the figure of Bernard Natan (1886–1941), the company's chief executive—to the point that changes in the company's status in the press seem linked with changes in assessments of its leader. During the boom years of the French film industry's conversion, when the company's numerous hit films played throughout its chain of first-run luxury theatres, the strategy of coordinating film production with a large theatre chain proved highly successful, and Natan himself showed up as a national hero.[6] As if leading the French cinema into its new, sound-defined future, Natan, as the Pathé-Natan company's high-profile leader, won credit for maintaining "the national cinema's standing" at an unusually uncertain time.[7] "Natan is not a businessman but a hero, a foot soldier during peacetime," according to one 1932 commentary.[8] Serious warnings regarding dealings between Pathé-Natan and Bauer and Marchal had sounded in newspapers, following the bank's failure in 1931. Nonetheless, reporting on the company in the film trade-press remained largely positive.[9] As late as December 1934, the trade journal *La technique cinématographique* attributed Pathé's sound-era success to Bernard Natan's unflagging effort and far-sighted vision for French cinema.[10]

Shortly afterward, however, in the wake of the company's official bankruptcy, press coverage of both the company and its leader changed definitively. In the increasingly right-wing and xenophobic popular press of the time, Natan came to exemplify the sort of crooked, foreign-born entrepreneur who allegedly ruled the French film industry during the upheaval of the early sound years. In the popular press, reference was sometimes made to Natan's Romanian Jewish origins.[11] After 1935, rumors circulated concerning Natan's conviction in 1911 for the making of pornographic films, an episode in Natan's past that had been kept out of public discourse until then.[12] After being jailed in 1936, Natan was put on trial for embezzlement in June 1939. He spent the next years in prison, stripped of his French nationality. During the German occupation of France, in September 1942, Natan was sent to die in Auschwitz.[13]

With respect to cultural history, the case of Bernard Natan opens out onto a diversity of difficult topics, from the knotty intricacies of media economics to the (enduring) national traumas of the wartime occupation and the Holocaust. Regarding a topic essential to this book, one historiographical point to be made regarding the heroization of Natan prior to 1935, and also the vilification afterward, is that both imply the same basic assumption concerning the nature of film-historical change. That is, in both cases, Natan's agency is assumed to have been so strong that his actions made, and then broke, the company, and, by extension, the entirety of the national film industry. In other words, much of what has been written on Pathé-Natan, beginning in the 1930s and continuing through the present, exemplifies the popular form of historical narrative that Braudel characterized as a history of the event, in which exceptional, individual human agents serve as history's primary causal force. In this chapter, the project is to bring about a shift in perspective by analyzing Pathé-Natan and its films in contexts that relate the actions of the company's leader to long-term historical continuities that had shaped, both explicitly and subliminally, the company's approach to sound-film practice. First, Pathé-Natan produced films solely for domestic consumption, a strategy whose beginnings took shape in the late 1910s, when the Pathé company began retreating from the export market and from film production generally. Second, Pathé-Natan was committed to theatre adaptations featuring popular French actors and singers, and hence to a conception of the scene as the recording of a performance—a conception whose beginnings lie in the national-film practices of the decade prior to World War I. These continuities, whose histories long preceded Bernard Natan's appointment as studio head, and whose impact during conversion may, in some respects, have passed unnoticed, were powerful in conditioning the national cinema's conversion.

## "Hollywoodization" at Joinville

A key context for making sense of Pathé-Natan during its formation in 1929 was the Pathé name's long and venerable history in world cinema. In key respects, the history of the Pathé company defined the history of French cinema. The touchstone was the period between 1904 and 1911, when Pathé Frères dominated the global film market as the world's largest film producer and exporter.[14] By 1912, however, the company's global preeminence had begun to fade, particularly in the lucrative American film market, where Pathé encountered increased competition from domestic film producers. Then, in 1914, a major setback occurred, when the outbreak of World War I severely curtailed film production in France, and Pathé's film output diminished radically. By the war's end, the company was producing less than a quarter of its prewar output. At the same time, Hollywood had emerged as the world's major production center, and American films, which had become popular in France during the war, entered the French film market in increasing numbers. Already a significant presence in France during the war, American films afterward reportedly outnumbered French productions by as much as eight to one—although native productions continued to rank very high in popularity with French viewers.[15]

Adding to the decline in production quantity was Charles Pathé's decision by 1920 to cease investing directly in the making of French films.[16] The withdrawal from production proved characteristic of Pathé's overall business strategy during the 1920s, as the old Pathé empire was divided into separate businesses, which were then sold off to pay creditors and to reap profits for key groups of shareholders. The trend began in 1918, when Pathé separated the company's phonograph manufacturing operation from its film business; and it increased throughout the next decade, as Pathé's film stock and equipment manufacturing operations, exhibition circuit, domestic and foreign film-distribution networks, and film laboratories were likewise divided into separate businesses and sold off.[17] Thus, at a time when major film companies in the United States were moving toward increasing industrial amalgamation, the Pathé company pursued a very different course, so as to become smaller and increasingly decentralized during the decade.

When Gaumont, Pathé's principal rival, also abandoned film production to distribute American films through a new, American-controlled, multinational company, Gaumont-Metro-Goldwyn (founded in 1925), film production in France was left to small and medium-sized firms, which were required to contract with Pathé and Gaumont for equipment and technical support. These production companies faced unprecedented competition in the home market from imports, particularly from the United States, and also from Germany. Beginning in 1926, the number of French-made films shown in France fell, while American imports increased to comprise nearly 80 percent of the domestic box office.[18] At the end of 1929, the position of French films on the home market had reached a record low: of the total of 437 feature-length films released in France during 1929 (both sound and silent), only 52 had been made there.[19] This figure represented less than 10 percent of the year's total, and a sharp decline from the previous year's 94 French films. Far more numerous in France were American and German films: of the total of 437 films, 220 came from the United States and 130 from Germany. Moreover, of the 52 French films, only a small handful had soundtracks, and these had been made not in France, where studios were not yet sound-equipped, but in England and Germany. Such was the case with Pathé-Natan's *Les trois masques* (*The Three Masks*, dir. André Hugon, 1929), made at Twickenham studios in England and marketed in fall 1929 as France's "first 100% talking film." These new French talkies, whatever the artistic limitations, proved stunningly popular with French audiences, recouping up to six times their production costs.

The sound-era re-creation of Pathé as a major film producer thus came during an unusually unsettled year for the French film industry—as well as for other national cinemas in Europe. The formation of Pathé-Natan in 1929 and Gaumont-Franco-Film-Aubert in 1930 occurred simultaneously with analogous events in other film-producing countries, where large, vertically integrated film-industrial combines were also created. Coinciding with the retirements of prominent French film-industry pioneers Léon Gaumont, Charles Pathé, Louis Aubert, and Jean Sapène, the formation of Pathé-Natan and Gaumont-Franco-Film-Aubert confirmed the impression that times had changed and a new era in national film history had arrived. The sense of renewal was especially strong concerning Pathé-Natan, with the ambitious and extraordinarily rapid remaking of the old Pathé firm into a vertically integrated company amounting to a total reversal of Charles Pathé's policy as leader of the company during the 1920s. In contrast to Pathé père's reduced "empire" of the late 1920s, the new Pathé-Natan was a media conglomerate whose scale invoked Pathé's prewar past as the powerhouse of world cinema. In July 1929, when Natan received the approval of Pathé-Cinéma's shareholders to expand and restructure through the purchase of dozens of expensive theatres and a new, large-scale commitment to film production, it looked like both an important step forward for the national film industry and a promise for a return to past glory.

During the next months, changes occurred quickly. In August 1929, after assuming official leadership of the company, Natan purchased a controlling interest in Cinéromans/Films de France, and took possession of the Cinéromans studio complex at Joinville, the largest and most modern film-production facility in the country. With the support of large loans from Bauer and Marchal, RCA Photophone was contracted to outfit Joinville for sound-film production, and also Natan's former Rapid-Film studio on rue Francoeur, which would soon consist of two sound stages. Beginning in October, new sound stages added at Joinville made Pathé-Natan's facility roughly equal in size to the neighboring Paramount-Paris operation in St. Maurice–Joinville. Industrial-scale film production began at Pathé-Natan in the summer of 1930, and by December of that year twelve feature-length sound films were released bearing the company's logo—a striking figure for a European company during 1930. Within one year of Natan's official entry as Pathé's director, the company's identity had undergone a total metamorphosis through its novel and ambitious transformation into a vertically integrated sound-film conglomerate.

### Vertical Integration in France: Theatre Chains and Sound-Film Exhibition

As noted in chapter 1, film-industrial concentration appears to have been universal during the conversion years, having happened in a diverse number of national film industries throughout the world. In entailing the marginalization of independent film production, this phenomenon can be taken to indicate the cinema's sound-era homogenization. But film-industrial concentration during this time, inflected by national differences in cognate media such as the gramophone, radio, and the popular stage, assumed multiple forms, and these sometimes varied significantly from country to country, with important consequences for the sorts of films that particular national film industries produced. In the case of Pathé-Natan, the company's production efforts must be seen relative to the market demand created by its large chain of luxury theatres. The chain invited comparison to the American precedent of the 1920s, when companies such as Paramount, Metro-Goldwyn-Mayer, and Fox combined ownership of production facilities, distribution net-works, and theatre chains.[20] Although vertical integration had a long his-tory in French cinema, and in the Pathé company, its incarnation at Pathé-Natan seemed novel, with Pathé-Natan's "chaining" of theatres comparable more to current American practice than to the Pathé com-pany's prewar past. In contrast to Pathé-Frères of the 1900s, Pathé-Natan, like the large Hollywood companies during the 1920s, had in-vested massively in first-run luxury theatres. In September 1931, when sound-film theatres were novel in France, Pathé-Natan was reported to own 62 in France and in Belgium, and to have gained de facto control of 150 others.[21] Estimated to accommodate up to 100,000 spectators per day, the Pathé-Natan chain—the largest in the country—made up the core of the conversion-era French cinema's exhibition sector, comprising roughly 15 percent of the total number of sound-equipped theatres in France in 1931.[22] Besides the quantity of theatres, also important was their quality: the majority were large, upscale houses, featuring from 1,000 to 3,000 seats and located in urban centers. In terms of national entertainment norms, these theatres were top of the line. Old facilities had been completely refurbished, and outfitted with new facades, plush new seats, air conditioning, and expensive RCA sound-film projection equipment.[23] Featuring rare and highly popular French-language re-leases in exclusive runs, at high admission prices, the rebuilt theatres re-ported doubling or tripling their receipts after Natan had wired and upgraded them.[24]

Although enormously costly to build and operate, these theatres gener-ated astonishing profits continuing through 1931, prior to the Depression-era slump in theatre attendance. During the boom of 1929–1931, the considerable theatre revenue allowed a quick amortization of the costs of industrial-scale sound-film production, allowing Pathé-Natan to make more films per year than any other French company. At the same time, the very existence of the theatres, with their entertainment-palace am-biance, stimulated demand in France for a certain stage-defined genre of sound film, made by the company's production facilities, and then dis-tributed by the company to the chain of flagship theatres. After playing exclusively in these theatres, the films were then distributed to the hun-dreds of additional sound-ready theatres in France clamoring to screen French-language films. Although the independent theatres sometimes waited until mid-1930 or later before showing a French-made talkie, the films were sufficiently popular that such theatres could make "excellent" profits from them anyway.[25]

### Pathé-Natan's "House Style"

In assessing the style of Pathé-Natan's films, it is useful to note a key difference in ambitions regarding distribution between Pathé-Natan and the Hollywood companies with which it is often compared. Unlike the Hollywood majors—which, like Pathé-Frères during the years before World War I, had made films for the global film market—Pathé-Natan made films primarily for domestic consumption. With the exception of experiments, such as the English-language version of *Mon gosse de Père* (dir. Jean de Limur, 1930) or the German, English, and Spanish versions of *Je t'adore mais pourquoi* (dir. Piére Colombier and René Pujol, 1931), Pathé-Natan did not produce multiple-language versions or other sorts of "international" films, nor did it dub its films for export to non-francophone markets. Pathé-Natan set its sight on the French market alone, and more so than any other production company, met the conversion-era need for French-language sound movies.

Given the French sound-film shortage of 1929–1931, Pathé-Natan, the country's main supplier, held a commanding position in the national film industry. Consolidating this position in the domain of movie production was the centrality of Pathé-Natan's Joinville studio facility for many of the country's numerous independent producers, who rented Joinville's soundstages, at a cost of 35,000 francs per day, and who also paid Pathé-Natan for the costs of film stock and for developing the negative.[26] According to government and film-industry estimates, such fees typically consumed from 40 to 50 percent of a film's total production costs.[27] To avoid paying these costs, independent producers such as Adolf Osso made French-language films in other countries, including at the Tobis-equipped studios in Hungary and Yugoslavia, while others avoided studio rental altogether by shooting entire films on location, as did André Hugon, Marcel Pagnol, Jacques de Baroncelli, and others. Besides the rental costs, producers working at Joinville often signed exclusive agreements to distribute the finished films with Paris Consortium Cinéma, the company's distribution office—otherwise the films might not have played in first-run venues. According to producer Pierre Braunberger, Pathé-Natan's refusal to rent out Joinville's stages unless guaranteed distribution of finished films motivated him and partner Roger Richebé to open their own studio at Billancourt in June 1930.[28]

The site of the production of a large portion of the national film output, the Joinville sound stages were a busy place during the early 1930s. Moreover, a fair number of the films can be located for study purposes. Of the fifty-four films that comprise my core sample for the statistics reported in chapter 4, more than one-fourth were made at Joinville. What sort of films were these? Can they be said to have exhibited a distinctive house style? In certain respects, generalizations concerning the studio's output are problematic. As with the national cinema generally, the Joinville films exhibit considerable stylistic diversity. For instance, with regard to statistics for average shot length, the range for these films (based on a sample of fifteen films made between 1930 and 1933, listed in the Filmography) is nearly as wide as that for the national output as a whole, from a low of 3.7 seconds to a high of 21.5. Nonetheless certain continuities across this rather varied body of work are evident, to the point that film-industry professionals recognized a "house style" characteristic of the studio.

Most fundamentally, Pathé-Natan was known for a wide range of theatre adaptations. Claiming to provide an alternative to "the standardized films that come to us from America," Pathé-Natan avoided categorizing its films in American film-genre terms, instead favoring genre labels that alluded to the films' popular-theatre sources. Thus, the production list for 1932 was divided into five categories, four of which— "great dramatic films," "boulevard comedies," "famous melodramas," and "cinematographic operettas"—alluded directly to the scenarios' theatrical origins.[29] Central to the appeal of these films were performances by stage-trained actors with prominent theatrical profiles, such as Jean Gabin, Charles Vanel, Elvire Popesco, Gaby Morlay, Victor Francen, and Gabriel Gabrio—all of whom had signed contracts with Pathé-Natan, as reported in the company's publicity.[30] The contracts were unusual in French cinema, and enhanced Pathé-Natan's identity as a modern-day French rejoinder to the major Hollywood studios, although film stardom in France differed in important respects from that in the United States.[31] With contracts rarely extending beyond two or three films, Pathé-Natan exercised far less control over actors' careers than did the Hollywood companies. Producer Emile Natan, Bernard's brother, reportedly prohibited Renée St. Cyr from appearing in *La maternelle* (dir. Jean Benoit-Levy and Marie Epstein, 1933) on the grounds that the role was inappropriately melodramatic, but such studio-initiated efforts to mold a star's image appear to have been exceptional.[32] Concerning the actors' work in theatre or other media, Pathé-Natan placed no restrictions whatsoever—on the basis perhaps that from the company's standpoint, the more active on stage, radio, and disc the actors were, the better. In fostering their familiarity with the French public, the actors' profiles in national entertainment—from the stage to radio, the electric phonograph, and illustrated magazines—distinguished Pathé-Natan's films, so rich in invocations of the national media culture, from the international appeal of dubbed American imports.

The importance to Pathé-Natan's films of stage-trained performers meant, in technical terms, that the films were cut to the measure of the actors rather than the other way around; hence the familiar characterization of the French cinema of the 1930s as an actor's cinema. Relevant in this regard is the extent to which actors at Pathé-Natan improvised their performances during shooting, which tended to impose technical limitations on the films as a whole. Describing his experience directing a film at Joinville, actor Charles Vanel complained about the amount of costly studio time lost because actors had not rehearsed their lines prior to shooting.[33] Vanel's observations are corroborated by other reports, such as an account of the production of *Le roi du cirage* (dir. Pière Colombier, 1932), which describes the shooting of a scene during which extras with speaking roles, unable to play their parts, were replaced after six unsuccessful takes.[34] A related problem concerned the generally minimal preproduction planning and scripting, with films routinely going into production prior to the script's completion. According to a report on the Pathé-Natan production *Sapho* (dir. Léonce Perret, 1933), the dialogue was not written out but improvised according to instructions in the "script," such as the following: "They exchange unpleasant remarks [*phrases bêtes*], but the tone of their voices reveals the true meaning of their words."[35] Actors and directors discussed what to say and how, while the crew waited and the studio's clock ticked. Similar practices of on-the-set script revision, with lines written and rewritten while the crew waited, were reported for the production of *Au nom de la loi* (*In the Name of the Law*, dir. Maurice Tourneur, 1931), another Joinville-made film.[36]

## Multiple-Camera Shooting

The improvised approach to shooting, along with the minimal pre-production planning and rehearsal, profoundly conditioned the peculiarities of the company's multiple-camera "house style." As proposed in chapter 5, the adaptation in French filmmaking of multiple-camera shooting reveals the extent to which the conversion-era French cinema had followed Hollywood's technical and industrial precedents while nonetheless diverging stylistically. Here Pathé-Natan's films are exemplary. Notwithstanding the reliance on multiple-camera shooting, these films feature 180-degree cuts, that is, straight jumps across the scene's axis of action. This sort of cutting endured at Joinville through mid-decade. As late as 1935, films such as *Justin de Marseilles* (dir. Maurice Tourneur) feature scenes constructed around violations of the 180-degree rule, in which the shot change entails a total, 180-degree jump across the scene's axis of action. (See Figures 6.1 through 6.4.)

This sort of discontinuous cutting appears congruent with the logic of the national popular approach to editing discussed in chapter 4, whereby cuts from shot to shot suggest not the demands of character psychology but rather the nature of the narrative or performance event, according to generic convention (e.g., chase scenes fast, romantic scenes slow). An intriguing feature of the Pathé-Natan examples, essential to the "liveness" of filmed theatre, is that the spatial fragmentation coincides with continuity in the actors' performances. That is, notwithstanding the unusual manner in which the scene's space is broken up, with unpredictable hops across the axis of action, the actors' performances maintain the unbroken momentum characteristic of a real-time stage or radio performance, with a constant vocal scale throughout the scene. (See Figure 6.5.)

Do the numerous 180-degree cuts in the films made at Pathé-Natan's Joinville facility imply a coherent, alternative film style, or are they best seen as random technical flaws, that is, "continuity violations" in Hollywood parlance? One factor complicating the case of the Joinville-made films is that the practice of filming scenes so as to produce 180-degree cuts, in light of its prevalence, seems to have been routine, as if it were the local, business-as-usual approach to shooting and cutting. That is,

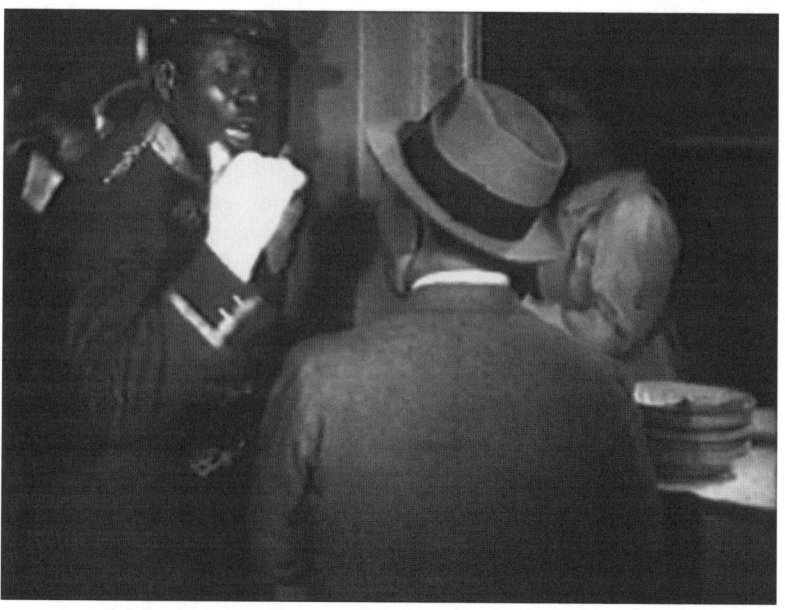

Figs. 6.1 and 6.2. The transgression of Hollywood's 180-degree rule in this two-shot sequence from *Le roi du cirage* (Pière Colombier, 1932) is typical of the often unorthodox use of multiple-camera shooting at Pathé-Natan's Joinville studio. Throughout *Le roi du cirage* dialogue exchanges between two characters are presented in series of 180-degree cuts that entirely reverse the positions of the actors, reveal the opposite sides of the sets, and generally serve to establish a 360-degree playing area alien to the Hollywood cinema's customary treatment of narrative space.

Figs. 6.3 and 6.4. Similar cutting patterns involving 180-degree cuts occur in other Joinville-made films, including independent productions involving the participation of personnel other than the house crew. In *Le prince de minuit* (René Guisart, 1934), for instance, straight jumps across the axis of action are featured in virtually all scenes. In this case, editing-related spatial disjunctions find a compensation of sorts in Garat's direct-recorded crooning, which remains unbroken across the shot changes.

Figure 6.5: This subsequent shot from the same scene in *Le prince de minuit* is telling with regard to production practice at Joinville. Hopping across the axis of action to a view of Garat and co-star Edith Méra from the exterior of the record shop, where a crowd has gathered to hear Garat sing, the change in camera position significantly expands the scene's physical scope. Positioned deep in the shot's space, Garat and Méra are now only barely visible through the shop window. Close examination of the scene reveals that Garat's performance has continued unbroken across the shot change, which points to an important circumstance regarding the film's production: rather than film this exceptional shot separately, and then insert it into the scene in post-production, the shot was taken by a third camera that had been running simultaneously with the others. In short, the entire scene had been filmed in a single multiple-camera take, with all the actors on the set at the same time. Although fraught with potential technical difficulties, this one-take approach to shooting and recording has powerfully conditioned familiar claims regarding the exceptional spontaneity of the French cinema of the 1930s.

insofar as continuity rules were flaunted, it appears to have been in a systematic, taken-for-granted manner, according to house practice, and an alternative conception of the playing space, in which changes in camera angles serve to set off individual shots as separate tableaux. Thus, to refer to these cuts as violations seems inappropriate, as if the wrong standard of judgment were being invoked. Unlike editing mistakes—technical flaws attributable to budget constraints, or to occasional negligence—

180-degree cuts in films produced at the Joinville studios imply an alternative set of norms altogether, intended less to absorb the viewer into a film's story than to inject a dynamism and mobility of sorts into a mise-en-scène that might otherwise seem excessively stage-derived. In this context, leaps across the scene's axis may be wholly functional, although in ways irrelevant to the drama's psychology.

A precedent for this sort of cutting existed in the national cinema's past, in the films produced at the Pathé company and at other French companies in the years before World War I, when, as Richard Abel notes, 180-degree cuts occurred in French films from this time, such as the Pathé productions directed by Léonce Perret.[37] Perret later worked at Pathé-Natan during the early 1930s, when he was among a number of directors working in France whose film careers began prior to the modernism of the 1920s. In the context of the continuity in practices and in personnel, the peculiar cutting evident in Pathé-Natan's films looks less like an avant-gardist violation of Hollywood norms than a continuation of national film-industry practices older than both the Hollywood style that took form in the late 1910s *and* the avant-garde and modernist styles that emerged during the next decade. From the standpoint of the established history of film style, at issue is a historiographical oddity: a European alternative to Hollywood style that owed little to the film modernism of the 1920s.

Conversion-era filmmakers often seemed to regard editing less as a storytelling tool than as a means of compensating for filmed theatre's tendency toward visual stasis, as noted in chapter 4. An intriguing aspect of many of the Joinville-made films is the apparent irrelevance of narrative considerations to editing decisions, as if shot choices were unrelated to the psychology of the drama. For instance, in *Chacun sa chance* (dir. Hans Steinhoff and René Pujol, 1931), certain cuts involve only minimal changes in camera angle and position and seem to carve up story-world space in ways irrelevant to the psychology of character interaction. In this context, the capacity of continuity violations, in strictly perceptual terms, to knock the viewer off balance, as it were, can be seen as advantageous. In requiring the viewer to adjust, again and again, to perpetual, unpredictable changes in camera position and sound perspective, a film can generate a sense of energy and movement—albeit in forms unrelated to the linear, narrative-defined movement associated with the Hollywood film—forms that, as in the case of the French cinema of the 1930s, invite description as spontaneous, open-ended, and off-the-cuff.

An alternative multiple-camera system, of this or any sort, would seem more likely to appear in the domain of the international art cinema, and at a later date in film history. In addition to Kurosawa, one might also cite French filmmakers such as Willy Rozier, François Truffaut, and 1930s veteran Jean Renoir, all of whom experimented with multiple-camera shooting in the decades after World War II.[38] But as the case of Pathé-Natan's multiple-camera house style suggests, alternative multiple-camera practice has a genealogy that goes back further historically, to the conversion years, when alternative styles emerged not only on the national cinema's avant-garde margins but also from within its commercial center.

The artistic quality of the French cinema of the 1930s has long been attributed to the French film industry's fragmented production sector, whose patchwork of small production companies, functioning largely independently of one another, provided an essential condition for the making of films in a wide variety of styles. In this context, the prominence during the conversion years of the short-lived conglomerates Gaumont-Franco-Film-Aubert and Pathé-Natan may seem too exceptional—or artistically unworthy—to merit scholarly interest. In fact, these large companies—particularly Pathé-Natan—have been regarded as obstacles to the national cinema's artistic progress, as if the nation's auteurs were made to wait until the crash of the conversion-era's film-industrial combines for conditions propitious for film art. The project of this chapter has been to reassess the period by clarifying Pathé-Natan's role in shaping a national film style for the sound era. This role can be difficult to recognize, given the anomalous status of the national popular films of companies such as Pathé-Natan. Made strictly for domestic consumption, such films seem excessively local, their historical significance wholly a function of the chaotic, multifaceted media culture in which they had taken form. In effect, the very qualities that had enabled the films' commercial success—their embeddedness in a national media culture encompassing stage, radio, and phonograph—has made them seem foreign to the spirituality of great art, that is, too occasional, too much a product of local and temporary circumstances, too commercial. Nevertheless, the sound-film techniques practiced at Pathé-Natan were distinctive relative to those of the other major national cinemas of the time, and would turn out to have an artistic significance in French filmmaking whose impact continues into the present, when direct-sound techniques still define the French cinema relative to other national cinemas. As discussed briefly in the conclusion that follows, sound-film techniques characteristic of France's conversion-era filmed theatre acquired a second life of sorts in the decades after World War II, when direct sound evolved into a definitive national film technique, and postwar filmmakers, while drawing on techniques familiar to the 1930s, explored direct sound's artistic potential in ways unimaginable during conversion.

# Conclusion: Sound and National Film Style—Past and Present

In this conclusion, the question posed in the introduction concerning the French cinema's status as an alternative model for sound-film practice is approached in terms of similarities between the cinema of the 1930s and that of today. As the intervening chapters have detailed, the French cinema's sound-film practices during the 1930s differed significantly from the American cinema's, despite use in the two countries' film industries of many of the same technologies and techniques, and emulation of some of the same films. Thus, in contrast to the familiar characterization of conversion as a homogenizing process, this book's examination of French filmmaking has shown that conversion's effects on national film styles took multiple forms, which varied substantially from one film-producing country to the next. Moreover, as the cases of both the American and French cinemas suggest, the national sound-film practices of the 1930s survived the conversion years to shape the national cinemas' subsequent histories.

The examination of sound-film history now opens out onto a basic question, raised in chapter 1, concerning the history of film style: the extent to which the established notion that the introduction of synchronous sound served to homogenize film style rests on the well-worn assumption that film is essentially a visual art. In other words, if sound conversion can be said to have produced a relative sameness at the level of image techniques such as editing and cinematography, does it necessarily follow that a homogenization of film style also occurred? By some accounts, there is overwhelming evidence to the contrary. As Michel Chion proposes, even a cursory consideration of the field of contemporary national cinema at the turn of the millennium reveals notable diversity at the level of sound technique, with Italian films differing significantly from French films, which differ from Hollywood films, which are unlike films from the Indian subcontinent, and so on: "Just as there exists a relative internationalism in the treatment of the film image, . . .

for film sound, each country has its own history and fashion of handling it."[1] Likewise, Alan Williams, in a recent survey of issues of film and nationalism, has suggested that important differences in national style today are more likely to be heard than seen.[2]

This book explores the history of sound's importance to national film style through a comparative study of the Hollywood cinema and one of the major national popular cinemas of Europe. In the closing remarks that follow, the objective is to suggest how an inquiry into national film practices today—not only American and French practices, but also (potentially) Italian, Indian, Japanese, and others—might benefit from the study of the cinema of the 1930s, when, in key respects, the foundations were laid for today's national differences in film style. The focus is on the enduring legacy of the sound-film techniques of the 1930s in filmmaking today, a legacy evident in both the American and French cinemas: just as the layered, multi-track approach to sound that began to define American cinema circa 1931 continues to do so, the direct-sound methods of the French cinema of the 1930s have survived into the present to become the definitive French film technique. How has the meaning of these techniques been transformed through their longevity in subsequent filmmaking history—a history whose effects extend into the present?

## Direct Sound since World War II and National Film Style

With regard to the present-day legacy of the sound-film techniques of the 1930s, the case of Hollywood practice seems relatively straightforward, with the contemporary cinema's multi-track approach continuous, in aesthetic principle, with the approach of the early 1930s. That is, at issue in both the American cinema of the 1930s and that of today is a layered approach to the soundtrack founded on the priority of story-world coherence. In the case of French cinema, however, the relation between technique and aesthetic function appears to have evolved historically. In French filmmaking, the technique of direct sound has become increasingly institutionalized, including in the curriculum of national film schools; but its aesthetic function has evolved considerably since the 1930s. The key development occurred in the years after World War II, when direct sound emerged in France as an alternative film practice. No longer a technique employed broadly throughout the mainstream film industry, direct sound during the 1950s and 1960s became essential to the styles of certain of the most ambitious alternative filmmakers of the time. This postwar history of direct-sound practice—which coincided with an important sound-technological change, the film-industrial adaptation of magnetic sound—is a topic sufficiently complex and multifaceted to require a book in itself. Also welcome would be thorough studies of the auteur practices of directors such as Rivette, Godard, Renoir, and others, whose films helped define direct-sound technique during the 1950s and 1960s.[3] The following observations are intended to outline basic changes in how direct sound was understood after World War II, when direct sound evolved from a technique into a style, from a mainstream film-industry practice to a feature of the work of certain of the national cinema's boldest auteur filmmakers.

Examples of postwar auteur practice include experiments with multiple-camera shooting by directors Willy Rozier, Jean-Pierre Melville, François Truffaut, and others. Jean Renoir, a veteran of the multiple-camera practices of the conversion years, returned to the technique in the 1950s in films such as *Le testament du Docteur Cordelier* (1959), which showcases a bravura performance by Jean-Louis Barrault as Dr. Jekyll/Mr. Hyde. Also during this time, Jean-Marie Straub and Danièle Huillet, in an extraordinary series of radically experimental films, drew on the expertise of sound personnel who had worked with prominent 1930s directors, including Renoir and Max Ophuls.[4] During the 1960s, in the wake of filmmaking's widespread adoption of magnetic sound technologies, new thresholds in sonic invention were heard in the films of Jean-Luc Godard, who employed both direct-sound and post-synchronization methods to striking effect—and, in the case of *Le mépris* (1963), with the help of sound technician Willem Sivel, a veteran of the French cinema during conversion. Also significant during this time were Jacques Rivette's films, such as *L'amour fou* (1969), which likewise featured direct-sound methods familiar to conversion-era filmmaking—improvised performances, location-recorded music, and direct-recorded tracking shots. According to sound technician Pierre Gamet, *son direct* serves as the "the very principle of the cinema of Rivette."[5] Similarly, director Jean Eustache, who claimed, "I know nothing other than direct sound," employed the technique exclusively in films such as *Le Père Noël a les yeux bleus* (*Father Christmas Has Blue Eyes*, 1966).[6]

The young auteurs of the postwar decades—often using magnetic rather than optical sound technologies—can be said to have adopted the earlier techniques in light of a self-conscious reflection on direct sound's artistic possibilities, which in key respects were alien to prewar film culture. While the techniques of the 1930s continued to be employed in later times, major changes in their artistic function are evident. This appears less true of the history of Hollywood's sound practice, which, notwithstanding numerous technical upgrades since the early 1930s, exhibits considerable continuity at the level of aesthetic function. An indication of the national difference can be found in the historiography, where the canon of important conversion-era Hollywood films has remained largely unchanged since conversion. That is, the work during the early 1930s of directors such as Mamoulian, Lubitsch, and Vidor, whatever its idiosyncrasies, is recognized today as foundational for the development of the contemporary Hollywood sound film. Radical exceptions, such as the enduring commitment to pantomime in Chaplin's *City Lights* (1931), seem to prove the rule, in that they were recognized at the time as one-off departures from the American film industry's sound-era norm.[7]

In this regard, the situation concerning the history of French filmmaking differs significantly, with today's canon of early French sound films amounting largely to a post–World War II invention that bears little resemblance to what conversion-era observers had regarded as the period's significant films. Indeed, in an important sense, today's French canon looks like the inverse of what had been celebrated then. On the one hand, major commercial directors of the time—such as Léon Mathot, Robert Florey, Jean Choux, Raymond Bernard, Pière Colombier, René Pujol, and André Hugon—have faded into historiographical invisibility. On the other hand, directors with relatively obscure profiles during conversion—that is, Jean Grémillon, Jean Renoir, Jean Vigo, Jean Cocteau, and Luis Buñuel—are today commonly regarded as the most significant filmmakers of the period, as if genuine sound-film talent were available only on the national film industry's margins. Emblematic here is the perhaps apocryphal anecdote concerning Bernard Natan's philistine reaction after a preview screening of Grémillon's *La petite Lise* (1930), when Natan, allegedly outraged by the extraordinarily inventive film, had banned Grémillon from future employment at Joinville.[8] Recall also the case of Vigo, whose brief career (1929–1934) coincided with the French film industry's conversion, but whose films found appreciative audiences and critical accolades only beginning in the 1940s, more than a decade after their initial release—or non-release, as in the case of the censored *Zéro de conduite* (1934), which played in Belgium but not in France. The circumstance was aptly summarized in the mid-1950s by P. E. Salles Gomes, Vigo's biographer: "Until 1940, Vigo's films were not thought of as a key element in the [early sound] period, whereas it is now very largely in relation to Vigo that the period interests us."[9]

The critical reception of the first sound films directed by René Clair, perhaps the only major conversion-era director whose renown during conversion endured into subsequent decades, also suggests the singularity of the early sound years relative to subsequent French film history. From the time of Clair's four breakthrough Tobis films in 1930–1932, up through the present, the magnitude of his conversion-era achievement has been unquestioned. But how the achievement is understood has changed. During the early 1930s, Clair's films pointed ahead to the future, demonstrating a sound-film style that might transcend the talkie's aesthetic limits, and in a commercially successful manner. After 1932, however, in the wake of filmed theater's undeniable dominance in the national film market, a consensus concerning the French cinema's aesthetic direction had taken form, and Clair's films were seen differently: although still much admired, they began to look like masterpieces of a bygone time—"museum pieces," as film historian Francis Courtade has suggested—rather than living exemplars for working filmmakers.[10]

Concerning this history of reception, something like the opposite situation could be said to have obtained for the early sound films of Jean Renoir, whose emergence as one of the national cinema's preeminent directors occurred subsequent to conversion. During conversion, *On purge bébé* (1930), *La nuit du carrefour* (*Night of the Crossroads,* 1932), *La chienne* (1931), *Boudu sauvé des eaux* (*Boudu Saved from Drowning,* 1932), and *Chotard et cie.* (1933) received modest critical and popular acclaim, and Renoir was becoming known as a talented film director sensitive to popular taste.[11] It wasn't until mid-decade, subsequent to conversion, that Renoir emerged as one of the national cinema's preeminent directors. After the war, Renoir's early sound films drew new interest, in light of an emerging "realist" cinema that included the work of Italian directors such as Roberto Rossellini and Vittorio De Sica. Ensuring the postwar status of Renoir's conversion-era films as realist was their use of direct sound, which distinguished them from the majority of films made during the 1940s—including the neorealist masterpieces, whose sounds, as Renoir observed, had been recorded separately and then post-synchronized.[12] Renoir's observation remains relevant to national cinema today, given the endurance of both the French cinema's preference for direct sound and the Italian cinema's reliance on post-synchronization. What has been forgotten, however, is that at the time that Renoir had directed films such as *La chienne*, direct-sound techniques, as detailed in the preceding chapters, had permeated the mainstream national cinema. For instance, inventive uses of location-recorded sound, and live rather than post-synchronized sound effects, are evident in other films made at the Braunberger-Richebé studio, such as *Le chien jaune* (dir. Jean Tarride, 1932), which features the work of certain of the same sound engineers who had worked with Renoir. Although Renoir's methods were remarkable in important respects (one can begin with the extreme use of long takes, manifest in an ASL nearly double the contemporaneous national norm), in terms of sound technique, they were less countercultural during the early 1930s than is often assumed.

## From Implicit to Explicit Practice

Dramatic postwar transformations in the canon of conversion-era films point to the need for caution in assessing direct sound's historical significance. While direct-sound techniques familiar to the French cinema of the 1930s have endured in French filmmaking today, they have done so in light of significant changes in aesthetic function. One way to specify the overall nature of the change lies in a consideration of what might be called a film technique's degree of explicitness, that is, the degree to which an explicit, self-aware consensus defines the film community's understanding of the technique's aesthetic implications in written statements and manifestos, and, most importantly, in films themselves.

In this regard, a considerable evolution in the artistic status of direct sound appears to have occurred subsequent to conversion. Direct sound had been imposed by industrial and technical necessity when introduced into French filmmaking in 1929 and 1930. At that point, there was little consensus, either explicit or implicit, concerning sound's impact on the cinema's future. Multiple alternative models for sound-film style, inflected by contemporaneous developments in radio, the gramophone, and other media, proliferated. Technologies that had been developed outside the film industry had to be adapted for filmmaking purposes and under economic, technological, and cultural conditions that varied, sometimes radically, from country to country. "L'empiricisme régnait," as director Henri Fescourt had put it, referring to the trial-and-error character of the sound-film production methods of the time.[13] While trade-press commentators sometimes stated a preference for direct-recorded over post-synchronized sound, and film producers and actors lobbied the government to ban the importation of dubbed films, such statements and efforts do not appear to have fed into a self-conscious stylistic program comparable to those undertaken in the 1950s and 1960s by filmmakers such as Straub and Huillet, Rivette, Godard, Eustache, Maurice Pialat, and numerous others. One might argue that it wasn't until the 1950s, and the self-conscious retrieval of direct-sound methods on the part of a young generation of filmmakers, that the stylistic implications of these methods became clear. In fact, attempts during the 1930s to theorize the aesthetics of film sound often appeared irrelevant to filmmaking's practical demands, as was the case, for instance, with avant-gardist attempts to ignore human perception's innate tendency to privilege voices over other types of sound. As Richard Abel observes, referring specifically to the early 1930s, "more often than not, French film theory and criticism hastened to catch up with rather than direct actual film practice."[14] In the event, direct-sound methods evolved less through deliberate choices made on aesthetic grounds than through ad hoc accommodation to technical and economic necessity. In sum, during the 1930s, film-sound methods typically lacked the artistic self-consciousness that critics such as Michel Chion properly attribute to direct-sound filmmaking in France today.[15]

In fact, direct-sound's emergence in conversion-era France as the principal film-sound technical norm occurred within a film community whose most prominent members advocated a post-synchronized alternative attuned to cinema's potential for spectacular formal manipulation rather than to its capacity for simulating theatrical or radio-broadcast liveness. As noted in chapter 3, many of the most prestigious filmmakers during the first years of the French cinema's conversion—including René Clair, Abel Gance, Charlie Chaplin, and Sergei Eisenstein—explicitly disparaged the direct-recorded *film parlant* in favor of the post-synchronized *film sonore*. For these eminent directors—and for many critics and commentators, both in France and in other countries—the mainstream sound cinema's direct-recorded performances of stage- and radio-defined actors had diminished the cinema as an art form.

The need for a "classical" alternative to direct sound, character- rather than actor-centered, and whose departure from filmed theatre would allow recovery of the international prestige of the art of cinema in the late silent era, began to be met in France during the late 1930s, when the technical quality, and exportability, of French films was improved via the use of re-recording and other multi-track techniques, and French films began winning international festival awards. By then, direct sound, with its sometimes unintelligible voices, had become associated with low technical quality, and also, given the many theatre-derived film scripts and performances, with aesthetic backwardness. Symptomatic of the film community's shift in perspective were demands in the film trade-press of the late 1930s for the mandatory re-recording of film sound, which presupposed use of a multi-track system. Exhortations of this sort became routine during the German occupation of France, when the technical quality of films from *Le corbeau* (dir. Henri-Georges Clouzot, 1943) to *Les enfants du paradis* (dir. Marcel Carné, 1944–1945) rested on the finesse of state-of-the-art, multi-track sound. With regard to the question of direct sound's degree of aesthetic explicitness, the situation after World War II clearly differed from that before. When a new, postwar generation of auteur filmmakers began retrieving direct-sound techniques familiar to the 1930s—while also creating new techniques, made possible by new magnetic-sound technologies—it was in the context of a self-conscious exploration of alternatives to the national quality cinema in the post-conversion period. Deliberately working against the tide of the cinema's mainstream, the auteurs comprising the postwar *nouvel avant garde* explored the potential of a sound-film technique that the commercial film industry, since the 1930s, had come to reject. Concerning direct sound's new status, a manifesto-like statement can be found in Straub and Huillet's claim that "direct sound is not merely a technical decision but a moral and ideological one."[16]

With respect to sound conversion's international or global dimension, an axiom suggests itself: just as a technique's aesthetic function changes when transplanted from one national film industry into another, it changes also over the course of historical time, as filmmakers in later periods draw on the cinema's past as a resource for innovation in the present and the technique's aesthetic implications become clear, manifest gradually in new films disclosing the aesthetic possibilities of new media technologies. Direct sound's ongoing endurance in French filmmaking provides a case in point: although the self-consciously alternative filmmakers of the decades after World War II employed direct-sound methods familiar to the theatre-cinema of the 1930s, they did so in light of an understanding of film aesthetics foreign in important regards to the film culture of the conversion years. This new aesthetic has, in turn, profoundly shaped today's understanding of the films of the 1930s, conditioning the historiography of the cinema's conversion to sound in ways that foreground certain aspects of the period's filmmaking while concealing others. Hence, the promise of an inclusive examination of the films of the period, which can newly illuminate today's national film styles, disclosing the latter's forgotten origins in the national popular cinemas of the 1930s. As this book has been concerned to demonstrate, to study conversion-era film practice is to gain insight into national cinema today.

# Notes

## Introduction

1. Concerning the importance of direct sound to contemporary French film-making, see the interviews with sound technicians in Claudine Nougaret and Sophie Chiabaut, *Le son direct au cinéma* [Direct Sound in the Cinema] (Paris: Femis, 1997).

2. In Jean-Pierre Frouard, "*doublage*" ("dubbing"), in *Dictionnaire du cinéma,* ed. Jean Loup Passek (Paris: Larousse, 1986), 195.

3. In Michel Chion, *Le cinéma et ses métiers* [The cinema and its crafts] (Paris: Bordas, 1990), 180.

4. See Michèle Deroyer, "Ce que Pirandello attend du cinéma" [What Pirandello expects from the cinema], *Pour vous,* no. 148 (17 September 1931), 3. Concerning Léger, see the remarks quoted in "Ce qu'ils pensent du son et de la couleur" [Thoughts on sound and color], *Pour vous,* no. 3 (6 December 1928), 2.

5. In Alexandre Arnoux, "Les auteurs dramatiques et les 'talkies'" [Dramatists and the talkies], *Pour vous,* no. 35 (18 July 1929), 2; see also André Berge, "Dira-t-on maintenant: êtes-vous phonogénique?" [Are you phonogenic?], *Pour vous,* no. 28 (30 May 1929), 2; and C. A. Gonnet, "Comment on devient star" [How to become a star], *Almanach de Mon Ciné* (1932), 24.

6. See, for instance, "Des film parfumés?" [Perfumed films?], *La cinématographie française,* vol. 12, no. 595 (29 March 1930), 16; Emile Roux-Parassac, "En écoutant le parlant" [While listening to the talkie], *Le cinéopse,* vol. 13, no. 141 (May 1931), 223.

7. See Martin Barnier, *En route vers le parlant: histoire d'une evolution technologique, économique et esthéthique du cinéma (1926–1934)* (Liège, Belgium: Ed. Du Céfal, 2002), 207–208.

8. See here remarks on sound conversion in Peter Wollen, "Cinema and Technology: A Historical Overview," *Readings and Writings: Semiotic Counter-Strategies* (London: Verso, 1982), 169–177.

9. See Alan Williams, *Republic of Images: A History of French Filmmaking* (Cambridge, Mass., and London: Harvard University Press, 1992), 138ff.

10. In Colin Crisp, *The Classic French Cinema, 1930–1960* (Bloomington: Indiana University Press, 1993), 109–110.

11. Regarding the filmic avant-garde's decline, see Leo Hirsch, "Film sonore et film muet" [Sound film and silent film], *La technique cinématographique,* vol. 4, no. 26 (February 1933), 79.

12. In Jean Fayard, "Acteurs de théâtre et acteurs de cinéma" [Theatre actors and film actors], *Pour vous*, no. 394 (4 June 1936), 2.

13. In Jean Mitry, *Histoire du cinéma, art et industrie*, vol. 4: *les années trentes* (Paris: J.-P. Delarge, 1980), 166–167.

14. In Jacques Vivien, "Broadway Melody," *Petit Parisien* (2 August 1929).

15. See Abel Gance, "Il y a le cinéma et il y a l'art du cinéma" [There is cinema and there is cinema art] (1934), in Roger Icart, *Abel Gance* (Lausanne: L'âge d'homme, 1983), 261; René Clair, "René Clair défend le parlant contre le parlant" [René Clair defends the talkie against the talkie], *Pour vous*, no. 56 (12 December 1929), 7; and Georges Charensol, "Panorama du cinéma," *Pour vous*, no. 61 (16 June 1930), 11.

16. Concerning the prodigious stylistic diversity engendered by sound cinema's relations with multiple media, see Martin Barnier, *En route vers le parlant: histoire d'une evolution technologique, économique et esthétique du cinéma (1926–1934)* (Liège, Belgium: Ed. Du Céfal, 2002), 137–195; and Christian Belaygue, ed., *La passage de muet au parlant: panorama mondial de la production cinématographique mondial, 1925–1935* (Toulouse: Cinémathèque de Toulouse/ Ed. Milan, 1988).


### 1. Sound's Impact on Film Style

1. See Martin Barnier, "Le Cinéphone et l'Idéal-Sonore, deux appareils sonores Gaumont des années 1920-1930," *1895*, no. 24 (June 1998), 37–53.

2. Concerning the formation of Tobis-Klangfilm, see Karel Dibbets, "L'Europe, le son, Tobis" [Europe, sound, Tobis], *Le passage du muet au parlant* [The passage from silent to speaking cinema], ed. Christian Belaygue (Toulouse: Cinémathèque de Toulouse/Ed. Milan, 1988), 38–41; on the "patents war," see Douglas Gomery, "Economic Struggle and Hollywood Imperialism: Europe Converts to Sound," *Yale French Studies*, vol. 60, no. 1 (1980), 80–93.

3. See Marcel Colin-Reval, "La répartition des teritoires Européens par les groupements Germano-Américains, Détenteurs des brevets sonores" [The division of European territories by German and American sound-patent-owning companies], *La technique cinématographique*, vol. 13, no. 660 (27 June 1931), 75.

4. See Francis Courtade, *Les Malédictions du cinéma français: une histoire du cinéma français parlant, 1928–1978* (Paris: Aláin Moreau, 1978), 39–43.

5. See Martin Barnier, *En route vers le parlant* (Liège, Belgium: Ed. Du Céfal, 2002), 150.

6. See David Bordwell, Janet Staiger, and Kristin Thompson, *The Classical Hollywood Cinema* (New York: Columbia University Press, 1985).

7. In Brian Winston, *Technologies of Seeing: Photography, Cinematography, and Television* (London: British Film Institute, 1996), 8.

8. See Douglas Gomery, "Technological Film History," in Robert Allen and Douglas Gomery, *Film History: Theory and Practice* (New York: Knopf, 1985).

9.  These figures are cited in James P. Kraft, *Stage to Studio: Musicians and the Sound Revolution, 1890–1950* (Baltimore and London: Johns Hopkins University Press, 1996), 49.

10. See Jean-Marie Lo Duca, *La technique du cinéma* (Paris: Presses Universitaires Françaises, 1948), 118.

11. A detailed analysis of these and other film-theatre receipts in Paris can be found in Reginald Ford, "Statistiques des cinémas de Paris," *La cinématographie française*, vol. 13, no. 629 (22 November 1930), 14.

12. See René Guy-Grand, "Debuts et avenir du film sonore" [The beginnings and future of the sound film], *Grand revue* (1 April 1930), 209–222. "The creation of the sound film is essentially an American effort."

13. In Paul Morand, "Les cinq sens de la terre," *Figaro* (15 April 1935), n.p.

14. In Ruth Vasey, *The World According to Hollywood* (Madison: University of Wisconsin Press, 1997), 63–99. According to a 1931 trade-press report, Paramount had decided to limit dialogue to 30 percent of a film's running time, so as to restore "the visual value and movement" that had been lost during conversion. See Marcel Colin-Reval, "La Convention Paramount à Berlin," *La cinematographie française*, vol. 13, no. 661 (4 July 1931), 9.

15. See "Braunberger-Richebé, specialists du 'parlant,'" *La cinématographie française*, vol. 12, no. 607 (21 June 1930), 7.

16. On vertical integration in Britain, see Ian Jarvie, *Hollywood's Overseas Campaign, The North Atlantic Movie Trade, 1920–1950* (Cambridge: Cambridge University Press, 1992), 135–143.

17. On Ufa's vertical structure, see Klaus Kreirmeier, *The Ufa Story*, trans. Robert and Rita Kimber (New York: Hill and Wang, 1996), 39–44, 61–73, 80–82.

18. On the formation of Tobis-Klangfilm, see "Une fusion sensationnelle: Tobis et Klang Film vont collaborer" [A sensational fusion: Tobis and Klangfilm begin to collaborate], *La cinématographie française*, vol. 11, no. 541 (16 March 1929), 11.

19. On the notion of intermediality, see Richard Abel and Rick Altman, eds., *The Sounds of Early Cinema* (Bloomington: Indiana University Press), xiii.

20. In Max Horkheimer and Theodor Adorno, "The Culture Industry: Enlightenment as Mass Deception," *Dialectic of Enlightenment* (New York: Continuum, 1989), 132ff.

21. See the report on Hollywood's music practice in Barrett O. Kiesling, "La musique de scène, adjuvant indispensable du film moderne" [Musical accompaniment: an indispensable element of the modern film], *Comoedia* (31 May 1930), 6. The American cinema's increasing abandonment of the popular song is contrasted to the song-oriented French approach to film music in Pierre Autré, "Trop d'enregistrements" [Too many recordings], *La cinématographie française*, vol. 13, no. 686 (26 December 1931), 110

22. On the "gramophone fever" of the late 1920s, see Pekka Gronow and Ilpo Saunio, *An International History of the Recording Industry*, trans. Christopher Mosely (New York: Cassell, 1998), 36–56.

23. See François Porcile, "Preface," in *La chanson française dans le cinéma des années trentes: Discographie*, ed. Guisy Basile and Chantal Gavouyère (Paris: Bibliothèque Nationale de France, 1996), 11.

24. See Pierre Autré, "Trop d'enrégistrements," 110.

25. According to figures in Porcile, "Preface," in *La chanson française dans le cinéma des années trentes: Discographie*.

26. The industrialization of entertainment radio in France occurred coincidentally with the French film industry's conversion to sound, circa 1929, some eight years later than in the United States. See Christian Brochard, *Histoire genérale de la radio et de la télévision en France*, vol. 1 *(1921–1944)* (Paris: La Documentation Française, 1994), 390–405.

27. In André Beucler, "Music-Hall et cinéma," *Pour vous*, no. 13 (14 February 1929), 3.

28. Concerning the film performances of the *chanteuses réalistes*, see Kelley Conway, "Les 'goualeuses' de l'écran" [The screen's great female personalities], in *Le cinéma au rendez-vous des arts: France, années 20 et 30*, ed. Emmanuelle Toulet (Paris: Bibliothèque Nationale de France, 1995), 162–171.

29. See the discussion of the aesthetic impact of synchronization in Michel Chion, *La musique au cinéma* (Paris: Fayard, 1995), 61–62.

30. On the topic of projection speed, see Paolo Cherchi Usai, *Burning Passions: An Introduction to the Study of Silent Cinema* (London: British Film Institute, 1994); and Jean Mitry, *Histoire du cinéma, art et industrie*, vol. 4: *les années trentes* (Paris: J.-P. Delarge, 1980), 19.

31. On projection practice in France during the 1920s, see observations by Vincent Pinel in "Dictionnaire du cinéma français des années vingt" [Dictionary of the French cinema of the 1920s], ed. F. Albera and Jean A. Gili, in *1895*, no. 33 (June 2001), 383–384.

32. In Marcel L'Herbier, "Devoir de la critique" [Criticism's duty], *La cinématographie française*, vol. 13, no. 642 (21 February 1931), 7; and Marcel Carné, "Comment on realize un film parlant française" [How a French talkie is made], *Cinémagazine* (July 1930), 16.

33. See the 1923 piece by Emile Vuillermoz, "Les impasses du synchronisme," reprinted in *Musiques d'écran: l'accompagnement musical du cinéma muet en France, 1918–1995*, ed. Emmanuelle Toulet (Paris: Réunion des Musées Nationaux, 1994), 89, which notes variations in projection speeds in Paris movie houses between thirteen and seventeen frames per second.

34. A discussion of sound-era changes in the projectionist's role can be found in Nino Frank, "Une cabine de projection en 1931" [A projection booth in 1931], *Pour vous*, no. 136 (25 June 1931), 6. Concerning the variety of live sound effects in the French cinema of the late silent era, see Blaise Cendrars, "Monsieur Nouvel-An, précurseur . . . " *Pour vous*, no. 40 (22 August 1929).

35. See Emile Vuillermoz, "Les trahisons du haut-parleur" [The betrayals of the loudspeaker], *Pour vous*, no. 365 (14 November 1935), 2. "A movie theatre is now worth exactly what its sound system is worth."

36. See, for instance, R. Berner, "Trop de bons fauteuils et pas assez de bons films"

[Too many good armchairs, not enough good films], *La technique cinématographique,* vol. 15, no. 745 (11 February 1933), 15; and Pierre Hémardinquer, "L'art et technique," *La technique cinématographique,* vol. 3, no. 1 (January 1932), 42.

37.  See remarks in Karel Dibbets, "The Introduction of Sound," in *The Oxford History of World Cinema,* ed. Geoffrey Nowell-Smith (Oxford: Oxford University Press, 1996), 214. "Without the mediation of a live orchestra, the thrill of watching a movie was transformed from a communal happening between four walls into an exclusive relation between the film(-maker) and the individual viewer."

38.  See Donald Crafton, *The Talkies: American Cinema's Transition to Sound, 1926–1931* (Berkeley and Los Angeles: University of California, 1997), 250–253.

39.  On the plight of film-theatre musicians, see James P. Kraft, *Stage to Studio: Musicians and the Sound Revolution, 1890–1950* (Baltimore and London: Johns Hopkins University Press, 1996), 38–56.

40.  See Raymond Berner, "Ce qu'est le circuit Pathé-Natan" [Pathé-Natan's theatre circuit], *La cinématographie française,* vol. 12, no. 596 (5 April 1930), 23.

41.  Concerning the scale and quality of live performances in Paris's top movie houses, see René Miquel, "La vie secrète d'un grand cinéma" [The secret life of a great moviehouse], *Pour vous,* no. 224 (2 March 1933), 8–9.

42.  According to M. Delannoy, director of the Marivaux, when *Les trois masques* played there in late 1929, "despite the complete soundtrack, we heard, at moments, a discrete accompaniment from the orchestra." Quoted in R. Régent, "Le musique enregistrée supprimera-t-elle les orchestras?" [Will recorded music suppress the orchestras?] *Pour vous,* no. 57 (19 December 1929). Additional examples of this sort of practice are discussed in Chion, *La musique au cinéma,* 76.

43.  On the inclusion of live performances in sound-era film programs in France during the mid-1930s, see Jean-Pierre Jeancolas, *Quinze ans des années trentes: le cinéma des français, 1929–1944* (Paris: Stock, 1983), 95–97.

44.  In Pierre Autré, "Depuis le début du film parlant, nos producteurs ont adapté 171 pièces de théâtre et 100 romans" [Since the talkies' debut, our producers have adapted 171 stage plays and 100 novels], *La cinématographie française,* vol. 15, no. 778 (30 September 1933), 87.

45.  In René Clair, "The Art of Sound," in *Film Sound: Theory and Practice,* ed. Elisabeth Weis and John Belton (New York: Columbia University Press, 1985), 95.

46.  See, for instance, remarks in Nino Frank, "Comment Jean de Limur conçoit le parlant français" [How Jean de Limur conceives the French talkie], *Pour vous,* no. 66 (20 February 1930), 3.

47.  On Shumyatsky's plans, see Jay Leyda, *Kino: A History of the Russian and Soviet Film* (New York: Collier Books, 1973), 323–324, 339–340; and Richard Taylor and Ian Christie, eds., *The Film Factory: Russian and Soviet Cinema in*

*Documents, 1896–1939* (London and New York: Routledge, 1988), 323–324, 339, 369.

48.     My use of the term "hegemony" is indebted to the geohistorical interpretation of Gramsci in Peter Taylor, *The Way the Modern World Works: World Hegemony to World Impasse* (Chichester, UK: John Wiley and Sons, 1996), 31ff.

49.     See P. A. Harlé, "Excellent accueil: le délégation Pathé-Natan en Amérique" [Excellent welcome: the Pathé-Natan delegation in America], *La cinématographie française*, vol. 11, no. 554 (15 June 1929), 11. See also Blaise Cendrars, *Hollywood, Mecca of the Movies,* trans. Garrett White (Berkeley and Los Angeles: University of California Press, 1995). Cendrars's text was published in French in 1936.

50.     See Roger Régent, "La colonie française est appréciée à Hollywood" [The French colony is appreciated in Hollywood], *Pour vous,* no. 109 (18 December 1930), 3; and Antoine de la Chevasnerie, "Avec la colonie française d'Hollywood," *Pour vous,* no. 198 (1 September 1932), 11.

51.     For an example, see P. A. Harlé, "Les secrets des américains," *La cinématographie française*, vol. 11, no. 552 (31 May 1929), 11.

52.     In J. G. Auriol, "L'importance des 'compagnies' dans le cinéma," *Pour vous,* no. 280 (29 March 1934), 2.

53.     See the discussion of frequent French appeals during the interwar years to "the individuality and creativity of the artisan, the small-scale craftsperson, over the industrialized machinery of the U.S. economy," in James Trumpbour, *Selling Hollywood to the World* (Cambridge: Cambridge University Press, 2002), 240ff.

54.     In Roger Leenhardt, "Continuité du cinéma français" (1945), *Chroniques de cinéma* (Paris: Ed. De l'Etoile, 1986), 131.

55.     In André Bazin, "The Evolution of the Language of Cinema," *What Is Cinema? Volume One* (Berkeley and Los Angeles: University of California, 1967), 28.

56.     In Arthur Knight, *The Liveliest Art: A Panoramic History of the Movies* (New York: Macmillan, 1957), 188–189.

57.     In Robert Sklar, *Film: An International History of the Medium,* 2d ed. (Upper Saddle River, N.J.: Prentice Hall, 2002), 208.

58.     See, for instance, remarks in Penelope Houston, *Keepers of the Frame: The Film Archives* (London: British Film Institute, 1994), 69–70.

59.     In Colin Crisp, *Genre, Myth and Convention in the French Cinema, 1929–1939* (Bloomington: Indiana University Press, 2002), xii.

60.     See, for instance, G. Sadoul, *Histoire d'un art: le cinéma des origines à nos jours* (Paris: Flammarion, 1949), 263; Jean Mitry, *Histoire du cinéma, art et industrie,* vol. 4: *les années trentes* (Paris: J.-P. Delarge, 1980), 16–17; and Paul Rotha, *The Film Till Now: A Survey of World Cinema* (Middlesex, UK: Hamlyn, 1967), 530.

61.     In Pierre Autré, "Depuis le début du film parlant, nos producteurs ont adapté

171 pièces de théâtre et 100 romans," *La cinématographie française*, 87. The figure cited for the number of French films based on prewar theatre sources is seventy-eight.

62. In Emile Vuillermoz, "Essai d'esthétique du sonore" [Essay on sound-film aesthetics], *La revue musicale*, no. 151 (December 1934), 52.

63. See Richard Dyer and Ginette Vincendeau, "Introduction," in *Popular European Cinema*, ed. Dyer and Vincendeau (London and New York: Routledge, 1992), 1–14.

64. See S. M. Eisenstein, V. I. Pudovkin, and G. V. Alexandrov, "A Statement," in *Film Sound: Theory and Practice*, ed. Elisabeth Weis and John Belton (New York: Columbia University Press, 1985), 84–86; and Rudolf Arnheim, *Film as Art* (Berkeley and Los Angeles: University of California Press, 1957).

## 2. Film History after Recorded Sound

1. See the survey of approaches to film-historical research and writing in Robert Allen and Douglas Gomery, *Film History: Theory and Practice* (New York: Knopf, 1985); and in Michèle Lagny, *De l'histoire du cinéma: méthode historique et histoire du cinéma* (Paris: Armand Colin, 1992).

2. In Charlie Chaplin, "Après le 'parlant' aurons-nous le film odorant?" [After the talkie, will we have the smellie?], *Pour vous*, no. 129 (7 May 1931), 3. Concerning Eisenstein, see "Les idées de M. Eisenstein sur le film sonore," *La cinématographie française*, vol. 12, no. 602 (17 May 1930), 15–16.

3. Regarding the promotion in the United States of sound cinema in terms of scientific progress in the electronics field, see Donald Crafton, *The Talkies: American Cinema's Transition to Sound, 1926–1931* (Berkeley and Los Angeles: University of California, 1997), 19–22.

4. Quoted in Roger Régent, "Point de vue d'un producteur français: M. Natan" [A French producer's point of view: Mr. Natan], *Pour vous*, no. 92 (21 August 1930), 2.

5. In Fernand Braudel, *On History*, trans. Sarah Matthews (Chicago: University of Chicago Press, 1980), 4.

6. For an account of the remarkable avant-garde film culture of 1920s France, with its web of theatres, journals, and ciné-clubs, see Richard Abel, "*Cinégraphie* and the Search for Specificity," in *French Film Theory and Criticism*, vol. 1: *1907–1929* (Princeton, N.J.: Princeton University Press, 1988), 194–223.

7. For a contemporary statement of this view of sound's effects on French film culture, see A. P. Richard, "Considérations théoriques sur le film sonore" [Theoretical considerations on the sound film], *La cinématographie française*, vol. 15, no. 751 (25 March 1933), i.

8. See, for instance, Scott Eyman, *The Speed of Sound: Hollywood and the Talkie Revolution, 1926–1930* (Baltimore and London: Johns Hopkins University), 1999.

9. In the editorial, "20e anniversaire du parlant" [Twentieth anniversary of the talkie], *La technique cinématographique*," vol. 17, no. 28 (3 October 1946), 1.

10. Concerning the impact on French film theory of Hollywood's adoption in the

late 1940s/early 1950s of widescreen and color, see David Bordwell, *On the History of Film Style* (Cambridge, Mass., and London: Harvard University Press, 1997), 60, 82.

11. In Georges Charensol, "Le film parlant," in *Le cinéma par ceux qui le font* [The cinema according to those who make it], ed. Denis Marion (Paris: Fayard, 1949), 54.

12. In André Bazin, "The Evolution of the Language of Cinema," *What Is Cinema? Volume One,* trans. Hugh Gray (Berkeley and Los Angeles: University of California, 1967), 23.

13. See Braudel, "History and the Social Sciences," in *On History,* esp. 27–31. On the Annales School of historiography, see Peter Burke, *The French Historical Revolution: The Annales School, 1929–1989* (Stanford, Calif.: Stanford University Press, 1990).

14. For a discussion of Braudel in the context of film historiography, and of multitemporal film history specifically, see Michèle Lagny, *De l'histoire du cinéma: méthode historique et histoire du cinéma* (Paris: Armand Colin, 1992), 32–35ff.

15. See here Barry Salt, "Statistical Style Analysis of Motion Pictures," in *Movies and Methods,* ed. Bill Nichols, vol. 2 (Berkeley and Los Angeles: University of California Press, 1985), 691–703. For a recent assessment of statistical film-style study, see Thomas Elsaesser and Warren Buckland, "Mise-en-scène Criticism and Statistical Style Analysis," in *Studying Contemporary American Film* (London: Arnold, 2002), 102–116.

16. In D. Crafton, *The Talkies,* 3.

17. In Alexander Walker, *The Shattered Silents: How the Talkies Came to Stay* (London: Elm Tree Books, 1978), vii.

18. See David Bordwell, Janet Staiger, and Kristin Thompson, *The Classical Hollywood Cinema: Film Style and Mode of Production to 1960* (New York: Columbia University Press, 1985), 298–308.

19. A similar claim concerning continuities between silent-era and sound-era Hollywood styles was also argued by Barry Salt, in the first edition of *Film Style and Technology: History and Analysis* (London: Starword, 1983).

20. On the a-classical character of conversion-era film comedy, see Henry Jenkins, *What Made Pistachio Nuts? Early Sound Comedy and the Vaudeville Aesthetic* (New York: Columbia University Press, 1992).

21. In Jan Mukarovsky, *Aesthetic Function, Norm and Value as Social Facts,* trans. Mark Suino (Ann Arbor: University of Michigan, 1979), 12–13.

22. Quoted in "Une révolution dans la technique du film sonore" [A revolution in sound-film technique], *Le cinéopse,* vol. 13, no. 141 (May 1931), 247.

23. In Dudley Andrew, *Mists of Regret: Culture and Sensibility in Classic French Film* (Princeton, N.J.: Princeton University Press, 1995), 119.

24. In Jacques Gerber, ed., *Pierre Braunberger, Producteur* (Paris: CNC/Centre Pompidou, 1987), 81–82. See also remarks in Ginette Vincendeau, *Stars and Stardom in French Film* (New York: Continuum, 2000), 5.

25. Quoted in Roger Régent, " 'Je joue pour le cinéma comme au theater,' dit

Raimu" ["I perform for the cinema as for the theater," says Raimu], *Pour vous*, no. 20 (22 September 1932), 3.

26. Concerning film's interconnectedness with theatre in conversion-era France, see the interviews with actors in "Peut-on faire à la fois du théâtre et du cinéma?" [Can one perform in theatre and in cinema at the same time?], a four-part article appearing in *Pour vous*, no. 105 (20 November 1930), 2; no. 106 (27 November 1930), 2; no. 107 (4 December 1930), 11; and no. 108 (11 December 1930), 11.

27. On the crossover of writers between film and theatre during this period see Olivier Barrot and Raymond Chirat, "Ciné-Boulevard," in *Jeux d'auteurs, mots d'acteurs: Scénaristes et dialogistes du cinéma français, 1930–1945* [Authors' performances, actors' words: scenarists and dialogists in French cinema, 1930–1945] (Lyon: Institut Lumière/Actes Sud, 1994), 81–130.

28. In Pierre Descaux, "Comment le film parlant a modifié le cinéma mondial" [How the talkie has changed world cinema], *Almanach de Mon Ciné* (1932), 40.

29. See Raymond Bernier, "Un extraordinaire conflit à propos de David Golder," *La cinématographie française*, vol. 13, no. 630 (29 November 1930), 17.

30. See Lucien Wahl, "Bouboule au Music-Hall," *Pour vous*, no. 160 (10 December, 1931), 2.

31. Quoted in an interview with Renoir apropos the making of *Toni* (dir. Jean Renoir, 1935), untitled publication available in the Fond Pierre Gaut at the Bibliothèque du Film in Paris, n.d.

32. In Michèle Lagny, Marie-Claire Ropars, and Pierre Sorlin, *Génériques des années trentes* (Vincennes: Presses Universitaires de Vincennes, 1986), 16.

33. See Ursula Hardt, *From Caligari to California: Erich Pommer's Life in the International Film Wars* (Providence, R.I.: Berghahn, 1996), 128.

34. In Léonce Perret, "*Enlevez-moi!* sera la première opérette vraiment française" [*Enlevez-moi!* will be the first truly French operetta], *La cinématographie française*, vol. 14, no. 721 (27 August 1932), 26.

35. See Jean Mitry, *Histoire du cinéma, art et industrie*, vol. 4: *les années trentes* (Paris: J.-P. Delarge, 1980), 23.

36. See Pierre Autré, "Au sujet des films américains," *La technique cinématographique*, vol. 15, no. 743 (28 January 1933), 35.

37. Cited in Jacques Kermabon, "Un cinéma pour le paradis," *Pathé, première empire du cinema*, ed. J. Kermabon (Paris: Centre Pompidou, 1994), 229.

38. See Richard Abel, *French Cinema: The First Wave, 1915–1929* (Princeton, N.J.: Princeton University Press, 1984), 64.

39. In Jean Renaitour, ed., *Où va le cinéma français?* [Where is the French cinema headed?] (Paris: Ed. Baudinière, 1937), 52.

40. See remarks from film distributor Marcel Spreher in Jean-Georges Auriol, "Opinions sur les causes d'un malaise," *Pour vous*, no. 171 (25 February 1932), 3.

41. See Jens Ulff-Møller, *Hollywood's Film Wars with France: Film-Trade Diplo-*

*macy and the Emergence of the French Film Quota Policy* (Rochester, N.Y.: University of Rochester Press, 2001), 38–39.

42.  See, for instance, statements made by the Minister of Fine Arts in "Déclaration prononcée par M. Maurice Petsch," *La cinématographie française,* vol. 13, no. 685 (19 December 1931), 5.

43.  In Jean Renaitour, ed., *Où va le cinéma français?* 45.

### 3. The Talkies in France

1.  In Andrew Higson, "The Concept of National Cinema," in *Film and Nationalism,* ed. Alan Williams (New Brunswick, N.J., and London: Rutgers University Press, 2002), 63.

2.  See the figures reported in Marcel Colin-Reval, "Seulement 52 films français" [Only 52 French films], *La cinématographie française,* vol. 12, no. 581 (21 December 1929), 36–37.

3.  See Donald Crafton, "Buying Broadway," in *Post-Theory: Reconstructing Film Studies,* ed. David Bordwell and Noel Carroll (Madison: University of Wisconsin Press, 1996).

4.  On the box-office performance of *The Jazz Singer* in France, see Francis Courtade, *Les malédictions du cinéma français* (Paris: Alain Moreau, 1978), 38.

5.  See R. Icart, *La révolution du parlant* (Perpignan, France: Institut Jean Vigo, 1988), 119–222; and Courtade, *Les malédictions du cinéma français,* 37–38.

6.  In Raymond Bernier, "Quelques considérations internationals sur le cinéma parlant" [A few international considerations on the talking cinema], *La cinématographie française,* vol. 12, no. 621 (29 September 1930), 162.

7.  The quotations appear in J. V.-B., "*Le chanteur de jazz,*" *Pour vous* (25 August 1929), n.p.; "*Le chanteur de jazz,*" *Le soir* (2 February 1929), n.p.; and Claude Jantel, "*Le chanteur de jazz,*" *Action française* (5 April 1929), n.p. These film reviews, along with others cited in this chapter, are available in dossiers in the Rondel Collection at the Bibliothèque Nationale in Paris, where they are indexed by film title.

8.  See Pierre Hémardinquer, *Le cinématographe sonore et la projection en relief* [The sound cinema and 3-D projection], 3d rev. ed. (Paris: Eyrolles, 1935), 137.

9.  See J. Bruno-Ruby, "Film sonore, film parlant?" *Ciné-miroir,* vol. 8, no. 239 (1 November 1929), 691.

10.  On the flood of *films sonores* in France, see P. A. Harlé, "Propos de fin d'année . . . et du début de l'autre" [Apropos of the end of one year . . . and the beginning of another], *La cinématographie française,* vol. 13, no. 633 (20 December 1930), 43.

11.  Accounts of the use of these techniques can be found in "Comment on 'fait' les bruits d'un film sonore" [How a sound film's noises are made], *Cinémonde,* vol. 4, no. 139 (18 June 1931), 387; and R. Vellard, *Le cinéma sonore et sa technique* (Paris: Etienne Cheron, 1933), 110–111.

12. Quoted in Jean Lenauer, "Pabst, lui aussi, croit au film parlant" [Pabst, too, believes in the talkie], *Pour vous*, no. 35 (18 July 1929), 11.

13. In J. Feyder, "Je crois au film parlant" [I believe in the talkie], *Pour vous*, no. 31 (20 June 1929), 3.

14. See "Les idées de M. Eisenstein sur le film sonore" [Mr. Eisenstein's ideas on the sound film], *La cinématographie française*, vol. 12, no. 602 (17 May 1930), 15–16.

15. See, for instance, P. A. Harlé, "Pas de guerre de brevets' en France" [No patents war in France], *La cinématographie française*, vol. 12, no. 602 (17 May 1930), 15.

16. In Emile Roux-Parassac, "Des paroles sur le 'parlant'" [A few remarks on the "talkie"], *Le cinéopse*, vol. 13, no. 142 (June 1931), 293.

17. These figures are cited in François Garçon, *Gaumont, un siècle de cinéma* (Paris: Gallimard, 1992), 39.

18. In P. A. Harlé, "Ne confondons pas films parlants et films sonorisés" [Do not confuse talkies with sonorized films], *La cinématographie française*, vol. 12, no. 600 (3 May 1930), 11.

19. In A. Arnoux, "A propos du *Chanteur de jazz*," *Pour vous*, no. 11 (31 January 1929).

20. See, for instance, Claude Lambert, "La Vitaphone à l'Aubert-Palace," *Ami du people* (1 February 1929), n.p. The same contrast between the two films is drawn in "*Le chanteur de jazz*," *Le journal* (1 February 1929), n.p., and also in Maurice Bex, "*Le chanteur de jazz*," *Volonté* (30 January 1929), n.p. According to Bex, *The Jazz Singer* was superior to *Ombres blanches* and to the Gaumont film *L'eau du nil* because it "uses not only orchestral music and the singing voice but dialogue."

21. Regarding the film's "documentary" quality, see L. Moussinac, "Un film parlant," *Le monde* (2 February 1929), n.p.; and "*Le chanteur de jazz*," *Le merle* (17 May 1929), n.p.

22. In Lucien Wahl, "Le miracle de la voix qu'on n'entend pas" [The miracle of the voice that can't be heard], *Oeuvre* (6 July 1929), n.p.

23. In Paul Gordeaux, "*Le chanteur de jazz*," *Le journal* (1 February 1929), n.p.

24. See the review published in *Le merle*, from an undated clipping in a file on *The Jazz Singer* in the Rondel Collection at the Bibliothèque Nationale. Similar remarks on Jolson's performance appear in Alexandre Arnoux, "Broadway Melody," *Nouveaux littéraires* (25 June 1929), n.p.; and in Claude Jantel, "Le chanteur de Jazz," *Action française* (5 April 1929), n.p.

25. See Raoul de Givrey, "Le chanteur de Jazz," *Ric à Rac* (26 March 1929), n.p.; and also A. Arnoux, "Muet contre parlant, premières escarmouches" [Speechless versus speaking, opening skirmishes], *Pour vous*, no. 51 (7 November 1929), 2.

26. See Pierre Braunberger's remarks on *La route est belle* in Jacques Gerber, ed., *Pierre Braunberger, Producteur* (Paris: CNC/Centre Georges Pompidou, 1987), 68–69. The film was made in record time, in seventeen afternoons, at the stu-

dios of British International Pictures in London. See "Robert Florey a terminé *La route est belle*" [Robert Florey has finished *La route est belle*], *La cinématographie française,* vol. 12, no. 576 (16 November 1929), 11.

27. In "Le film sonore, entre le théâtre et le cinéma" [Sound film, between theatre and cinema], *La cinématographie française,* vol. 12, no. 604 (31 May 1930), ii.

28. In Jean Fayard, "*Le chemin du paradis,*" *Candide* (21 November 1930), n.p.

29. In Emile Vuillermoz, "*Le chemin du paradis,*" *Nouvelles Littéraires* (22 November 1930), n.p.

30. See the interview with Clair in Suzanne Chantal, "René Clair dirige une scène de *Million*" [René Clair directs a scene from *Le million*], *Cinémonde,* vol. 4, no. 124 (5 May 1931), 147. "When I saw this film [*Le chemin du paradis*], I had just finished the script for *Le million,* and was led to reconsider some of the situations and effects I had planned. I was thus obliged to return to my scenario and modify several scenes."

31. In Alexandre Arnoux, "Une journée aux studios de Neubabelsberg" [A day at the studios in Neubabelsberg], *Pour vous,* no. 113 (15 January 1931), 3.

32. In François Porcile, "Preface," in *La chanson française dans le cinema des années trentes: Discographie,* ed. Guisy Basile and Chantal Gavouyère (Paris: Bibliothèque Nationale de France, 1996), 11.

33. See Jean Vincent-Bréchignac, "Ce que nous dit M. Erich Pommer" [What Mr. Erich Pommer tells us], *Pour vous,* no. 148 (17 September 1931), 3; and also Guisy Basile and Chantal Gavouyère, eds., *La chanson française dans le cinéma des années trentes: Discographie,* 42.

34. See Jean Vincent-Bréchignac, "Ce que nous dit M. Erich Pommer," 3; and also remarks by music publisher Francis Salabert in Philippe Roland, "Une visite aux Studios Salabert," *La technique cinématographique,* vol. 4, no. 34 (October 1933), 521.

35. In Vuillermoz, "*Le chemin du paradis,*" n.p.

36. In an anonymous review, publication unidentified, dated 18 November 1930. Located in a dossier of press clippings on *Le chemin du paradis* in the Rondel Collection in the Bibliothèque Nationale.

37. See Pierre Leprohon, "Cinéma allemand et opérettes françaises" [German cinema and French operettas], *Le cinéopse,* vol. 4, no. 150 (3 September 1931), 566.

38. In J.-M. Aimot, "Film opérette," *Le soir* (22 November 1930), n.p.

39. In Pierre Autré, "En France, triomphe du théâtre photographié" [Triumph of the filmed stage production in France], *La cinématographie française,* vol. 15, no. 782 (28 October 1933), 95.

40. In Dudley Andrew, *Mists of Regret,* 54.

41. Quoted in Claude Vermorel, "Pour faire des films vraiment français?" [How to make truly French films], *Pour vous,* no. 235 (18 May 1933), 11.

42. Quoted in Pierre Bret., "Quand René Clair tourne *Quatorze juillet*" [When René Clair shoots *Quatorze juillet*], *Pour vous,* no. 204 (13 October 1932), 4.

43. In an interview conducted after his retirement from filmmaking, Clair commented as follows on *Quatorze Juillet*: "I wanted to make a very simple film [after *A nous la liberté* (1931)], simpler and more realistic than the previous ones, with less fantasy . . . a film for and about the popular audience, the ordinary people, from whom I felt I was gradually and unintentionally slipping away." In R. C. Dale, *The Films of René Clair*, vol. 1 (Metuchen, N.J., and London: Scarecrow, 1986), 205.

44. See "*Le chemin du paradis*," *Echo* (10 October 1930), n.p.

45. In Erich Pommer, "Sur le film sonore et sa technique" [On the sound film and its technique], *Comoedia* (22 April 1930), 6. Describing production of a scene from *Mélodie du coeur* (dir. Hans Schwarz, 1930), featuring dialogue between Willy Fritsch and Dita Parlo, Pommer comments as follows: "All the scenarios now for our sound films are spoken and rehearsed watch-in-hand, prior to shooting, in order to avoid in advance any potential slowdowns in the production." For further discussion of this approach, whereby each of a scene's shots is rehearsed and timed so as to match the rhythm of a pre-recorded song, see Marcel Carné, "Comment on réalise un film parlant français," *Cinémagazine* (July 1930), 15–16. Carné appears to be referring to practices at Tobis Films Sonores, in Paris.

46. On Clair's use of a metronome during shooting, see R. C. Dale, *The Films of René Clair*, 178.

47. The scenario for *Vive la liberté* is available at the Bibliothèque du Film in Paris.

48. See, for instance, the script for *Sous les toits de Paris*, available at the Bibliothèque Nationale, at the Arsenal, in the Department des Arts at Spectacles.

## 4. Sound-Era Film Editing

1. In Ernest Lindgren, *The Art of the Film* (London: Allen and Unwin, 1948), 55.

2. See, for instance, V. I. Pudovkin, *Film Technique and Film Acting*, Memorial ed., trans. Ivor Montagu (New York: Grove Press, 1970), 23.

3. Regarding synchronous sound's impact on editing practice, see, for instance, Karel Reisz and Gavin Millar, *The Technique of Film Editing* (London and New York: Focal Press, 1968), 41–66.

4. In S. M. Eisenstein, V. I. Pudovkin, and G. V. Alexandrov, "A Statement," in *Film Sound: Theory and Practice*, ed. Elisabeth Weis and John Belton (New York: Columbia University Press, 1985), 84.

5. In André Bazin, "The Evolution of the Language of Cinema," *What Is Cinema? Volume One* (Berkeley and Los Angeles: University of California, 1967), 28.

6. In Barry Salt, *Film Style and Technology: History and Analysis*, 2d ed. (London: Starword, 1992), 218.

7. In Colin Crisp, *The Classic French Cinema, 1930–1960* (Bloomington: Indiana University Press, 1993), 410.

8.   See Salt, *Film Style and Technology*, 174, 190–191.

9.   See Jill Forbes and Sarah Street, *European Cinema: An Introduction* (Hampshire, UK, and New York: Palgrave, 2000), 44ff.

10.  See, for instance, the discussion of art cinema in David Bordwell, *Narration in the Fiction Film* (Madison: University of Wisconsin Press, 1985), 228–229.

11.  In Erich Pommer, "Peut-on faire des films internationaux" [Can international films be made?], *La cinématographie française*, vol. 11, no. 542 (23 March 1929), 35.

12.  In Kristin Thompson, "National or International Films? The European Debate During the 1920s," *Film History*, vol. 8, no. 3 (1996), 289.

13.  See Ben Brewster and Lea Jacobs, *Theatre to Cinema* (Oxford: Oxford University Press, 1997), 4.

14.  Concerning surrealist enthusiasm for Hollywood over the national cinemas of Europe, see, for example, Luis Buñuel, "Buster Keaton's *College*" (1927), in *The Shadow and Its Shadow: Surrealist Writings on the Cinema*, 2d ed., ed. Paul Hammond (Edinburgh: Polygon, 1991), 64–65.

15.  See Richard Dyer and Ginette Vincendeau, eds., "Introduction," *Popular European Cinema* (London and New York: Routledge, 1992), 1.

16.  For a helpful overview of questions regarding the emergence of national film styles in the late 1900s, see Tom Gunning, "Notes and Queries about the Year 1913 and Film Style: National Style and Deep Staging," *1895* (October 1993), 195–204.

17.  See Barry Salt, *Film Style and Technology: History and Analysis*, 2d ed. (London: Starword, 1992), 214–226; and Colin Crisp, *The Classic French Cinema* (Bloomington: Indiana University Press, 1993), 400–414. My statistics are based on an analysis of the films listed in this book's Filmography and are presented here in this chapter.

18.  Greatly facilitating this sort of work are computer software such as Microsoft's SPSS. See Thomas Elsaesser and Warren Buckland, *Studying Contemporary American Film* (London: Arnold, 2002), 106–116.

19.  See Salt, *Film Style and Technology*, 214–216.

20.  Salt doesn't provide an ASL average for French films during 1930–1933. My figures here are based on my own analysis of a sample of fifty-four feature films made during these years. A list of titles can be found in the Filmography.

21.  ASL figures for films viewed on PAL video were multiplied by 1.04 to correct for PAL's one-frame-per-second increase in running time.

22.  In Arthur Hoerée, "Le travail du film sonore" [The work of the sound film], *La revue musicale*, no. 151 (December 1934), 64.

23.  This figure for the average shot number was generated from a sample of twenty French films made during 1930–1933 whose running times exceeded seventy minutes. The titles are among those listed in the Filmography.

24.  Concerning the rapidity of French films of the early 1930s relative to those of

the latter half of the decade, consider my figures relative to those reported in Salt, *Film Style and Technology*, 216. In his sample of sixty-four films for 1934–1939, Salt finds only two with ASLs below seven seconds, whereas my sample of sixty films for 1930–1933 includes nine such films. For a different ASL estimate for French films of the early 1930s, see Crisp, *The Classic French Cinema, 1930–1960*, 401. Crisp's graph suggests a national mean ASL of roughly 14 for French films of the early 1930s, which is several seconds higher than what I've come up with. The difference may be an effect of what appears to be a relatively small sampling of films, which allows the exceptionally high figures included for films directed by Jean Renoir to skew the outcome upward.

25. See the remarks on method in Barry Salt, "Statistical Style Analysis of Motion Pictures," in *Movies and Methods*, vol. 2, ed. Bill Nichols (Berkeley and Los Angeles: University of California Press, 1985), 694.

26. Salt explains the decision to examine thirty-minute samples rather than entire films with reference to scriptwriting practices since the 1920s, which ensured a relatively standardized cutting across a film's running time. See Salt, *Film Style and Technology*, 226.

27. My figures for total running times refer to titles made in France only.

28. In Raymond Bernier, "Quelques considérations internationales du cinéma parlant" [Some international considerations of the talkie], *La cinématographie française*, vol. 12, no. 621 (29 September 1930), 162.

29. Quoted in Nino Frank, "Les confidences de M. Julien Duvivier" [Mr. Julien Duvivier's confidences], *Pour vous*, no. 117 (12 February 1931), 11.

30. Quoted in R. de Thomasson, "Mon ambition est de distraire et d'amuser le public dit M. René Pujol" [My ambition is to distract and amuse the public, Mr. René Pujol tells us], *Pour vous*, no. 257 (19 October 1933), 11.

31. Quoted in Nino Frank, "Pierre Colombier, metteur-en-scène des 'Rois'" [Pierre Colombier, director of the *Rois*], *Pour vous*, no. 118 (19 February 1931), 6.

32. In Crisp, *The Classic French Cinema*, 406–414.

33. In A. P. Richard, "Où en est la technique américaine?" [What's happening with American technique?], *La cinématographie française*, no. 699 (26 March 1932), ii; see also Jean Morienval, "Les lois de l'art" [The laws of the art], *Le cinéopse*, vol. 16, no. 176 (April 1934), 111: "It is not the succession of images that counts but their necessity."

34. The quote is from Hitchcock's article "On Direction" (1937), cited in Elisabeth Weis, *The Silent Scream: Alfred Hitchcock's Soundtrack* (London and Toronto: Associated University Press, 1982), 37.

35. In Kermabon, *Pathé, première empire du cinéma*, 245.

36. See the quote regarding parallel cuts from the 1944 British Film Institute pamphlet cited in K. Reisz and G. Millar, *The Technique of Film Editing*, 271.

37. In J.-G. Auriol, "La chienne" (from *Revue du cinéma*, 1931), in R. Abel, ed.,

*French Film Theory and Criticism,* vol. 2 (Princeton: Princeton University Press, 1988), 87.

38. In Michel Chion, *Audio-Vision: Sound on Screen,* trans. Claudia Gorbman (New York: Columbia University Press, 1994).

39. A discussion of scale-matching can be found in J. P. Maxfield, "Technic of Recording Control for Sound Pictures," *American Cinematographer,* vol. 11, no. 1 (May 1930), 11–12, 18, 24, 44. For an analysis of Maxfield's theory, see Rick Altman, "Sound Space," in *Sound Theory/Sound Practice* (New York and London: Routledge, 1992), 46–64.

40. See J. Lastra, "Standards and Practices: Aesthetic Norm and Technological Innovation in the American Cinema," in *The Studio System,* ed. Janet Staiger (New Brunswick, N.J.: Rutgers University Press, 1995).

41. In Constant Mic., "Comment on monte un film sonore" [How a sound film is edited], *Pour vous,* no. 81 (5 June 1930), 2.

42. In Emile Vuillermoz, "Essai d'esthéthique du sonore" [Essay on sound-film aesthetics], *La revue musicale,* no. 151 (December 1934), 52.

43. In Jean Epstein, "Découpage (construction sonore)," *La technique cinématographique,* vol. 18, no. 46 (12 June 1947), 1065.

44. Quoted in Michel Chion, *Le cinéma et ses métiers* (Paris: Bordas, 1990), 125.

45. Concerning point-of-audition sound, see Altman, "Sound Space," 60.

46. In Pangloss, "Films parlés," *Comoedia* (14 November 1930), 6. See also Jean Marguet, "Le dialogue à l'écran" [Dialogue on the screen], *Cinémonde,* vol. 2, no. 84 (29 May 1930), 343.

47. In Barry Salt, *Film Style and Technology,* 214. Regarding the effect of editing technology on American film style, see also Richard Maltby, *Hollywood Cinema,* 2d ed. (London: Blackwell, 2003), 258.

48. See Suzanne Albarran, "Les travailleurs obscures du cinéma" [The cinema's obscure laborers], *Pour vous,* no. 173 (10 March 1932), 9.

49. See A. Richard, "Les milles et un métiers du film parlant" [The talkies' thousand-and-one crafts], *Pour vous,* no. 343 (13 June 1935), 14.

50. See Pierre Autré, "L'association des monteurs de films vient de se créer" [The Association of Film Editors is created], *La cinématographie française,* vol. 15, no. 767 (29 July 1933), 28.

51. See A. P. Richard, "Le montage exige un véritable métier" [Film editing demands true craftsmanship], *La cinématographie française,* vol. 15, no. 756 (29 April 1933), 43–44.

52. In Emile Vuillermoz, "Essai d'esthétique du sonore."

53. In Crisp, *The Classic French Cinema,* 405–406.

54. On the problem of technological determinism, see Crisp, *The Classic French Cinema,* 405.

55. In Henri-Diamant Berger, "Technique de Hollywood et technique de Paris," *Pour vous,* no. 560 (9 August 1939), 2.

## 5. Shooting and Recording in Paris and Hollywood

1. See, for instance, James Lastra, *Sound Technology and the American Cinema* (New York: Columbia University Press, 2000); and Donald Crafton, *The Talkies: American Cinema's Transition to Sound, 1926–1931* (Berkeley and Los Angeles: University of California, 1997), 236.

2. Quoted in Raymond Barkan, "M. Willem Sivel: ingénieur du son" [Mr. Willem Sivel, sound engineer], *La technique cinématographique*, vol. 19, no. 74 (2 September 1948), 368.

3. In Crafton, *The Talkies*, 355–380.

4. For an account by a film-sound engineer, see the historical overview in James R. Cameron, "Historical—Sound Transmission," in *Sound Motion Pictures: Recording and Reproducing* (Coral Gables, Fla.: Cameron Publishing, 1959), 33–58.

5. See the discussion of French commentary on *The Jazz Singer* in chapter 3.

6. See the illuminating discussion of this point in Lastra, *Sound Technology and American Cinema*, 206ff.

7. In Nathan Levinson, "Rerecording, Dubbing or Duping," *American Cinematographer*, vol. 13, no. 11 (March 1933), 6–7.

8. See, for instance, S. Silka, "Comment placer le microphone au studio" [How to position the microphone in the studio], *La technique cinématographique*, vol. 3, no. 4 (April 1932), 188–189.

9. In P. A. Harle, "La qualité du son" [Sound quality], *La cinématographie française*, vol. 20, no. 1013 (1 April 1938), 6; see also R. Singer, "Quelques idées nouvelles en Amérique" [Some new ideas from America], *La technique cinématographique*, vol. 10, no. 96 (December 1938), 1320.

10. On the separation of sound from image production, see Rick Altman, "Evolution of Sound Technology," *Film Sound: Theory and Practice*, ed., Elisabeth Weis and John Belton (New York: Columbia University Press, 1985), 44–53.

11. See P. Thomas, "Les studios moderne et son traitement acoustique" [Modern studios and their acoustic treatment], *La technique cinématographique*, vol. 5, no. 37 (January 1934), 33.

12. The quotation is from a published interview with Lang, apropos of his work on *Liliom*, in the file on *Liliom* in the Rondel Collection at the Bibliothèque Nationale, no title, date, or publication credit.

13. See A. P. Richard, *Cinématographie française*, no. 965 (30 April 1937), ix. "Filmmakers now increasingly neglect the static shot in favor of the more dynamic moving camera, which imposes on the engineers and their assistants veritable acrobatics for the proper recording of sound. . . . "

14. See "La technique du *travelling* dans les films d'André Hugon" [Moving-camera technique in André Hugon's films], *La cinématographie française*, vol. 15, no. 769 (29 July 1933), 22.

15. See, for instance, the numerous quotations from filmmakers concerning location-recorded sound in Claude Vermorel, "Le cinéma peut-il s'affranchir du

studio" [Can the cinema escape from the studio?], *Pour vous,* no. 216 (5 January 1933).

16. See O. Blemmec, "A propos de l'enregistrement avec bandes de fréquences multiples" [Apropos of recording with multiple frequency tracks], *Le cinéopse,* vol. 21, no. 238 (June 1939), 119.

17. In Barkan, "M. Willem Sivel, ingénieur du son," 368. "Even in the case of delicate scenes, we are rarely able to practice postsynchronization. We don't have the actors available for a long enough time."

18. See, for instance, A. Lovichi, "La technique du réenregistrement" [The technique of re-recording], *La technique cinématographique,* vol. 2, no. 6 (July 1931), 9–12.

19. For a discussion of re-recording, see Arthur Hoerée, "La travail du film sonore," *La revue musicale,* no. 151 (December 1934), 73.

20. The figure concerning re-recording is cited in David Bordwell, Janet Staiger, and Kristin Thompson, *The Classical Hollywood Cinema* (New York: Columbia University Press, 1985), 303.

21. See Pierre Autré's addendum to Maurice Pivar, "Le montage du film sonore" [Editing the sound film], *La cinématographie française,* vol. 14, no. 725 (24 September 1932), ix.

22. See, for instance, "La technique en 1932" [Technique in 1932], *La cinématographie française,* vol. 14, no. 743 (28 January 1932), 27.

23. In Pierre Autré, "High Fidelity," *La cinématographie française,* vol. 15, no. 747 (25 February 1933), 8.

24. See A. P. Richard, "La qualité du son," *La cinématographie française,* vol. 15, no. 750 (18 March 1933), 7.

25. In Autré, "High Fidelity," 7.

26. See A. P. Richard, "La technique 1938, une marche constante vers le progrès" [Technique in 1938: a steady course toward progress], *La cinématographie française,* vol. 20, no. 1052 (30 December 1938), iv.

27. In O. Blemmec, "La situation des opérateurs au cinéma" [The situation regarding film projectionists], *Le cinéopse,* vol. 16, no. 178 (June 1934), 150. "Some propose that re-recording should be used in all cases, but it seems better to use it only when one can't do otherwise."

28. See, for instance, "Le son et l'art," *Le film français,* no. 87 (22 April 1944), 6.

29. See Bordwell, Staiger, and Thompson, *The Classical Hollywood Cinema,* 302.

30. In Michel Chion, *The Voice in Cinema* (New York: Columbia University Press, 1999), 5.

31. Quoted in Barkan, "M. Willem Sivel, ingénieur du son," 368

32. From an interview with cinematographer Michel Kelber, quoted in Colin Crisp, *The Classic French Cinema, 1930–1960* (Bloomington: Indiana University Press, 1993), 383.

33. See the informative discussion of relations between the French cinema of the 1930s and the popular stage in Dudley Andrew, *Mists of Regret,* 114–147.

34. Regarding parameters of voice quality and timbre in the context of sound-media practice, see Theo van Leeuwen, *Speech, Music, Sound* (London: Macmillan, 1999), 125–155.

35. Quoted in André Arnyvelde, "En marge de *Quatorze Juillet*: entretien avec René Clair" [A footnore to *Quatorze Juillet*: an interview with René Clair], *Pour vous*, no. 213 (15 December 1932), 3.

36. Extracts from the report include: "the door shuts while Edwige speaks," "a glass clinks during dialogue," "words are unclear," "bad sound, the machine makes too much noise," "good performance, but not so good for the sound," "sound is less good than for take 2; if necessary synchronize the sound for take 2 onto take 3," "no good, error in the dialogue," "bad sound, too much difference in tone," and "noise covers the dialogue." This report can be found in a dossier of production-related documents pertaining to *Feu!* in the Bibliothèque du Film in Paris.

37. Once electrical recording was introduced into the gramophone industry in 1925, classical music began to be recorded in famous concert halls, on the grounds that the spatial characteristics of such places registered on the recording. See Timothy Day, *A Century of Recorded Music: Listening to Musical History* (New Haven, Conn., and London: Yale University Press, 2000), 18.

38. See Crafton, *The Talkies*, 360–370.

39. See A. P. Richard, "La technique de l'année 1936" [Technique in the year 1936], *La cinématographie française*, no. 947 (26 December 1936), ii. "American technique tends, if not toward the disappearance of ambient sound, at least toward its diminution, so that the principal noises and words will not be covered over."

40. In Arthur Hoerée, "La travail du film sonore," *La revue musicale*, no. 151 (December 1934), 64.

41. In Barkan, "M. Willem Sivel, ingénieur du son," 368. By some accounts, this particular national difference endures today. See, for instance, remarks by sound technician Michel Durande, quoted in Claudine Nougaret and Sophie Chiabaut, *Le son direct au cinéma* (Paris: Femis, 1997), 151: "The French shoot in ways that capture a lot of ambient sound. The Americans capture only the voices, and are content with that."

42. See remarks in P. Jacquin, "Considérations générales sur l'enregistrement du son" [General considerations on sound recording], *La technique cinématographique*, vol. 18, no. 47 (26 June 1947), 1083.

43. In Michel Chion, *Le cinéma et ses métiers* (Paris: Bordas, 1990), 124–125.

44. See, for instance, remarks on French film style in Michel Chion, *La musique au cinéma* (Paris: Fayard, 1995).

45. For examples of such methods, see the interview with sound-effects specialist Cutelli in Michel Ferry, "Le 'roi du micro' est à Paris" [The microphone king is in Paris], *Pour vous*, no. 218 (19 January 1933), 6.

46. In Henry Hamelin, ed., *L'industrie du cinéma* (Paris: Société Nouvelle Mercure, 1954).

47. On the "multiple version" phenomenon of the early 1930s, see Nataša

Ďurovičová, "Translating America: The Hollywood Multilinguals 1929–1933," in Altman, *Sound Theory/Sound Practice*, 138–153; see also the chapters by Ginette Vincendeau, Martine Danan, and Joseph Garncarz in *"Film Europe" and "Film America": Cinema, Commerce, and Cultural Exchange, 1920–1939*, ed. Andrew Higson and Richard Maltby (Exeter, UK: University of Exeter Press, 1999).

48.  Regarding the situation in the United States, see Harold Lewis, "Getting Good Sound Is an Art," *American Cinematographer*, vol. 15, no. 2 (June 1934), 65, 73–74.

49.  See, for instance, characterizations of the single-microphone dialogue recording as "an absolute law" in Gilles Frenais, *Son, musique et cinéma* (Québec: Gaëtan Morin, 1980), 40; and also in Paul Honoré, *A Handbook of Sound Recording* (South Brunswick, N.J.: A. S. Barnes, 1980), 41.

50.  See remarks in W. R. Sivel, "Vive le son!" *Paris-cinéma, grandeur et servitudes du cinéma français*, no. 1 (1945): "Just think that in 1935, in order to record certain scenes, four to five microphones were necessary. Moreover, these microphones were supported by all sorts of very awkward tripods and booms. Today, rare are the scenes utilizing more than one microphone." See also W. Sivel, "Le son et le micro" [Sound and the microphone], *L'écran français*, vol. 5, no. 91 (25 March 1947), 13, 14.

51.  See O. Blemmec, "A propos de l'enregistrement avec bandes de frequencies multiples," *Le cinéopse*, vol. 21, no. 238 (June 1939), 119. See also R. Singer, "Quelques idées nouvelles en Amérique," *La technique cinématographique*, vol. 10, no. 96 (December 1938), 1319–1320.

52.  In Pierre Hémardinquer, *Le cinématographe sonore et la projection en relief*, 3d rev. ed., corrected (Paris: Eyrolles, 1935), 164–165. The author specifies "at least three or four microphones in different positions and orientations which are activated at will according to the movement of the artists within the cinematographic 'scene.'"

53.  See O. Blemmec, "Les microphones," *Le cinéopse*, vol. 16, no. 176 (April 1934), 116.

54.  See O. Blemmec, "Variétés sur les studios" [Observations on the studios], *Le cinéopse*, vol. 20, no. 222 (February 1938), 43. "A highly directional microphone authorizes a greater reverberation in the studio."

55.  See, for instance, "L'évolution de la technique cinématographique en 1933" [Evolution of cinematography techniques in 1933], *Le cinéopse*, vol. 16, no. 173 (January 1934), 15.

56.  Concerning Vitaphone technique, see, for instance, Edwin Schallert, "Vitaphone Activity in Hollywood," *Motion Picture News* (8 July 1927), 35–36; and "How Vitaphone Enters In," *New York Times* (28 August 1927), 7: 4. Both pieces are reprinted in Robert Carringer, ed., *The Jazz Singer* (Madison: University of Wisconsin Press, 1979), 175–181. See also the important collection on Vitaphone, *The Dawn of Sound*, ed. Mary Lea Bandy (New York: Museum of Modern Art, 1989).

57.  A description of multiple-camera shooting can be found in Robert Florey,

"Comment on met en scène un film sonore, parlant, et chantant" [How a talking and singing film is made], *Cinémagazine,* no. 36 (6 September 1929), pt. 1, and *Cinémagazine,* no. 37 (13 September 1929), pt. 2.

58. See, for instance, the interviews with Jeanne Boitel, Meg Lemoinnier, Helena Manson, and René Sylviano in Christian Gilles, ed., *Le cinéma des années trentes par ceux qui l'ont fait,* I (Paris: L'Harmattan, 2000). Such work conditions were catalogued in the Petsche Report (1935), which informed later government policy concerning the film industry.

59. Concerning the talkies' "grossly overlit sets," see Bert Glennon, "Cinematography and the Talkies: Some Honest Criticism from a Former Cameraman," *American Cinematographer,* vol. 10, no. 11 (February 1930), 7, 45.

60. In Bordwell, Staiger, and Thompson, *The Classical Hollywood Cinema,* 305.

61. Quoted in the interview with Kevin Macdonald, "From Vigo to the Nouvelle Vague: A Cameraman's Career," in *Projections 6* (London: Faber and Faber, 1996), 232. An intriguing counterexample to the practices that Kelber describes is *Marius* (dir. Alexander Korda, 1931), in which Pierre Fresnay is occasionally photographed from behind while speaking.

62. See the discussion of multiple-camera shooting in Bordwell, Staiger, and Thompson, *The Classical Hollywood Cinema,* 305; and in Crafton, *The Talkies,* 244.

63. See Bordwell, Staiger, and Thompson, *The Classical Hollywood Cinema,* 305.

64. See Fernand Vincent, "Les studios Pathé-Natan de Joinville," *La cinématographie française,* vol. 12, no. 594 (22 March 1930), 57.

65. An account of the shooting of a four-camera scene, made on location at the Trocadero casino in Paris, can be found in A.-P. Barancy, "George Milton a gagné hier soir un million" [George Milton won a million yesterday evening], *L'intransigeant* (26 April 1934), n.p.

66. On multiple-camera shooting's role in mid-century television in enabling "the television image to recreate the perceptual continuity of the theatre," see Philip Auslander, *Liveness: Performance in a Mediatized Culture* (New York and London: Routledge, 1999), 19–22.

67. See Léon Moussinac, *Panoramique du cinéma* (Paris: Le Sans Pareil, 1929). See also P.-A. Harlé, "Des technicians du scènario et du découpage" [Technicians of the shooting script], *La cinématographie française,* vol. 11, no. 542 (23 March 1929), 32. See also Crisp, *The Classic French Cinema,* 107, referring to scriptwriters as "almost nonexistent in France in the twenties."

68. In H. Fescourt, *La foi et les montagnes, ou le septième art au passé* (Paris: Paul Montel, 1959), 385–386.

69. Charles-Felix Tavano, quoted in D. Marion, ed., *Le cinéma par ceux qui le font* (Paris: Fayard, 1949), 90.

70. This assessment is based on the examination of some fifteen shooting scripts for French films of the 1930s (*découpages techniques*), available in Paris at the Bibliothèque du Film and at the Dept. des Arts et Spectacles of the Bibliothèque Nationale.

71. In Pierre Desclaux, "Comment le film parlant a modifié le cinéma mondial," *Almanach de Mon Ciné* (1932), 39.

72. See L'Herbier, "Devoir de la critique," 8.

73. See Desclaux, "Comment le film parlant a modifié le cinéma mondial," 39: "In practice, [the actors] trust in their own inspiration and often arrive at the studio ignorant of the scene they are to shoot."

74. See, for instance, P. Michaut, "Le rôle de l'ingénieur du son" [The role of the sound engineer], *La cinématographie française,* vol. 21, no. 1065 (31 March 1939), 84.

75. See P. Leprohon, *Les milles et un métiers du cinéma* (Paris: Melot, 1947), 162.

76. In A.-P. Richard, "Petites questions techniques importantes: à propos du parler 'susurré'" [Important little technical questions: apropos of speaking in a whisper], *Cinématographie française,* vol. 19, no. 965 (30 April 1937), ix.

77. See Pierre Autré, "Les technicians français sont trop modestes" [French technicians are too modest], *La cinématographie française,* vol. 15, no. 764 (24 June 1933), viii.

78. In Marcel Pagnol, *Cinématurgie de Paris* (Paris: Editions de Fallois, 1991), 43.

79. For a sound engineer's assessment, see L. E. Clark, "Sound Recording: Art or Trade," *American Cinematographer,* vol. 13, no. 2 (June 1932), 17: "We knew little or nothing of conditions within the motion picture industry—and cared little about them. We were engineers—and proud of it. Our business was to install and operate the recording equipment, not to make pictures per se."

80. See Carl Dreher, "Sound Personnel and Organization," *American Cinematographer,* vol. 10, no. 13 (April 1930), 18.

81. See "Sound Men and Cinematographers Discuss their Mutual Problems," *American Cinematographer,* vol. 10, no. 5 (August 1929), 8, 39.

82. See Bordwell, Staiger, and Thompson, *The Classical Hollywood Cinema,* 299–301.

83. See J. Lastra, "Standards and Practices: Aesthetic Norm and Technological Innovation in the American Cinema," in *The Studio System,* ed. Janet Staiger (New Brunswick, N.J.: Rutgers University Press, 1995).

84. See P. Michaut, "Un musicien: M. Maurice Thiriet," *Cinématographie française,* no. 1077 (24 June 1939), xii. "In the absence of any special teaching, in the conservatory or in an official institute, microphone techniques are learned through empiricism and individual experience."

85. In G. Gérardot, "L'importance du rôle de l'ingénieur du son dans une production" [The sound engineer's important role in a production], *La cinematographie française* (22–29 December 1934), 149.

86. See Pierre Autré, "Le film parlant à reconquis le plein air" [The talkie conquers the outdoors], *La technique cinématographique,* vol. 14, no. 738 (24 December 1932), 173.

87. See Blemmec, "Variétés sur les studios," 43.

88. In P. Thomas, "Le studio moderne et son traitement acoustique" [The modern

studio and its acoustic treatment], *La technique cinématographique,* vol. 5, no. 37 (January 1934), 33. For the alternative perspective, see Ken Cameron, *Sound and the Documentary Film* (London: Isaac Pitman and Sons, 1947), 30: "For ideal recording of dialogue, the room should be . . . absolutely 'dead.'"

89.  See Colin Crisp, *The Classic French Cinema, 1930–1960* (Bloomington: Indiana University Press, 1993), 95.

90.  In A. P. Richard, "Tendances actuelles de la technique sonore américaine: comparaison avec méthodes françaises" [Current trends in American sound technique: a comparison with French methods], *La cinématographie française,* vol. 27, no. 1137 (29 December 1945), 7.

91.  Quoted in G. Sadoul, "En marge de l'affaire Pathé-Natan" [A footnote to the Pathé-Natan Affair], *Regards,* no. 262 (19 January 1939).

## 6. Hollywood Indigenized

1.  The topic of Pathé-Natan's similarities to its Hollywood counterparts is taken up in Gilles Willems, "Les origines du groupe Pathé-Natan et le modèle américain" [Origins of the Pathé-Natan group and the American model], *Vingtième siècle,* no. 46 (April–June, 1995), 98–106; Kermabon, *Pathé, première empire du cinéma,* 224–227; and Martin Barnier, *En route vers le parlant* (Liège, Belgium: Ed. du Céfal, 2002), 142–144.

2.  Figures reported for the total number of films made at Joinville, year by year, are as follows: ten for 1929, fifteen for 1930, twenty-four for 1931, twenty-three for 1932, and forty for 1933. In "Les studios Pathé-Natan de Joinville," *Technique cinématographique,* vol. 5, nos. 43–44 (July–August 1934), 187. Gaumont-Franco-Film-Aubert, Pathé-Natan's main rival, produced 32 films total during this time, twenty of which were made by independent producers. See Philippe d'Hughes and Dominique Muller, *Gaumont, 90 ans de cinéma* (Paris: Ramsey/La cinematheque françaises, 1986), 84.

3.  See the discussion of the Natan Affair in Jens Ulff-Møller, *Hollywood's Film Wars with France: Film-Trade Diplomacy and the Emergence of the French Film Quota Policy* (Rochester, N.Y.: University of Rochester Press, 2001), 116ff. Regarding the politics of the Stavisky Affair, see Maurice Chavardès, *Une Campagne de presse: la droite française et le 6 février 1934* (Paris: Flammarion, 1970).

4.  In Roger Manvell, *Film* (London: Pelican Books, 1944), 148.

5.  In G. Sadoul, *Histoire d'un art: le cinéma des origins á nos jours* (Paris: Flammarion, 1949), 265.

6.  See, for instance, "Les affaires de Cinéma-Pathé prospèrent" [Cinéma-Pathé's business prospers], *La cinématographie française,* vol. 12, no. 590 (22 February 1930), 11.

7.  In Louis D'Herbeumont, "Film parlant et sonore," *Le cinéopse,* vol. 11, no. 124 (1 December 1929), 955.

8.  Examples of favorable trade-press coverage of Natan in the face of scandal include "A la societé Pathé-Natan," *Le cinéopse,* vol. 17, no. 189 (May 1935), 108–109.

9. In Ilya Ehrenbourg, *Usine de rêves* [Industry of dreams] (Paris: Gallimard, 1936), 106. According to a publisher's note, this book was written in 1932, and thus predates the collapse of Pathé-Natan and Gaumont-Franco-Film-Aubert.

10. Quoted in Christian Brieu, Laurent Ikor, and J. Michel Viguier, *Joinville le cinéma: le temps des studios* (Paris: Ramsey, 1985), 58, 60.

11. See André Rossel-Kirschen and Gilles Willems, "Bernard Natan à la direction de Pathé-Cinéma," *1895*, no. 21 (December 1996), 163.

12. Regarding the pornography conviction, which was erased in 1919 in light of Natan's favorable military record, see André Rossel-Kirschen and Gilles Willems, "Bernard Natan à la direction de Pathé-Cinéma," 168–169.

13. Concerning these events, see Marc-Antoine Robert, "L'affaire Natan," in Jacques Kermabon, ed., *Pathé, première empire du cinéma* (Paris: Centre Pompidou, 1994), 260–267.

14. See Richard Abel, *The Ciné Goes to Town* (Berkeley and Los Angeles: University of California Press, 1994), 9–58.

15. According to Richard Abel, French films in 1919 made up only 10 percent of the French film market. In R. Abel, "Survivre à un nouvel ordre mondial" [To survive in a new world order], in Jacques Kermabon, ed., *Pathé, première empire du cinéma* (Paris: Centre Pompidou, 1994), 163. See also remarks in D. Gomery, *Movie History: A Survey* (Belmont, Calif.: Wadsworth, 1991), 113.

16. See Charles Pathé, *De Pathé Frères à Pathé Cinéma* (Lyon: SERDOC, 1970). These memoirs were first published in 1940.

17. See Abel, "Survivre à un nouvel ordre mondial," 158–189.

18. See F. Garçon, *Gaumont, un siècle de cinéma* (Paris: Gallimard, 1992), 34–35.

19. Concerning these figures, see "De ci, de là, dans le corporation" [In the film business, here and there], *Le cinéopse,* vol. 12, no. 126 (February 1930), 88. A compilation of such reports, covering the period from 1924 to 1938, appears in a table in Paul Leglise, *Histoire de la politique du cinéma français, vol. 2: entre deux républiques, 1940–1946* (Paris: Pierre L'Herminier, 1977), 213.

20. See Raymond Berner, "Le circuit Pathé-Natan," *La cinématographie française,* vol. 13, no. 672 (19 September 1931), 97: "The working principle resembles that of the great programmers of the American circuits who contract with producers like Paramount or Metro and furnish films to hundreds of theatres."

21. See Marc-Antoine Robert, "La naissance d'un grand circuit" [The birth of a great theatre chain], in Jacques Kermabon, ed., *Pathé, première empire du cinéma,* 280–285.

22. See Raymond Bernier, "Le circuit Pathé-Natan," 97; R. Bernier, "Les grands circuits français," *La cinématographie française,* vol. 13, no. 634 (27 December 1930), 105–106; and André Rossel-Kirschen and Gilles Willems, "Bernard Natan à la direction de Pathé-Cinéma," 170.

23. See R. Bernier, "Une opération monstre" [An enormous operation], *La ciné-matographie française*, vol. 12, no. 614 (9 August 1930).

24. See R. Bernier, "Ce qu'est le circuit Pathé-Natan," *La cinématographie française*, vol. 12, no. 596 (5 April 1930), 23.

25. See Roger Régent, "Les indépendants contre les circuits" [Independents versus the chains], *Pour vous*, no. 90 (7 August 1930), 2.

26. The figure of 35,000 francs is cited in R. Régent, "Charles Vanel met en scène son premier parlant" [Charles Vanel directs his first talkie], *Pour vous*, no. 164 (7 January 1932), 6.

27. Cited in Jacques Choukroun, "Contrôler les studios, un atout majeur pour les grandes compagnies françaises des années trente?" [To control the studios, a major goal for the large French film companies of the 1930s?], in *Une histoire économique du cinéma français (1895–1995): regards croisés franco-américains*, ed. Pierre-Jean Benghozi and Christian Delage (Paris: L'Harmattan, 1997), 117–119.

28. See Jacques Gerber, ed., *Pierre Braunberger, producteur* (Paris: CNC/Centre G. Pompidou, 1987), 66.

29. In Louis Saurel, "Le nouveau programme de production Pathé-Natan" [Pathé-Natan's new production program], *La cinématographie française*, vol. 14, nos. 715–716 (23 July 1932), 19. The fifth category on the production list for 1932 was "properly original scenarios" (e.g., *Mirages de Paris* [dir. Fédor Ozep, 1932]).

30. See R. Régent, "Point de vue d'un producteur français: M. Natan," *Pour vous*, no. 92 (21 August 1930), 2.

31. See Ginette Vincendeau, *Stars and Stardom in French Film* (London and New York: Continuum, 2000).

32. See Kermabon, "Un cinéma pour le paradis," in *Pathé, première empire du cinéma*, 232–236.

33. In R. Régent, "Charles Vanel met en scène son premier parlant," *Pour vous*, no. 164 (7 January 1932), 6. "How much time is squandered in the studios because a small role is not ready, because one must rehearse it three times more than should be needed."

34. In André Arnyvelde, "Quand G. Milton tourne *Le roi du cirage*" [When G. Milton shoots *Le roi du cirage*], *Pour vous*, no. 123 (26 March 1931), 6.

35. See André Arneyville, "Léonce Perret tourne *Sapho* avec Mary Marguet" [Léonce Perret shoots *Sapho* with Mary Marguet], *Pour vous*, no. 258 (26 October 1933), 6.

36. See S. Chantal, "A Joinville, on tourne *Au nom de la loi*" [*Au nom de la loi* is being shot in Joinville], *Cinémonde*, vol. 4, no. 150 (3 September 1930), 564.

37. On Perret's use of 90- and 180-degree cutting during the early 1910s, see Abel, *The Ciné Goes to Town*, 382, 386, 387, 423.

38. See remarks in Bordwell, Staiger, and Thompson, *The Classical Hollywood Cinema*, 306: "[N]ot until Akira Kurosawa's films (e.g., *Record of a Living*

*Being*, 1955; *High and Low*, 1963), does an alternative aesthetic of multiple-camera filming emerge."

## Conclusion

1.  In Michel Chion, "Problèmes et solutions pour developer l'étude du son, en Europe et dans le monde" [Problems and solutions for the development of sound-film study in Europe and in the world], *Iris*, no. 27 (spring 1999), 21–22.

2.  In Alan Williams, "Introduction," *Film and Nationalism* (New Brunswick, N.J.: Rutgers University Press), 19–20.

3.  For Godard, a place to begin is with issues raised in Alan Williams's "Godard's Use of Sound," in *Film Sound: Theory and Practice*, ed. Elisabeth Weis and John Belton (New York: Columbia University Press, 1985), 332–345.

4.  See Barton Byg, *Landscapes of Resistance: The German Films of Danièle Huillet and Jean-Marie Straub* (Berkeley and Los Angeles: University of California Press, 1995), 22–23.

5.  Regarding Rivette's direct-sound practices, see the interview with sound technician Pierre Gamet, in François Thomas, "L'image du son: entretien avec Pierre Gamet," in *Jacques Rivette, la règle du jeu*, ed. Danièla Guiffrida (Turin: Centre culturel française de Turin/Musée nazionale del cinema di Torino, 1992), 77.

6.  Quoted in the interview with sound technician Bernard Aubouy, in Claudine Nougaret and Sophie Chiabaut, *Le son direct au cinéma* (Paris: Femis, 1997), 105.

7.  On the reception of *City Lights* in the United States, see Crafton, *The Talkies*, 374–377.

8.  See Andrew, *Mists of Regret*, 106, 111.

9.  In P. E. Salles Gomes, *Jean Vigo* (London: Faber and Faber, 1998), 233.

10. In F. Courtade, *Les malédictions du cinéma français* (Paris: Alain Moreau, 1978), 79.

11. Concerning Renoir's career during conversion, see Andrew, *Mists of Regret*, 277–283.

12. In Jean Renoir, *Ma vie et mes films* (Paris: Flammarion, 1974), 141.

13. In H. Fescourt, *La foi et les montagnes* (Paris: Paul Montel, 1959), 378.

14. In R. Abel, *French Film Theory and Criticism*, vol. 2 (Princeton, N.J.: Princeton University Press, 1988), 5.

15. See Michel Chion, *Audio-Vision: Sound on Screen*, trans. C. Gorbman (New York: Columbia University Press, 1994), 95.

16. In Jean-Marie Straub and Danièle Huillet, "Direct Sound: An Interview," in *Film Sound: Theory and Practice*, 152.

# Filmography:
# French Films, 1930–1933

The sixty-one films listed below encompass titles used for the statistical analysis reported in chapter 4. The list does not include all of the films mentioned in the book, and includes others not mentioned but that nonetheless factored into the statistics. In any case, these films constitute the core corpus for the book's investigation into conversion-era French film style.

Listed after each title is the director, the studio facility (if known), and the average shot length (ASL) for the film's first thirty minutes, when available (not available = N.A.).

## 1930

*Au nom de la loi*
>       dir. Maurice Tourneur
>       studio Pathé-Natan at Joinville
>       ASL = 8.5 seconds

*L'affaire classée*
>       dir. Charles Vanel
>       studio Pathé-Natan at Joinville
>       ASL = 13.4 seconds

*L'âge d'or*
>       dir. Luis Buñuel
>       studio Braunberger-Richebé at Billancourt
>       ASL = 6.1 seconds

*La petite Lise*
>       dir. Jean Grémillon
>       studio Pathé-Natan at Joinville
>       ASL = 18.2

*La poignard malais*
>       dir. Roger Goupillières
>       studio Pathé-Natan at Joinville
>       ASL = 12.3

*Le blanc et le noir*
>       dir. Robert Florey
>       studio Braunberger-Richebé at Billancourt
>       ASL = 13.6 seconds

*Le chemin du paradis*
>       dir. Wilhelm Thiele and Max de Vaucorbeil
>       studio Ufa in Neubabelsberg, Germany

ASL = 8.8 seconds

*Le fin du monde*
  dir. Abel Gance
  studio Gaumont at La Victorine in Nice
  ASL = 5.2 seconds

*Le sang d'un poète*
  dir. Jean Cocteau
  studio Pathé-Natan at Joinville
  ASL = 11.2 seconds

*L'opéra de quat' sous*
  dir. Georg-Wilhelm Pabst
  studio Nero Film in Berlin and Tobis Films Sonores at Epinay
  ASL = 15.8 seconds

*On purge bébé*
  dir. Jean Renoir
  studio Braunberger-Richebé at Billancourt
  ASL = 26 seconds

*Paris la nuit*
  dir. Henri Diamant-Berger
  studio N.A.
  ASL = 15.1 seconds

*Prix de beauté*
  dir. Augusto Genina
  studio Tobis Films Sonores at Epinay
  ASL = 6.1 seconds

*Sous les toits de Paris*
  dir. René Clair
  studio Tobis Films Sonores at Epinay
  ASL = 8.6 seconds


## 1931

*A nous la liberté*
  dir. René Clair
  studio Tobis Films Sonores at Epinay
  ASL = 8.2 seconds

*Chacun sa chance*
  dir. Hans Steinhof and René Pujol
  studio Pathé-Natan at Joinville
  ASL = 12.2 seconds

*Cinq gentlemen maudit*
  dir. Julien Duvivier
  studio Tobis at Epinay
  ASL = 5.9 seconds

*Dactylo*
  dir. Wilhelm Thiele
  studio N.A.
  ASL = 17.6 seconds

*Faubourg Montmartre*
  dir. Raymond Bernard
  studio Pathé-Natan at Joinville
  ASL = 11.4 seconds
*Il est charmant*
  dir. Louis Mercanton
  studio Paramount at St. Maurice
  ASL = 9.4 seconds
*Je serai seule après minuit*
  dir. Jacques de Baroncelli
  studio Braunberger-Richebé at Billancourt
  ASL = 11.7 seconds
*La chienne*
  dir. Jean Renoir
  studio Braunberger-Richebé at Billancourt
  ASL = 21.2 seconds
*L'aiglon*
  dir. Victor Tourjansky
  studio Pathé-Natan at Joinville
  ASL = 12.7 seconds
*Le million*
  dir. René Clair
  studio Tobis Films Sonores at Epinay
  ASL = 8.7 seconds
*Le parfum de la dame en noir*
  dir. Marcel L'Herbier
  studio Pathé-Natan at Joinville
  ASL = 6.1 seconds
*Marius*
  dir. Alexander Korda
  studio Paramount at St. Maurice
  ASL = 9.2 seconds
*Paris-Beguin*
  dir. A. Genina
  studio Pathé-Natan at Joinville
  ASL = 10.1 seconds
*Pour un sou d'amour*
  dir. Jean Grémillon
  studio PhotoSonor at Courbevois
  ASL = 11.5 seconds
*Tu m'oublieras*
  dir. Henri Diamant-Berger
  studio N.A.
  ASL N.A.
*Le chien qui rapporte*
  dir. Jean Choux
  studio N.A.
  ASL = 4.3 seconds

1932

*Boudu sauvé des eaux*
>dir. Jean Renoir
>studio Braunberger-Richebé at Billancourt
>ASL = 14.9 seconds

*Coeur de Lilas*
>dir. Anatole Litvak
>studio Pathé-Natan at Joinville
>ASL = 7.3 seconds

*Fanny*
>dir. Marc Allégret
>studio Paramount at St. Maurice
>ASL = 11.1 seconds

*Fantômas*
>dir. Paul Féjos
>studio Braunberger-Richebé at Billancourt
>ASL = 4.4 seconds

*La chanson d'une nuit*
>dir. Anatole Litvak
>studio Hunnia in Budapest, Hungary
>ASL = 6.2 seconds

*L'affaire est dans le sac*
>dir. Pierre Prévert
>studio Pathé-Natan at Joinville
>ASL = 17.6

*La nuit du carrefour*
>dir. Jean Renoir
>studio Braunberger-Richebé at Billancourt
>ASL = 13.2 seconds

*La tête d'un homme*
>dir. Julien Duvivier
>studio Braunberger-Richebé at Billancourt
>ASL = 15.9 seconds

*Le chien jaune*
>dir. Jean Tarride
>studio Braunberger-Richebé at Billancourt
>ASL = 14.4 seconds

*Le roi du cirage*
>dir. Pière Colombier
>studio Pathé-Natan at Joinville
>ASL = 3.8 seconds

*Le rosier de Madame Husson*
>dir. Bernard Deschamps
>studio Tobis Films Sonores at Epinay
>ASL = 9.8 seconds

*Les gaîtés de l'escadron*
>dir. Maurice Tourneur
>studio Pathé-Natan at Joinville

ASL = 9.2 seconds

*Les trois mousequetaires*
>dir. Henri Diamant-Berger
>studio N.A.
>ASL = 7.4 seconds

*Le triangle de feu*
>dir. Edmond Gréville
>studio N.A.
>ASL = 6.2 seconds

*Marie, légende hongroise*
>dir. Paul Féjos
>studio Hunnia in Budapest, Hungary
>ASL = 5.6 seconds

*Poil de carotte*
>dir. Julien Duvivier
>studio Pathé-Natan at Joinville
>ASL = 11.8 seconds

*Quatorze juillet*
>dir. René Clair
>studio Tobis Films Sonores at Epinay
>ASL = 11.6 seconds

*Rouletabille aviateur*
>dir. Istvan Szekely
>studio Hunnia in Budapest, Hungary
>ASL = 6.7 seconds

*Topaze*
>dir. Louis Gasnier
>studio Paramount at St. Maurice
>ASL = 10.4 seconds

## 1933

*Ces messieurs de la santé*
>dir. Pière Colombier
>studio Pathé-Natan at Joinville
>ASL = 19.4 seconds

*Chotard et cie.*
>dir. Jean Renoir
>studio Pathé-Natan at Joinville
>ASL = 25 seconds

*Joffroi*
>dir. Marcel Pagnol
>Filmed on location in Provence
>ASL = 18.2 seconds

*L'agonie des aigles*
>dir. Roger Richebé
>studio Braunberger-Richebé at Billancourt
>ASL = 14.2 seconds

*La maternelle*
> dir. Jean Benoit-Lévy and Marie Epstein
> studio PhotoSonor at Courbevois
> ASL = 8.6

*Le grand jeu*
> dir. Jacques Feyder
> studio Tobis Films Sonores at Epinay
> ASL = 18

*Le sexe faible*
> dir. Robert Siodmak
> studio Tobis Films Sonore at Epinay
> ASL = 12.8 seconds

*Les misérables*
> dir. Raymond Bernard
> studio Pathé-Natan at Joinville
> ASL = 11.2

*L'illustre Maurin*
> dir. André Hugon
> studio N.A.
> ASL = 30.5 seconds

*Mauvais graine*
> dir. Billy Wilder
> Filmed on location in Paris and Marseilles
> ASL = 6.9 seconds

*Miquette et sa mère*
> dir. Henri Diamant-Berger
> studio N.A.
> ASL 7.0

*Zéro de conduite*
> dir Jean Vigo
> studio Gaumont at La Villette, Paris
> ASL = 8.6 seconds

# Index

*Italicized page numbers indicate illustrations.*

CHARLES O'BRIEN teaches film studies at Carleton University in Ottawa, Canada. He is co-translator of Francesco Casetti's *Inside the Gaze: The Fiction Film and Its Spectator* (Indiana University Press, 1998), and has published articles on diverse topics in film and media history.